PARENTS AND EDUCATORS PRAISE THE CORE KNOWLEDGE SERIES

"Though I have twenty-five years teaching experience, this is my first year as a Core Knowledge teacher. Now, for the first time in a long time, I am excited about teaching again. As for my students, I seriously believe that many of them would eliminate summer vacation to get on with the business of learning!"

—*Joan Falbey, teacher, Three Oaks Elementary School, Fort Myers, Florida*

"Thank you for writing such wonderful books! My children and I have thoroughly enjoyed them. Your books have been a great source and a guide to us. I have a degree in elementary education and I think this is the best curriculum I have encountered."

—*Barbara de la Aguilera, parent, Miami, Florida*

"For three years, we have been using elements of the Core Knowledge program, and I have watched as it invigorated our students. These books should be in every classroom in America."

—*Richard E. Smith, principal, Northside Elementary School, Palestine, Texas*

"Hirsch made it quite clear (in *Cultural Literacy*) that respect for cultural diversity is important but is best achieved when young people have adequate background knowledge of mainstream culture. In order for a truly democratic and economically sound society to be maintained, young people must have access to the best knowledge available so that they can understand the issues, express their viewpoints, and act accordingly."

—*James P. Comer, M.D., professor, Child Study Center, Yale University (in* Parents *magazine)*

The CORE KNOWLEDGE Series

Resource Books for
Kindergarten Through Grade Six

Bantam Books

New York

Core Knowledge®

What Your Fourth Grader Needs to Know

Fundamentals of a Good Fourth-Grade Education

(Revised Edition)

Edited by E. D. Hirsch, Jr.

Published in the United States by Bantam Books, an imprint of Random House,
a division of Penguin Random House LLC, New York.

BANTAM BOOKS and the HOUSE colophon are registered trademarks of
Penguin Random House LLC.

CORE KNOWLEDGE is a trademark of the Core Knowledge Foundation.

Originally published in hardcover in the United States in 1992. A revised hardcover
edition was published in 2004 by Doubleday, an imprint of the Knopf Doubleday
Publishing Group, a division of Random House LLC, a Penguin Random House
Company and subsequently in trade paperback in 2005 by Delta Books, an imprint of
The Random House Publishing Group, a division of Random House LLC,
a Penguin Random House Company.

Library of Congress Cataloging-in-Publication Data
Names: Hirsch, E. D. (Eric Donald) editor.
Title: What your fourth grader needs to know : fundamentals of a good fourth-grade
education / edited by E.D. Hirsch, Jr.
Description: Revised edition; 2016 Bantam Books trade paperback edition. |
New York : Bantam, 2016. | Includes bibliographical references and index.
Identifiers: LCCN 2016000522 (print) | LCCN 2016012596 (ebook) |
ISBN 9780553394672 (paperback) | ISBN 9780553394696 (ebook) |
ISBN 9780553394696 ()
Subjects: LCSH: Fourth grade (Education)—Curricula—United States. | Curriculum
planning—United States. | BISAC: EDUCATION / Elementary. | EDUCATION /
Curricula. | EDUCATION / Reference.
Classification: LCC LB1571 4th .W48 2016 (print) | LCC LB1571 4th (ebook) |
DDC 372.24/2—dc23
LC record available at http://lccn.loc.gov/2016000522

Printed in the United States of America on acid-free paper

randomhousebooks.com

2 4 6 8 9 7 5 3 1

Book design by Diane Hobbing

Editor-in-Chief of the Core Knowledge Series: E. D. Hirsch, Jr.

Editors, Revised Edition: John Holdren, Susan Tyler Hitchcock

Project Manager and Art Editor: Alice Wiggins, Emma Earnst

Writers: John Hirsch (math), Michele Josselyn (visual arts),
Mary Beth Klee (American history), Barbara Lachman (music),
Deborah Mazzotta Prum (world history), Christiana Whittington (music),
Words and Numbers (all)

Artists and Photographers: Steve Henry, Bob Kirchman, Gail McIntosh,
Jane Sickon

Art and Photo Research, Art and Text Permissions: Emma Earnst, Alice Wiggins,
Words and Numbers

Acknowledgments

This series has depended on the help, advice, and encouragement of some two thousand people. Some of those singled out here already know the depth of our gratitude; others may be surprised to find themselves thanked publicly for help they gave quietly and freely for the sake of the enterprise alone. To helpers named and unnamed we are deeply grateful.

Advisors on Multiculturalism: Minerva Allen, Barbara Carey, Frank de Varona, Mick Fedullo, Dorothy Fields, Elizabeth Fox-Genovese, Marcia Galli, Dan Garner, Henry Louis Gates, Cheryl Kulas, Joseph C. Miller, Gerry Raining Bird, Connie Rocha, Dorothy Small, Sharon Stewart-Peregoy, Sterling Stuckey, Marlene Walking Bear, Lucille Watahomigie, Ramona Wilson

Advisors on Elementary Education: Joseph Adelson, Isobel Beck, Paul Bell, Carl Bereiter, David Bjorklund, Constance Jones, Elizabeth LaFuze, J. P. Lutz, Sandra Scarr, Nancy Stein, Phyllis Wilkin

Advisors on Technical Subject Matter: Marilyn Jager Adams, Karima-Diane Alavi, Richard Anderson, Judith Birsh, Cheryl Cannard, Barbara Foorman, Paul Gagnon, David Geary, Andrew Gleason, Ted Hirsch, Henry Holt, Blair Jones, Connie Juel, Eric Karell, Morton Keller, Joseph Kett, Charles Kimball, Mary Beth Klee, Barbara Lachman, Karen Lang, Michael Lynch, Diane McGuinness, Sheelagh McGurn, Joseph C. Miller, Jean Osborn, Vikas Pershad, Margaret Reed, Donna Rehorn, Gilbert Roy, Nancy Royal, Mark Rush, Janet Smith, Ralph Smith, Keith Stanovich, Paula Stanovich, Nancy Strother, Nancy Summers, Marlene Thompson, James Trefil, Patricia Wattenmaker, Nancy Wayne, Christiana Whittington, Linda Williams, Lois Williams

Conferees, March 1990: Nola Bacci, Joan Baratz-Snowden, Thomasyne Beverley, Thomas Blackton, Angela Burkhalter, Monty Caldwell, Thomas M. Carroll, Laura Chapman, Carol Anne Collins, Lou Corsaro, Henry Cotton, Anne Coughlin, Arletta Dimberg, Debra P. Douglas, Patricia Edwards, Janet Elenbogen, Mick Fedullo, Michele Fomalont, Mamon Gibson, Jean Haines, Barbara Hayes, Stephen Herzog, Helen Kelley, Brenda King, John King, Elizabeth

La-Fuze, Diana Lam, Nancy Lambert, Doris Langaster, Richard LaPointe, Lloyd Leverton, Madeline Long, Allen Luster, Joseph McGeehan, Janet McLin, Gloria McPhee, Marcia Mallard, William J. Maloney, Judith Matz, John Morabito, Robert Morrill, Roberta Morse, Karen Nathan, Dawn Nichols, Valeta Paige, Mary Perrin, Joseph Piazza, Jeanne Price, Marilyn Rauth, Judith Raybern, Mary Reese, Richard Rice, Wallace Saval, John Saxon, Jan Schwab, Ted Sharp, Diana Smith, Richard Smith, Trevanian Smith, Carol Stevens, Nancy Summers, Michael Terry, Robert Todd, Elois Veltman, Sharon Walker, Mary Ann Ward, Penny Williams, Charles Whitten, Clarke Worthington, Jane York

Schools: Special thanks to Three Oaks Elementary for piloting the original *Core Knowledge Sequence* in 1990. And thanks to the schools that have offered their advice and suggestions for improving the *Core Knowledge Sequence*, including (in alphabetical order): Academy Charter School (CO); Coleman Elementary (TX); Coral Reef Elementary (FL); Coronado Village Elementary (TX); Crooksville Elementary (OH); Crossroads Academy (NH); Gesher Jewish Day School (VA); Hawthorne Elementary (TX); Highland Heights Elementary (IN); Joella Good Elementary (FL); Mohegan School-CS 67 (NY); The Morse School (MA); Nichols Hills Elementary (OK); North East Elementary (MD); Ridge View Elementary (WA); R. N. Harris Elementary (NC); Southside Elementary (FL); Thomas Johnson Elementary (MD); Three Oaks Elementary (FL); Vienna Elementary (MD); Washington Core Knowledge School (CO). And to the many other schools teaching Core Knowledge—too many to name here, and some of whom we have yet to discover—our heartfelt thanks for "sharing the knowledge"!

Benefactors: The Brown Foundation, The Challenge Foundation, Mrs. E. D. Hirsch, Sr., The Walton Family Foundation.

Our grateful acknowledgment to these persons does not imply that we have taken their (sometimes conflicting) advice in every case, or that each of them endorses all aspects of this project. Responsibility for final decisions must rest with the editors alone. Suggestions for improvements are very welcome, and we wish to thank in advance those who send advice for revising and improving this series.

This book is dedicated, gratefully, to
Linda and Gerald

A Note to Teachers

We hope you will find this book useful, especially those of you who are teaching in the growing network of Core Knowledge schools. Throughout the book, we have addressed the suggested activities and explanations to "parents," since you as teachers know your students and will have ideas about how to use the content of this book in relation to the lessons and activities you plan. If you are interested in the ideas of teachers in Core Knowledge schools, please write or call the Core Knowledge Foundation (801 East High Street, Charlottesville, VA 22902; 434-977-7550) for information on ordering collections of lessons created and shared by teachers in Core Knowledge schools. Many of these teacher-created lessons are available through the Core Knowledge website at the following address: www.coreknowledge.org.

Author's earnings from sales of the Core Knowledge Series go to the nonprofit Core Knowledge Foundation. E. D. Hirsch, Jr., receives no remuneration for editing the series nor any other remuneration from the Core Knowledge Foundation.

Contents

I. Language and Literature

II. Geography and History

III. Visual Arts

IV. Music

V. Mathematics

VI. Science

General Introduction to the Series

Schools and Your Child

If Charles Dickens were alive today and observing the state of American schools, he might be tempted to note anew that it is the best of times and the worst of times. Seldom has there been more attention and energy aimed at our nation's education system. Unacceptable inequities in achievement between income and ethnic groups, long viewed with alarm, are being addressed with unprecedented urgency and resources. Years of dismay over lackluster performance have created a sense of crisis, even fear, that if we do not set our educational house in order, American competitiveness, our economy, and even our way of life are at risk. The response has been an unprecedented era of educational dynamism and innovation. Seen through this lens, it might seem to be the best of times for American education.

Yet for all our admirable focus, urgency, and investment, we have surprisingly little to show for it. Reading test scores for American seventeen-year-olds, the ultimate report card for our schools, have hardly budged in forty years. That's two generations with no discernible progress. How can this be? We have tried testing every child and holding teachers accountable. We have built charter schools and filled classrooms with computers. We have even made it the law of the land that every child read at grade level, but to no avail. Surely, it is the worst of times.

Do not blame teachers. They are among our most committed and generous-spirited citizens. We have not lacked urgency, idealism, or even resources. What we have lacked is a coherent plan for educating all children to proficiency.

The book you hold in your hands exemplifies an essential building block of that coherent plan.

Why Knowledge Matters in the Era of Google

American public education sprang from the nineteenth-century idea of the common school. We sent our children to learn reading and writing, but also a common curriculum of history, geography, math, and other subjects. Such schools also strived to create virtuous, civic-minded citizens for the new nation. As the United States matured and became more diverse, the idea of a common curriculum gradually melted away. Today, we have all but abandoned the idea that there is a body of knowledge that every child should learn in school, and that the broad mission of education is to maximize each individual's potential. However, there is good reason to believe that the idea of common schooling is even more relevant and effective today than ever before.

Ask yourself: Would I rather have my child go to school to gain knowledge of history, science, art, or music? Or should schools emphasize skills such as critical thinking and problem solving? The answer should ideally be both. Knowledge and skills are not two different things; they are two sides of the same coin. Thinking skills are what psychologists call "domain specific." In plain English, this means that you cannot think critically about a subject you know little about. If we want our children to be broadly competent readers, thinkers, and problem solvers, they must have a rich, broad store of background knowledge to call upon, enabling them to flex those mental muscles.

Unfortunately, too many of our schools have lost touch with this critical insight. It is commonly believed to be a fool's errand to think we can teach children all they need to know—far better simply to spark in children a lifelong love of learning. Indeed, many well-intentioned educators believe that the in-depth study of a few topics, practice with a variety of "thinking skills," and access to the Internet are all anyone needs today. Why clutter our minds with facts and trivia when you can just Google them? Today's classroom and curriculum, it is commonly argued, should be built around "twenty-first-century skills" such as media literacy and working cooperatively to solve "authentic" problems. These are the skills that will ensure them a lifetime of learning, productivity, and engaged citizenship. The rest is mere trivia. Right?

On its surface, the idea that skills are more important than knowledge has a basic, commonsense appeal. Why should your child learn about the American Revolution, the parts of an atom, or who painted the *Mona Lisa*? What child hasn't asked, "Why do we need to know this?" Unfortunately, this benign, even obvious-sounding idea contains a great paradox: it takes knowledge to gain knowledge. Those who repudiate a coherent, knowledge-rich curriculum on the grounds that you can always look things up have failed to learn an important lesson from cognitive science: deemphasizing factual knowledge prevents children from looking things up effectively. When you have just a little bit of information about a subject, you cannot evaluate the importance of new knowledge. When you know nothing, you're flying blind, like reading a book whose words you don't know. Thus, emphasizing procedural skill at the expense of factual knowledge hinders children from learning to learn. Yes, the Internet has placed a wealth of information at our fingertips. But to be able to use that information—to absorb it, to add to our knowledge—we must already possess a storehouse of knowledge. That is the paradox disclosed by cognitive research.

Common Knowledge, Not "One Size Fits All"

All children are different. Like the idea that skills are more important than knowledge, there is a warm, intuitive appeal to the idea that we should tailor schooling to allow every child to find what most excites and engages him and let those interests drive his "child-centered" education. But again, this ignores some fundamental facts about how we learn.

Language and vocabulary—like critical thinking and problem solving—also depend a great deal on a broad base of shared knowledge. When a sportscaster describes a surprising performance by an underdog basketball team as "a Cinderella story," or when a writer compares an ill-fated couple to Romeo and Juliet, they are making an assumption that their audience will know and understand the reference. So much of our language depends on a shared body of knowledge. Yes, you must know the words. But you must also understand the context in order to understand and be understood. The word "shot," for example, means something different in a doctor's office, on a basketball court, or when a technician says your dishwasher is beyond fixing. Fluency depends on context, and context is largely a function of shared background knowledge.

Yet it remains all too easy to deride a knowledge-rich curriculum as "mere facts" and "rote learning." The idea that there is a common body of knowledge that all children should know to enable them to read, communicate, and work cooperatively with others does sound old-fashioned. But the overwhelming evidence argues that this is precisely the case. Learning builds on learning: children (and adults) gain new knowledge only by building on what they already know. It is essential to begin building solid foundations of knowledge in the early grades, when children are most receptive, because for the vast majority of children, academic deficiencies from the first six grades can permanently impair the success of later learning. Poor performance of American students in middle and high school can be traced to shortcomings inherited from elementary schools that have not imparted to children the knowledge and skills they need for further learning.

All of the highest-achieving and most egalitarian elementary school systems in the world (such as those in Sweden, France, and Japan) teach their children a specific core of knowledge in each of the first six grades, thus enabling all children to enter each new grade with a secure foundation for further learning. U.S. schools, with their high student mobility rates, would especially benefit from a carefully sequenced core curriculum in the elementary and middle school years.

Commonly Shared Knowledge Makes Schooling More Effective

We know that the one-on-one tutorial is the most effective form of schooling, in part because a parent or teacher can provide tailor-made instruction for the individual child. But in a non-tutorial situation—in, for example, a typical classroom with twenty-five or more students—the instructor cannot effectively impart new knowledge to all the students unless each one shares the background knowledge upon which the instructor is building the lesson.

Consider this scenario. In third grade, Ms. Franklin is about to begin a unit on early explorers—Columbus, Magellan, and others. In her class, she has some students who were in Mr. Washington's second-grade class last year and some students who were in Ms. Johnson's second-grade class. She also has a few students who have moved in from other towns. As Ms. Franklin begins the unit on explorers, she asks the children to look at a globe and use their fingers to trace a route across the Atlantic Ocean from Europe to North America. The students who had Mr. Washington look blankly at her: they didn't learn that last year. The students who had Ms. Johnson, however, eagerly point to the proper places on the globe, while two of the students who came from other towns pipe up and say, "Columbus and Magellan again? We did that last year."

When all the students in a class share the relevant background knowledge, a classroom can begin to approach the effectiveness of a tutorial. Even when some children in a class do not have elements of the knowledge they were supposed to acquire in previous grades, the existence of a specifically defined core makes it possible for the teacher or parent to identify and fill the gaps, giving all students a chance to fulfill their potentials in later grades.

Commonly Shared Knowledge Makes Schooling Fairer and More Democratic

When all the children who enter a grade can be assumed to share some of the same building blocks of knowledge, and when the teacher knows exactly what those building blocks are, then all the students are empowered to learn. In our current system, children from disadvantaged backgrounds too often suffer from unmerited low expectations that translate into watered-down curricula. But if we specify the core of knowledge that all children should share, then we can guarantee equal access to that knowledge and compensate for the academic advantages some students are offered at home. In a Core Knowledge school, all children enjoy the benefits of important, challenging knowledge that will provide the foundation for successful later learning.

Commonly Shared Knowledge Helps Create Cooperation and Solidarity in Our Schools and Nation

Diversity is a hallmark and strength of our nation. American classrooms are usually made up of students from a variety of cultural backgrounds, and those different cultures should be honored by all students. At the same time, education should create a school-based culture that is common and welcoming to all because it includes knowledge of many cultures and gives all students, no matter what their background, a common foundation for understanding our cultural diversity.

Commonly Shared Knowledge Creates the Conditions That Make Higher-Order Thinking Possible

"We don't just read about science. We do science," a teacher in New York City recently wrote. One of the greatest misconceptions in contemporary education is the idea that in order to best prepare students for college and careers, we should train them to "think like an expert." In other words, we should help them understand and practice what scientists, historians, and other highly skilled professionals do. But it is clear from cognitive science that to think like an expert, you must know what the expert knows. Unfortunately, there are no shortcuts to expertise. Deep knowledge and practice are essential. Yet our schools, under the mistaken idea that knowledge is less important than skills, try to teach children to engage learning by doing, under the assumption that skills trump knowledge. They do not. You cannot have one without the other.

All of our most cherished goals for education—reading with understanding, critical thinking, and problem solving—are what psychologists call "domain-specific" skills. Simply put, there is no such thing as an all-purpose critical thinker or problem solver. Such skills are a function of your background knowledge.

What Knowledge Needs to Be Taught?

One of the primary objections to a content-rich vision of education is that it offends our democratic sensibilities. The title of this book—*What Your Fourth Grader Needs to Know*—can easily be viewed as presumptuous: "Who are you to say what knowledge matters? Why do you get to decide what goes in my child's curriculum and what gets left out?" Deciding what we want our children to know can be a politically and emotionally charged minefield. No grade-by-grade sequence of knowledge or course of study will satisfy everyone. But it is educationally reckless to ignore what we know about the importance of a broad knowledge base. The effort may be difficult, but we are duty-bound to try.

The content in this and other volumes in the Core Knowledge Series is based on a document called the *Core Knowledge Sequence*, a document of specific grade-by-grade content guidelines in history, geography, mathematics, science, language arts, and fine arts. As the core of a school's curriculum, it offers a solid, coherent foundation of learning while allowing flexibility to meet local needs. The entire sequence, from preschool to eighth grade, can be downloaded for free at the Core Knowledge Foundation's website, www.coreknowledge.org/download-the-sequence.

The Core Knowledge Foundation invested a considerable amount of time, energy, and resources in an attempt to find a consensus on the most enabling knowledge—the content that would most enable all children to read, write, listen, and speak with understanding.

Shortly after the establishment of the Core Knowledge Foundation in 1987, we analyzed the many reports issued by state departments of education and by professional organizations—such as the National Council of Teachers of Mathematics and the American Association for the Advancement of Science—that recommend general outcomes for elementary and secondary education. We also tabulated the knowledge and skills, through grade 6, specified in the successful educational systems of several other countries, including France, Japan, Sweden, and Germany.

In addition, we formed an advisory board on multiculturalism that proposed a specific knowledge of diverse cultural traditions that all American children should share as part of their school-based common culture. We sent the resulting materials to three independent groups of teachers, scholars, and scientists across the country, asking them to create a master list of the knowledge children should have by the end of grade 6. About 150 education professionals (including college professors, scientists, and administrators) were involved in this initial step.

These items were amalgamated into a master plan, and further groups of teachers and specialists were asked to agree on a grade-by-grade sequence of the items. That sequence was then sent to some one hundred educators and specialists who participated in a national conference to hammer out a working agreement on an appropriate core of knowledge for the first six grades; kindergarten, grades 7 and 8, and preschool were subsequently added to the sequence.

This important meeting took place in March 1990. The conferees were elementary school teachers, curriculum specialists, scientists, science writers, officers of national organizations, representatives of ethnic groups, district superintendents, and school principals from across the country. A total of twenty-four working groups decided on revisions in the *Core Knowledge Sequence.* The resulting provisional sequence was further fine-tuned during a year of implementation at a pioneering school, Three Oaks Elementary, in Lee County, Florida.

In only a few years, many more schools—urban and rural, rich and poor, public and private—joined in the effort to teach Core Knowledge. Based largely on suggestions from these schools, the *Core Knowledge Sequence* was revised in 1995; separate guidelines were added for kindergarten, and a few topics in other grades were added, omitted, or moved from one grade to another to create an even more coherent sequence for learning. Because the sequence is intended to be a living document that provides a foundation of knowledge that speakers and writers assume their audiences know, it has been—and will continue to be—periodically updated and revised. In general, however, there is more stability than change in the sequence.

The purpose of the *Core Knowledge Sequence* is not to impose a canon. It is an attempt to *report* on a canon—to identify the most valuable, empowering knowledge across subject areas, and to create a plan for imparting it from the first days of school.

Knowledge Still Matters

This book, as well as the work of the Core Knowledge Foundation and the efforts of Core Knowledge teachers in hundreds of schools nationwide, swims strongly against the anti-knowledge tide of mediocrity that threatens to drag down our schools, our children, and ultimately our nation.

A broad, rich store of background knowledge is not merely nice to have. Knowledge is the essential raw material of thinking. Cognitive scientist Daniel Willingham observes, "Knowledge is not only cumulative, it grows exponentially. Those with a rich base of factual knowledge find it easier to learn more—the rich get richer. In addition, factual knowledge enhances cognitive processes such as problem solving and reasoning. The richer the knowledge base, the more smoothly and effectively these cognitive processes—the very ones that teachers target—operate. So, the more knowledge students accumulate, the smarter they become."

If all of our children are to be fully educated and participate equally in civic life, then we must provide each of them with the shared body of knowledge that makes literacy and communication possible. This concept, so central to the new Common Core State Standards adopted by more than forty states, and to the Core Knowledge Foundation's goal of equity and excellence in education, manifests itself in the *Core Knowledge Sequence*—and in these popular grade-by-grade books. It is a pleasure to introduce this latest refinement of them to a new generation of readers.

E. D. Hirsch, Jr.
Charlottesville, Virginia

I
Language and Literature

Reading, Writing, and Your Fourth Grader: A Note to Parents

In this chapter, you and your child will learn to appreciate the magic of words, travel to other worlds without leaving the room, and understand how words work together to create meaning. This chapter presents a rich and varied selection of literature, including poems and stories. You will also read brief discussions of grammar and writing and explanations of common sayings and phrases.

By the end of fourth grade, students should be able to engage in the mental process of turning letters into sounds automatically. This year, they will focus more on meaning as they read, extending their vocabulary and understanding of the texts. Asking questions is a good way to draw your children into a story. Here are a few that work well:

"What do you think is going to happen next?"

"How might the story have turned out differently if . . . ?"

"What did you hear/read that makes you believe that . . . ?"

"What does the author mean by the statement . . . ?"

"How is this story similar to . . . ?"

You might also ask your child to retell the story. You can even encourage your child to change events or characters: this is a rich tradition of storytelling and explains why there are so many versions of traditional stories.

You may also encourage your child to write and illustrate her own stories. Some children may be interested in beginning to keep a journal or writing letters to friends or relatives—these are both fine ways for children to cultivate their writing skills. Another way to build vocabulary and foster language skills is by playing word games such as Scrabble, Boggle, or hangman and doing crossword puzzles. You can download many of these popular word games on tablet devices and computers.

Experts say our children already know more about grammar than we can ever teach them. But standard written language does have special characteristics that children need to learn. The treatment of grammar and language conventions in this book is an overview. It needs to be supplemented and rounded out by giving your child opportunities to read and write and to discuss reading and writing in connection with grammar and spelling.

At school, children should be working on vocabulary and spelling in the fourth grade. They should enjoy a rich diet of fiction, poetry, drama, biography, and nonfiction. They should be involved in the writing process, inventing topics, discovering ideas in early drafts, and revising toward "publication" of polished final drafts—all with encouragement and guidance along the way. They should practice writing in many modes, including stories, poetry, journal entries, formal reports, dialogues, and descriptions.

For some children, the section on sayings and phrases may not be needed; they will have picked up these sayings by hearing them in everyday speech. But this section will be useful for children from homes where American English is not spoken.

For additional resources to use in conjunction with this section, visit the Core Knowledge Foundation's website at www.coreknowledge.org.

Literature

Introduction

This selection of poetry, stories, and myths can, in most cases, be read independently by fourth graders. We hope you'll take this as a starting point in your search for more literature for your child to read and enjoy.

We have included both poetry and prose. The best way to help children appreciate the spirit of poetry is to read it aloud to them and encourage them to speak it aloud so that they can experience the music in the words. Until children take pleasure in the sound of poetry, there is little reason to analyze it technically.

Most of the stories in this book are either excerpts from longer works or abridged versions of those works. If a child enjoys a particular story, he should be encouraged to read a longer version. Several of the novels excerpted here are available in child-friendly versions as part of the Core Knowledge Foundation's *Core Classics* series, available for purchase through the foundation's website, www.coreknowledge.org.

This book continues the effort, begun in previous books, to allow you to coordinate readings about literature and other subjects, including history, visual arts, music, and science. These stories and poems also give you the opportunity to discuss the value of virtues, such as friendship, courage, and honesty, with your child.

Poetry

Monday's Child Is Fair of Face
(author unknown)

Monday's child is fair of face,
Tuesday's child is full of grace,
Wednesday's child is full of woe,
Thursday's child has far to go,
Friday's child is loving and giving,
Saturday's child works hard for a living,
But the child that is born on the Sabbath day
Is fair and wise and good and gay.

Humanity

by Elma Stuckey

If I am blind and need someone
To keep me safe from harm,
It matters not the race to me
Of the one who takes my arm.

If I am saved from drowning
As I grasp and grope,
I will not stop to see the face
Of the one who throws the rope.

Or if out on some battlefield
I'm falling faint and weak,
The one who gently lifts me up
May any language speak.

We sip the water clear and cool,
No matter the hand that gives it.
A life that's lived worthwhile and fine,
What matters the one who lives it?

Talk and Think

Explain to your child that a theme is a central idea or message that an author hopes the reader will take away from a story or poem. Ask your child: "What do you think is the theme of Elma Stuckey's poem 'Humanity'?"

Fog

by Carl Sandburg

The fog comes
on little cat feet.

It sits looking
over harbor and city
on silent haunches
and then moves on.

Clouds

by Christina G. Rossetti

White sheep, white sheep
On a blue hill,
When the wind stops
You all stand still.
When the wind blows,
You walk away slow.
White sheep, white sheep,
Where do you go?

Make a Connection
Clouds can look like sheep in the sky! After reading the poem "Clouds" with your child, turn to pages 424–425 to teach her about the science of clouds.

the drum

by Nikki Giovanni

daddy says the world is
a drum tight and hard
and i told him
i'm gonna beat
out my own rhythm

Things

by Eloise Greenfield

Went to the corner
Walked in the store
Bought me some candy
Ain't got it no more
Ain't got it no more

Went to the beach
Played on the shore
Built me a sandhouse
Ain't got it no more
Ain't got it no more

Went to the kitchen
Lay down on the floor
Made me a poem
Still got it
Still got it

Dreams

by Langston Hughes

Hold fast to dreams
For if dreams die
Life is a broken-winged bird
That cannot fly.

Hold fast to dreams
For when dreams go
Life is a **barren** field
Frozen with snow.

New Word

Does your child know the word **barren**? Explain to your child that "barren" means not able to produce life. In the poem "Dreams," Langston Hughes uses the line "Life is a barren field" to help the reader imagine the emptiness of a life without dreams.

Afternoon on a Hill

by Edna St. Vincent Millay

I will be the gladdest thing
Under the sun!
I will touch a hundred flowers
And not pick one.

I will look at cliffs and clouds
With quiet eyes,
Watch the wind bow down the grass,
And the grass rise.

And when lights begin to show,
Up from the town,
I will mark which must be mine,
And then start down.

The Rhinoceros

by Ogden Nash

The rhino is a homely beast,
For human eyes he's not a feast.
But you and I will never know
Why Nature chose to make him so.
Farewell, farewell, you old rhinoceros,
I'll stare at something less prepoceros.

Talk and Think

Point out the word "prepoceros" to your child in the poem "The Rhinoceros." Explain that the poet has invented a new spelling for a real word. "Prepoceros" resembles the word "preposterous." Does your child know what the word "preposterous" means? "Preposterous" can mean "ridiculous" or "unbelievable." Ask your child:
Why might the poet think the rhinoceros is a preposterous sight?
Why might he have chosen to spell "preposterous" in such an unusual way?

The Pobble Who Has No Toes

by Edward Lear

The Pobble who has no toes,
  Had once as many as we;
When they said, "Some day you may lose them all";
  He replied, "Fish Fiddle de-dee!"
And his Aunt Jobiska made him drink,
Lavender water tinged with pink;
For she said, "The World in general knows
There's nothing so good for a Pobble's toes!"

The Pobble who has no toes,
  Swam across the Bristol Channel;
But before he set out he wrapped his nose
  In a piece of scarlet flannel.
For his Aunt Jobiska said, "No harm
Can come to his toes if his nose is warm;
And it's perfectly known that a Pobble's toes
Are safe—provided he minds his nose."

The Pobble swam fast and well.
  And when boats or ships came near him,
He tinkledy-binkledy-winkled a bell,
  So that all the world could hear him.
And all the Sailors and Admirals cried,
When they saw him nearing the further side—
"He has gone to fish, for his Aunt Jobiska's
Runcible Cat with crimson whiskers!"

But before he touched the shore—
    The shore of the Bristol Channel,
A sea-green Porpoise carried away
    His wrapper of scarlet flannel.
And when he came to observe his feet,
Formerly garnished with toes so neat,
His face at once became forlorn,
On perceiving that all his toes were gone!

And nobody knew,
    From that dark day to the present,
Whoso had taken the Pobble's toes,
    In a manner so far from pleasant.
Whether the shrimps, or crawfish gray,
Or crafty Mermaids stole them away—
Nobody knew; and nobody knows
How the Pobble was robbed of his twice five toes!

The Pobble who has no toes
    Was placed in a friendly Bark,
And they rowed him back, and carried him up
    To his Aunt Jobiska's Park.
And she made him a feast at his earnest wish
Of eggs and buttercups fried with fish,
And she said, "It's a fact the whole world knows,
That Pobbles are happier without their toes."

A Tragic Story

by William Makepeace Thackeray

There lived a **sage** in days of yore,
And he a handsome pigtail wore;
But wondered much, and sorrowed more,
   Because it hung behind him.

He mused upon this curious case,
And swore he'd change the pigtail's place,
And have it hanging at his face,
   Not dangling there behind him.

Says he, "The mystery I've found—
I'll turn me round,"—he turned him round;
   but still it hung behind him.

Then round, and round, and out and in,
All day the puzzled sage did spin;
In vain—it mattered not a pin—
   The pigtail hung behind him.

And right and left, and round about,
And up and down, and in and out
He turned; but still the pigtail stout
   Hung steadily behind him.

And though his efforts never slack,
And though he twist, and twirl, and tack,
Alas! Still faithful to his back,
   The pigtail hangs behind him.

> **New Word**
> Does your child know two meanings of the word **sage**? Tell your child that a sage is a wise person. Sage is also an herb used in cooking.

The Ecchoing Green

by William Blake

The sun does arise,
And make happy the skies.
The merry bells ring
To welcome the Spring.
The sky-lark and thrush,
The birds of the bush,
Sing louder around,
To the bells' cheerful sound.
While our sports shall be seen
On the Ecchoing Green.

Old John, with white hair
Does laugh away care,
Sitting under the oak,
Among the old folk,
They laugh at our play,
And soon they all say.
"Such, such were the joys.
When we all girls & boys,
In our youth-time were seen,
On the Ecchoing Green."

Till the little ones weary
No more can be merry
The sun does descend,
And our sports have an end:
Round the laps of their mothers,
Many sisters and brothers,
Like birds in their nest,
Are ready for rest;
And sport no more seen,
On the darkening Green.

Talk and Think

The poet, William Blake, spells "echoing" a bit different than we do today. You may wish to show your child, explain the difference, and also explain that before dictionaries became popular, many people spelled words in different ways. Ask your child how he would have spelled the word "echoing" based on the sounds that make up the word.

Paul Revere's Ride

by Henry Wadsworth Longfellow

Listen, my children, and you shall hear
Of the midnight ride of Paul Revere,
On the eighteenth of April, in Seventy-five;
Hardly a man is now alive
Who remembers that famous day and year.

He said to his friend, "If the British march
By land or sea from the town to-night,
Hang a lantern aloft in the belfry arch
Of the North Church tower as a signal-light,—
One, if by land, and two, if by sea;
And I on the opposite shore will be,
Ready to ride and spread the alarm
Through every Middlesex village and farm,
For the country folk to be up and to arm."

Then he said "Good night!" and with muffled oar
Silently rowed to the Charlestown shore,
Just as the moon rose over the bay,
Where swinging wide at her moorings lay
The *Somerset*, British man-of-war:
A phantom ship, with each mast and spar
Across the moon like a prison bar,
And a huge black hulk, that was magnified
By its own reflection in the tide.

Meanwhile, his friend, through alley and street,
Wanders and watches with eager ears,
Till in the silence around him he hears
The muster of men at the barrack door,

The sound of arms, and the tramp of feet,
And the measured tread of the grenadiers,
Marching down to their boats on the shore.

Then he climbed to the tower of the Old North Church,
By the wooden stairs, with stealthy tread,
To the belfry-chamber overhead,
And startled the pigeons from their perch
On the somber rafters, that round him made
Masses and moving shapes of shade—
By the trembling ladder, steep and tall
To the highest window in the wall,
Where he paused to listen and look down
A moment on the roofs of the town,
And the moonlight flowing over all.

Beneath, in the churchyard, lay the dead,
In their night-encampment on the hill,
Wrapped in silence so deep and still
That he could hear, like a sentinel's tread,
The watchful night-wind, as it went
Creeping along from tent to tent,
And seeming to whisper, "All is well!"
A moment only he feels the spell
Of the place and the hour, and the secret dread
Of the lonely belfry and the dead;
For suddenly all his thoughts are bent
On a shadowy something far away,
Where the river widens to meet the bay,—
A line of black, that bends and floats
On the rising tide, like a bridge of boats.

Meanwhile, impatient to mount and ride,
Booted and spurred, with a heavy stride,
On the opposite shore walked Paul Revere.
Now he patted his horse's side,
Now he gazed at the landscape far and near,
Then, impetuous, stamped the earth,
And turned and tightened his saddle-girth;
But mostly he watched with eager search
The belfry-tower of the Old North Church,
As it rose above the graves on the hill,
Lonely and spectral and somber and still.

And lo! as he looks, on the belfry's height
A glimmer, and then a gleam of light!
He springs to the saddle, the bridle he turns,
But lingers and gazes, till full on his sight
A second lamp in the belfry burns!
A hurry of hoofs in a village street,
A shape in the moonlight, a bulk in the dark,
And beneath, from the pebbles, in passing, a spark
Struck out by a steed flying fearless and fleet:
That was all! And yet, through the gloom and the light,
The fate of a nation was riding that night;
And the spark struck out by that steed, in his flight,
Kindled the land into flame with its heat.

He has left the village and mounted the steep,
And beneath him, tranquil and broad and deep,
Is the Mystic, meeting the ocean tides;
And under the alders that skirt its edge,
Now soft on the sand, now loud on the ledge,
Is heard the tramp of his steed as he rides.

It was twelve by the village clock

When he crossed the bridge into Medford town.

He heard the crowing of the cock,

And the barking of the farmer's dog,

And felt the damp of the river fog,

That rises after the sun goes down.

It was one by the village clock,

When he galloped into Lexington.

He saw the gilded weathercock

Swim in the moonlight as he passed,

And the meeting-house windows, blank and bare,

Gaze at him with a spectral glare,

As if they already stood aghast

At the bloody work they would look upon.

It was two by the village clock,

When he came to the bridge in Concord town.

He heard the bleating of the flock,

And the twitter of birds among the trees,

And felt the breath of the morning breeze

Blowing over the meadows brown.

And one was safe and asleep in his bed

Who at the bridge would be first to fall,

Who that day would be lying dead,

Pierced by a British musket-ball.

You know the rest. In the books you have read,

How the British Regulars fired and fled,—

How the farmers gave them ball for ball,

From behind each fence and farm-yard wall,

Chasing the red-coats down the lane,

Make a Connection

Read the poem "Paul Revere's Ride" with your child. Then, turn to page 169 and read "The Redcoats Are Coming!" Ask your child to compare the two stories. In what ways are they similar and different? Help your child to consider why "Paul Revere's Ride" is in the Literature section. Did the author know everything he wrote to be true, or was he trying to write a good story?

Then crossing the fields to emerge again
Under the trees at the turn of the road,
And only pausing to fire and load.

So through the night rode Paul Revere;
And so through the night went his cry of alarm
To every Middlesex village and farm,—
A cry of defiance and not of fear,
A voice in the darkness, a knock at the door,
And a word that shall echo forevermore!
For, borne on the night-wind of the Past,
Through all our history, to the last,
In the hour of darkness and peril and need,
The people will waken and listen to hear
The hurrying hoof-beats of that steed,
And the midnight message of Paul Revere.

Concord Hymn
by Ralph Waldo Emerson

By the rude bridge that arched the flood,
    Their flag to April's breeze unfurled,
Here once the embattled farmers stood,
    And fired the shot heard round the world.

The foe long since in silence slept;
    Alike the conqueror silent sleeps;
And Time the ruined bridge has swept
    Down the dark stream which seaward creeps.

On this green bank, by this soft stream,
    We set to-day a **votive** stone;
That memory may their deed redeem,
    When, like our sires, our sons are gone.

Spirit, that made those heroes dare
    To die, and leave their children free,
Bid Time and Nature gently spare
    The shaft we raise to them and thee.

New Word
Does your child know the word **votive**? The word describes something dedicated in the carrying out of a vow. Reread the third stanza and ask your child why the narrator sets a votive stone. What vow might the narrator be carrying out?

Lines and Stanzas

Poetry is made up of lines. Sometimes the lines of a poem are grouped into clusters called stanzas. In Ralph Waldo Emerson's "Concord Hymn," for example, there are four stanzas, each of which contains four lines. The first and third lines of each stanza rhyme, and so do the second and fourth.

George Washington

by Rosemary Benét and Stephen Vincent Benét

Sing hey! for bold George Washington,

That jolly British tar,

King George's famous admiral

From Hull to Zanzibar!

No—wait a minute—something's wrong—

George *wished* to sail the foam.

But, when his mother thought, aghast,

Of Georgie shinning up a mast,

Her tears and protests flowed so fast

That George remained at home.

Sing ho! for grave Washington,
The staid Virginia squire,
Who farms his fields and hunts his hounds
And aims at nothing higher!
Stop, stop, it's going wrong again!
George *liked* to live on farms,
But, when the Colonies agreed
They could and should and would be freed,
They called on George to do the deed
And George cried, "Shoulder arms!"

Sing ha! for Emperor Washington,
That hero of renown,
Who freed his land from Britain's rule
To win a golden crown!
No, no, that's what George *might* have won
But didn't, for he said,
"There's not much point about a king,
They're pretty but they're apt to sting,
And, as for crowns—the heavy thing
Would only hurt my head."

Sing ho! for our George Washington!
(At last I've got it straight.)
The first in war, the first in peace,
The goodly and the great.
But, when you think about him now,
From here to Valley Forge,
Remember this—he might have been
A highly different specimen,
And, where on earth would we be, then?
I'm glad that George was George.

Make a Connection

After reading the poem, turn to page 238 and identify George Washington in the painting. Ask your child to compare Washington's portrayal in the painting to his description in the poem. What is alike? What is different?

Stories and Myths

The Fire on the Mountain*

This story comes from an old Ethiopian folktale.

People say that in the old days in the city of Addis Ababa there was a young man by the name of Arha. He had come as a boy from the country of Guragé, and in the city he became the servant of a rich merchant, Haptom Hasei.

Haptom Hasei was so rich that he owned everything that money could buy, and often he was very bored because he had tired of everything he knew, and there was nothing new for him to do.

One cold night, when the damp wind was blowing across the plateau, Haptom called to Arha to bring wood for the fire. When Arha was finished, Haptom began to talk.

"How much cold can a man stand?" he said, speaking at first to himself. "I wonder if it would be possible for a man to stand on the highest peak, Mount Sululta, where the coldest winds blow, through an entire night without blankets or clothing and yet not die?"

"I don't know," Arha said. "But wouldn't it be a foolish thing?"

"Perhaps, if he had nothing to gain by it, it would be a foolish thing to spend the night that way," Haptom said. "But I would be willing to bet that a man couldn't do it."

"I am sure a courageous man could stand naked on Mount Sululta throughout an entire night and not die of it," Arha said. "But as for me, it isn't my affair since I've nothing to bet."

"Well, I'll tell you what," Haptom said. "Since you are sure it can be done, I'll make a bet with you anyway. If you can stand among the rocks on Mount Sululta for an entire night without food or water, or clothing or blankets or fire,

---

* "The Fire on the Mountain" from *The Fire on the Mountain and Other Stories from Ethiopia and Eritrea* by Harold Courlander and Wolf Leslau. Copyright © 1978 by Harold Courlander and Wolf Leslau. Reprinted by permission of The Emma Courlander Trust.

"Then I will give you ten acres of good farmland for your own, with a house and cattle."

and not die of it, then I will give you ten acres of good farmland for your own, with a house and cattle."

Arha could hardly believe what he had heard.

"Do you really mean this?" he asked.

"I am a man of my word," Haptom replied.

"Then tomorrow night I will do it," Arha said, "and afterward, for all the years to come, I shall till my own soil."

But he was very worried, because the wind swept bitterly across the peak. So in the morning Arha went to a wise old man from the Guragé tribe and told him of the bet he had made. The old man listened quietly and thoughtfully, and when Arha had finished he said:

"I will help you. Across the valley from Sululta is a high rock which can be seen in the daytime. Tomorrow night, as the sun goes down, I shall build a fire there, so that it can be seen from where you stand on the peak. All night long you must watch the light of my fire. Do not close your eyes or let the darkness creep

upon you. As you watch my fire, think of its warmth, and think of me, your friend, sitting there tending it for you. If you do this you will survive, no matter how bitter the night wind."

Arha thanked the old man warmly and went back to Haptom's house with a light heart. He told Haptom he was ready, and in the afternoon Haptom sent him, under the watchful eyes of other servants, to the top of Mount Sululta. There, as night fell, Arha removed his clothes and stood in the damp, cold wind that swept across the plateau with the setting sun. Across the valley, several miles away, Arha saw the light of his friend's fire, which shone like a star in the blackness.

The wind turned colder and seemed to pass through his flesh and chill the marrow in his bones. The rock on which he stood felt like ice. Each hour the cold numbed him more, until he thought he would never be warm again, but he kept his eyes upon the twinkling light across the valley, and remembered that his old friend sat there tending a fire for him. Sometimes wisps of fog blotted out the light, and then he strained to see until the fog passed. He sneezed and coughed and shivered, and began to feel ill. Yet all night through he stood there, and only when the dawn came did he put on his clothes and go down the mountain back to Addis Ababa.

Haptom was very surprised to see Arha, and he questioned his servants thoroughly.

"Did he stay all night without food or drink or blankets or clothing?"

"Yes," his servants said. "He did all of these things."

"Well, you are a strong fellow," Haptom said to Arha. "How did you manage to do it?"

"I simply watched the light of a fire on a distant hill," Arha said.

"What! You watched a fire? Then you lose the bet, and you are still my servant, and you own no land!"

"But this fire was not close enough to warm me, it was far across the valley!"

"I won't give you the land," Haptom said. "You didn't fulfill the conditions. It was only the fire that saved you."

Arha was very sad. He went again to his old friend of the Guragé tribe and told him what happened.

"Take the matter to the judge," the old man advised him.

Arha went to the judge and complained, and the judge sent for Haptom. When Haptom told his story, and the servants said once more that Arha had watched a distant fire across the valley, the judge said:

"No, you have lost, for Haptom Hasei's condition was that you must be without fire."

Once more Arha went to his old friend with the sad news that he was doomed to the life of a servant, as though he had not gone through the ordeal on the mountaintop.

"Don't give up hope," the old man said. "More wisdom grows wild in the hills than in any city judge."

He got up from where he sat and went to find a man named Hailu, in whose house he had been a servant when he was young. He explained to the good man about the bet between Haptom and Arha, and asked if something couldn't be done.

"Don't worry about it," Hailu said after thinking for a while. "I will take care of it for you."

Some days later Hailu sent invitations to many people in the city to come to a feast at his house. Haptom was among them, and so was the judge who had ruled Arha had lost the bet.

When the day of the feast arrived, the guests came riding on mules with fine trappings, their servants strung out behind them on foot. Haptom came with twenty servants, one of whom held a silk umbrella over his head to shade him from the sun, and four drummers played music that signified the great Haptom was here.

The guests sat on soft rugs laid out for them and talked. From the kitchen came the odors of wonderful things to eat: roast goat, roast corn and durra, pancakes called *injera* and many tantalizing sauces. The smell of the food only **accentuated** the hunger of the guests. Time passed. The food should have been served, but they did not see it, only smelled vapors that drifted from the kitchen. The evening came, and still no food was served. The guests began to whisper among themselves. It was very curious that the honorable Hailu had not had the food brought out. Still the smells came from the kitchen. At last one of the guests spoke out for all the others:

"Hailu, why do you do this to us? Why do you invite us to a feast and then serve us nothing?"

"Why, can't you smell the food?" Hailu asked with surprise.

"Indeed we can, but smelling is not eating; there is no nourishment in it!"

"And is there warmth in a fire so distant that it can hardly be seen?" Hailu asked. "If Arha was warmed by the fire he watched while standing on Mount Sululta, then you have been fed by the smells coming from my kitchen."

The people agreed with him; the judge now saw his mistake, and Haptom was shamed. He thanked Hailu for his advice and announced that Arha was then and there the owner of the land, the house, and the cattle.

Then Hailu ordered the food brought in, and the feast began.

Make a Connection

After reading "The Fire on the Mountain" with your child, turn to page 143 and read the passage "Aksum" about Ethiopia, where the story takes place.

The Wonderful Chuang Brocade

This folktale is from a region in southern China called Chuang. For thousands of years the people of China have been famous for their rich art in silken brocades. The Chuang people of Kwangsi province are especially well known for their beautiful designs and pictures. Some of them tell stories such as this one.

In this province, at the foot of high peaks, in a thatched cottage, lived an old widow with her three sons: Lemo, Letui, and Leju. The old mother was a most wonderful weaver of brocades, which merchants and folks bought from her to make vests, bedcovers, and blankets. Her sons were woodcutters.

One day the old mother went to sell a fine brocade she had made. In the merchant's shop hung a painting of wondrous beauty. It showed a village with a rich, tall palace with colorful gardens around it. Beautiful flowers and ripe vegetables were everywhere; ducks, chickens, and cows were all over. Never had she seen a more beautiful scene. Quickly she sold her brocade and bought the painting, forgetting the rice and other foods she needed.

At home she proudly showed the painting. "How happy I would be to live in that palace with its gardens," she said to her sons.

"That is a dream, *Ah-mee*," spoke Lemo, the oldest son.

"Maybe we will live in such a place in our next life," said Letui, her second son.

Then Leju, the youngest, said, "*Ah-mee*, you must weave a brocade just like the painting, and when you look at your work you will think you are living in the palace with those gardens."

"You are right, son," said the old mother, and she set to work at once.

Day in, day out, and nights as well, she worked at the wooden loom with silk threads, and the scenes of the painting grew in beauty on the brocade.

She never stopped working. Her old eyes hurt from the smoke of the pine-oil lamps, but she did not stop. After one year, tears filled her eyes, but instead of stopping, she put her tears into the brocade and made of them a singing river and a shining pool full of fishes. After two years, drops of blood fell from her eyes onto the brocade. Out of these she wove bright red flowers and a glowing sun.

So the old, near-blind mother worked for three years until she finished putting the painting into the brocade. The sons were so proud of her work, they took it out of their dark hut and put it in front of the door, where there was enough daylight to see and admire it. Everyone who saw it exclaimed, "What a wonderful Chuang brocade!"

All of a sudden a weird whirring wind came along and . . . *whisht!* it picked up the brocade and carried it high, high up into the sky and . . . the brocade disappeared.

The old mother fainted, everyone shouted . . . but the brocade was gone. The mother became very ill and no doctor could help her. She was forever crying for her brocade!

Seeing this, Lemo said, "Mother, stop grieving! I will find your beautiful brocade and bring it back to you."

"Go, son, and may good fortune go with you."

Lemo set out over mountains and across rivers. One day he came to a mountain pass, on one side of which stood a stone house. To the right was a stone horse, its mouth wide open, bent over an arbutus bush full of red berries.

At the door sat an old white-headed woman.

"Who are you and where are you going, young man?" she asked Lemo.

He told her the tale of his mother's beautiful brocade—how hard and long she had worked at it and how the wind had carried it away and how very ill she had become.

"Young Lemo, I know all this. The winds of the mountains tell me many things. Your brocade is now in the Sun Mountain of the East with the beautiful fairies who live there. They saw the brocade and sent the wind for it. They are

Make a Connection

In this story, the old mother weaves beautiful paintings called brocades, using silk fabric and threads. The use of silk to weave beautiful designs and pictures is a traditional Chinese art form. To learn more about Chinese art, turn to page 233.

now copying your mother's beautiful work, and you can get it back only with the help of the stone horse. But the horse will help you only if you give him two of your teeth for the ones he is missing in his mouth so that he can eat the berries from the arbutus bush. Then he will take you far and wide to the Sun Mountain in the East.

"On the way you will come to a mountain of leaping flames through which you must pass. You must do it in silence and without fear. If you cry out even once, you will turn into charcoal.

"Then you will come to a sea full of jagged ice with knife-cutting cold winds tearing at you, but you must not cry out or even shiver with cold. If you do, you will be crushed by the wild tossing ice and buried in the icy water.

"If you go through these trials, you will get your mother's brocade."

Lemo was silent. His face turned blue with fear and he hung his head and thought—for a long time. To lose his teeth and endure such terrible trials!

The old woman watched him. Then she said, "Son, your face tells your thoughts. It says: It is too much! But you tried, so there is a little iron box full of gold nuggets. Go back home and live well."

Lemo took the box and thanked her and left. But he was thinking hard. "If I go home I must share the gold with all my family! There will be little for me. . . . No! I will go to the city and live on my wealth!" So he turned his steps toward the big city.

The old mother waited and waited, pining for her beautiful brocade. "If only I could see it before I die," she cried continually.

Letui, her second son, said, "Mother, I will bring you your brocade," and he set off at once.

He, too, came to the stone house with the old lady and her stone horse, and she told him just what she had told Lemo.

Letui also thought and thought, and the old woman knew what was in his mind. "Son," she said, "I can tell you think the trials are too much for you, but you started bravely, so here is a little iron box with gold nuggets. Go back and live happily." But Letui thought as did Lemo, so instead of going home, he too turned toward the city.

At home the old mother waited, crying for her handiwork until her eyes gave out and she became completely blind!

Leju, the youngest son, said, "Mother, I will go on the road to find your beautiful brocade and bring it back to you. You will be with kind neighbors who will take care of you while I am away."

He bade her good cheer and went off. Like his brothers, he came to the stone house with the stone horse and the old woman. She told him how he could get the brocade only with the help of the horse, and of the dangers he must face.

Instead of thinking long as his brothers had, Leju gave two of his teeth to the horse and mounted it. The horse ate the berries and then went off swift as the wind. Horse and rider went through the burning mountain and the icy sea. But Leju sat firm on the horse, thinking only of helping his mother, and so he reached the Sun Mountain and the palace where the lovely fairies were busy copying *Ah-mee*'s masterpiece.

Leju spoke to them, telling them of his mother's sickness and blindness and of how she continued to cry for her lost brocade.

"We will finish copying your mother's wonderful work by tomorrow morning," said one of the maidens. "Then you can take it back to your *ah-mee*."

They gave him delicious fruits to eat, and he fell asleep. But during the night the fairies hung a big glowing pearl on the rafter and wove by its light.

A maiden in a red dress finished first. She looked at her own work and then at *Ah-mee*'s. She sighed, "I am afraid mine is not nearly as fine. I wish I could live in the beautiful place that is on her brocade." So she began weaving her own image right near the fish pond that *Ah-mee* had woven.

Leju slept in the palace of the fairies, but the next morning, before the maidens arose, he took his mother's brocade, mounted the stone horse, and in the wink of time they were back at the stone house, where the white-haired woman sat waiting for him.

"Leju, your mother is very ill," she said. "Hurry back. The sight of her brocade will bring her health." Then she took the two teeth from the horse's mouth and put them back into Leju's. Next she put a pair of magic deerskin shoes on his feet and bade him good luck.

The shoes were like wings and took him swiftly to his home, where his mother was lying in bed, thin as a stick and barely alive.

"Ah-mee," he shouted, "I have brought you your brocade. Here!"

No sooner did she touch it than she began to feel well again. Her eyes opened wide and once again she could see! She got up and took her beloved work out into the open sunshine and then . . . a miracle happened! The embroidery of her brocade became a real place. Trees! Flowers! All were there before the rich palace, and by the fish pond stood the lovely maiden in her red dress.

Leju married the maiden, and the two lived happily all their lives.

One day two beggars came to their village. They were Lemo and Letui. They had spent all their gold, drinking, eating, and making merry in the city, and now they were dressed in rags and begging for food. When they saw the beautiful garden where *Ah-mee*, Leju, and his wife were walking and singing, they quietly slipped away, too ashamed to face their mother and brother.

King Arthur and the Knights of the Round Table

Old legends tell of an ancient British king named Arthur and of his queen, Guinevere. The legends tell how they held court at Camelot, where they were attended by the famous Knights of the Round Table. These knights upheld the code of chivalry, defending the defenseless and fighting for justice.

Arthur himself was the son of King Uther Pendragon. To protect his son, King Pendragon put Arthur in the care of Merlin, a sorcerer. Merlin could cast magic spells and change his appearance to look like an animal or another person. He was also called a seer because he could see the future—for everyone except himself. Merlin allowed Arthur to be raised by a knight, Sir Ector. Sir Ector did not know that Arthur was the king's son, and Arthur did not know this, either.

When Arthur was still a very young man, King Pendragon died, leaving no other heir to the throne. The British lords began to feud with each other over who should be king. The feuding went on until one Christmas day something amazing happened. As the lords came out of church, they found a square marble stone in the churchyard. In the middle of it was an anvil and into the anvil was thrust a sword. The stone gripped the naked sword by the point, and on the blade was written in gold letters: *Whosoever pulls out this sword from this stone and anvil is the true-born king of Britain.*

All of the great lords tried to pull out the sword, but all failed. When all of the great men had tried, Arthur grasped the sword by the hilt and gave it a light, quick pull—and out it came. The great men of the kingdom were astonished, and they knelt before Arthur and acknowledged him as the rightful king of Britain.

A few weeks later, Arthur and Merlin were out riding when they came to a lake in the middle of which Arthur saw a sight as strange as the stone and anvil in the churchyard. Rising out of the water was an arm clothed in soft white silk holding a sword. Farther off, Arthur saw a boat move across the water with a damsel in it.

"That is the Lady of the Lake," said Merlin. "Speak well to her and she will give you her sword."

The boat approached the land, and the lady greeted Arthur.

"Damsel," he replied, "what sword is that, that yonder arm holds above the water? I wish it were mine, for at the moment I have none."

"Sir Arthur, king," she answered, "that sword is mine, and if you will give me a gift when I ask, you shall have it."

Arthur replied, "I will give you whatever gift you shall ask for."

"Very well," she said, "get into the boat and row to the sword. Take it with you."

So Arthur and Merlin tied up their horses and rowed across the lake to the mysterious arm. As soon as Arthur grasped the hilt of the sword, the hand let go and the arm sank back into the water. As they rowed back to the shore, the king examined the sword and saw that it was truly magnificent. Its name was carved into the blade—Excalibur. It would be Arthur's sword in many battles to come.

Arthur chose the Lady Guinevere as his wife and queen and received his famous round table as a gift from Guinevere's father. Arthur's knights met at the round table to discuss important affairs.

Talk and Think

Ask your child why she thinks that the Round Table was made to be round.

Of all the Knights of the Round Table, Sir Lancelot was the bravest and strongest. No knight had ever defeated Lancelot in combat. On horse or on foot, he was the champion. He was the king's dear friend. He would help any woman in need, but he had sworn a special, lifelong vow of service to Guinevere.

One night Lancelot was staying in a castle where an elderly couple had given him shelter. After dinner, Lancelot put his armor and sword beside him and soon fell asleep in his upstairs room.

During the night a violent knocking on the gate below woke him. He ran to the window and, by the light of the moon, saw a knight being chased by other knights. Lancelot donned his armor, tied his bedsheet to the window, and slid down. He strode right into the middle of the fighting knights. To his surprise, he noticed the single knight's shield to be that of Sir Kay, the king's steward. Lancelot leaped at the three knights and in seven strokes he beat them all to the ground.

"Sir knight," they said, "we yield to you as to a champion of unmatched strength."

He answered, "I will not accept your yielding to me. You must yield to this knight or else I will kill you."

"Fair knight, we cannot do that, because we would have beaten that knight if you had not come," the three knights said.

"Well, you can choose whether you will die or live," said Sir Lancelot. "If you yield, it must be to Sir Kay."

So the three yielded to Sir Kay, and Sir Lancelot ordered them to go to the court at Camelot and beg the queen for mercy, saying that Sir Kay sent them there as her prisoners.

Over the years Lancelot sent many a defeated knight to Camelot, commanding each to bow down before Guinevere. Eventually, however, the love between Lancelot and Guinevere helped tear Camelot apart. Lancelot and Arthur, who had once been best friends, fought many battles against each other, and the kingdom again descended into turmoil. During one battle, Arthur was mortally wounded.

Although Camelot ended unhappily, people still remember it as a time of peace and nobility, when chivalry shone as brightly as a polished suit of armor and adventure was always waiting around the next turn in the road.

Saint George and the Dragon

Saint George, the patron saint of England, traveled around the world doing chivalrous deeds. Once, in Africa, he spent a night at an old hermit's house.

"Sir knight," said the hermit, "I am sorry that it is your destiny to arrive in our country at a time when we are in great distress. We are cursed with a terrible dragon. Every day we must present this monster with a young girl, whom the beast devours. If we fail to do this, the dragon blows such a horrible stench from its nostrils that disease sweeps through the land. This dragon has devoured almost all of the young girls in our country, and tomorrow the king's own daughter is to be sacrificed to the monster. Therefore the king has proclaimed that if any knight is so adventurous as to combat with this dragon and preserve his daughter's life, that man shall have great rewards."

New Word

Does your child know the word **enterprise**? Explain to your child that it is an activity that is often difficult.

Hearing this, Saint George made a solemn vow that he would either save the king's daughter or lose his life in that honorable **enterprise**. In the morning he buckled on his armor, mounted his horse, and had the old hermit guide him to the place where the sacrifices were made. As they approached the spot, the knight saw a beautiful damsel, dressed like a bride in pure Arabian silk, being led to the sacrifice. He told the princess to return to her father's palace. He would fight the dragon and save her from her cruel fate.

Then the noble knight rode into the valley where the dragon had its lair. When the dragon saw him, it made a hideous roaring noise, loud as thunder. The dragon was fearful to behold. It was fifty feet long with scales of glittering silver. The beast swung its powerful tail and smote the knight so hard that both horse and rider were thrown to the ground. Two of Saint George's ribs were broken in the fall, but the brave knight did not give up. He prayed to God to give him the strength and agility to slay the monster. Then with a bold, courageous heart, he charged the beast and drove his spear into a soft spot under the dragon's wing, where there were no scales. The spear found its way to the dragon's heart, and the dying beast sent forth a gushing stream of purple gore.

When the king heard what the knight had done, he offered him a large reward. But Saint George refused to take the money. He encouraged the king to give the money to the poor. Then he mounted his horse and rode away, in search of further noble adventures.

Robin Hood

(Excerpt from the novel by J. Walker McSpadden)

English legends tell of a great outlaw hero named Robin Hood, who is said to have lived in England in the Middle Ages. Robin Hood lived in Sherwood Forest with his band of merry men, hunting for deer with his bow and arrow, stealing from the rich and giving to the poor, and doing battle with the wicked Sheriff of Nottingham.

One day Robin Hood was walking along a path in Sherwood Forest when he saw a little footbridge that led across a stream. As he drew near the bridge, he saw a tall stranger coming from the other side. Robin quickened his pace, and the stranger did likewise, each thinking to cross first. They met at the middle of the log, and neither would yield an inch.

"Give way, fellow!" roared Robin.

The stranger smiled. He was almost a head taller than Robin. "Nay!" he retorted. "I give way only to a better man than myself."

"Give way, I say," repeated Robin, "or I shall have to show you a better man."

His opponent budged not an inch but laughed loudly. "Now," he said good-naturedly, "I'll not move after hearing that speech, even if I might have before. I have sought this better man my whole life long. Therefore show him to me."

"That I will right soon," said Robin. "Stay

Talk and Think

In the story, Robin's opponent speaks to him good-naturedly. Point out the word "good-naturedly" in the story and ask your child to think about how it hints at the outcome of the story.

here while I cut a cudgel like that you have been twiddling in your fingers." So saying, he leapt to his own bank again and cut a stout staff of oak, a good six feet in length. Then back he came boldly, whirling the staff above his head and calling, "Make ready for the tune I am about to play upon your ribs! One! Two!"

"Three!" roared the giant, striking at Robin mightily.

The fight was fast and furious. It was strength pitted against skill. The mighty blows of the stranger went whistling around Robin's ducking head, while his own swift undercuts gave the stranger an attack of indigestion. Yet each stood firmly in his place, not moving backward or forward a foot for a good half hour. The giant's face was getting red, and his breath came snorting forth like a bull's. Robin dodged his blows lightly, then sprang in swiftly and unexpectedly and gave the stranger a wicked blow upon the ribs.

The stranger reeled and nearly fell but regained his footing.

"By my life, you can hit hard!" he gasped, giving back a blow as he staggered.

That blow was a lucky one. It caught Robin off his guard, striking him on the head and dropping him neatly into the stream.

The cool, rushing current quickly brought him to his senses. But he was still so dazed that he groped blindly for the swaying reeds to pull himself up on the bank. His opponent could not help laughing heartily, but he also thrust down his long staff to Robin, crying, "Lay hold of that!"

Robin took hold and was hauled to dry land like a fish. He lay on the warm bank awhile to regain his senses; then he sat up and rubbed his head.

"By all saints," said he, "my head hums like a beehive on a summer morning."

Then he picked up his horn, which lay nearby, and blew three **shrill** notes that echoed among the trees. A moment of silence followed, then the rustling of leaves and crackling of twigs could be heard, and from the glade two dozen yeomen burst, all clad in Lincoln green like Robin.

"Good master," cried the man named Will Stutely, "how is this? There is not a dry thread on you."

"This fellow would not let me pass the footbridge," replied Robin, "and

> **New Word**
>
> Does your child know what the word **shrill** means? Explain to her that a shrill sound is one that is high-pitched or piercing and usually unpleasant.

when I tickled him on the ribs, he answered with a pat on my head that sent me into the stream."

"Then shall he taste some of his own porridge," said Will. "Seize him, lads!"

"Nay, let him go free," said Robin. "The fight was a fair one. Are you ready to quit?" he continued, turning to the stranger with a twinkling eye.

"I am content," said the other, "for I like you well and wish to know your name."

"My men, and even the Sheriff of Nottingham, know me as Robin Hood the outlaw."

"Then am I right sorry that I beat you," exclaimed the man, "for I was on my way to join your company. But now that I have used my staff on you I fear you will not have me."

"Nay, never say it," cried Robin. "I am glad you fell in with me, though I did all the falling!"

As the others laughed, the two men clasped hands, and the strong friendship of a lifetime began.

Robinson Crusoe

(Retold from the novel by Daniel Defoe)

The English writer Daniel Defoe wrote Robinson Crusoe *(1719) after hearing the story of a Scottish man who lived alone on a deserted island for almost five years. Defoe began with the factual story, imagined how such a character must have felt, and added elements of danger and adventure to make a fictional story that readers would enjoy.*

What About You?

Ask your child: "What would you do to survive if you were stranded on an island like Robinson Crusoe was?"

I, Robinson Crusoe, was born in the year 1632 in England. As a young lad I took to the sea, against the wishes of my father. In times to come I would often recall his warnings that I would live to regret my decision, for in September of 1659, I was shipwrecked off the coast of South America during a dreadful storm and washed up on the shore of a deserted island, all the rest of the ship's company being drowned, and myself almost dead.

My initial joy at finding myself alive soon gave way to wild despair as I looked about me and realized that I was alone, with no means of sustaining myself. I soon discovered, however, that the bulk of the ship remained intact some distance from shore, and by fashioning a raft from pieces of the wreckage, I was able to carry away some provisions and tools.

Among these were a tin of biscuits, some dried meat, a bit of rum and tobacco, a spyglass, several axes and other implements, and several guns with a quantity of gunpowder and shot that had luckily not been dampened by the sea. With these last I managed to shoot enough birds and wild goats to provide myself with food when my supplies began to give out. And when my clothes fell to pieces, I made myself a short jacket and breeches of goatskin, as well as a cap to protect my head from sun and rain. With my hairy attire, my sunburned skin, and my growing beard, I would have caused fright or else raised a great deal of laughter had any Englishman been there to see me.

I protected myself from wild beasts and any savages who might roam the island by building a small fort. This was of great comfort to me, for I feared being discovered by the fierce cannibals known to inhabit that part of the world.

With continual labor, I was in time able to fashion almost everything needed to make my dwelling comfortable, including a table and shelves for storing my possessions and some clay pots. I managed to trap and tame a she-goat and her kid, and in time I acquired an entire flock. For companionship I had a dog and two cats, the only other survivors of the wreck. To these I added two parrots, which I tamed and taught to speak a few words. With these subjects about me, I thought myself quite the master of my little kingdom.

One day I discovered corn growing near the entrance to my cave. I carefully watered the plants until they ripened, then I saved all the grain for planting season. After the next harvest, I again saved all for planting, continuing in this manner until I had an ample crop to eat.

I explored the island and found wild grapes in abundance, which I gathered and dried as raisins. I also built a small canoe out of a tree trunk, and this I used to explore the coast.

For fifteen years, I busied myself with caring for my crops and flocks, maintaining my fort, and exploring the island. Then one day as I went to my boat, I was surprised to see the print of a man's naked foot very plain in the sand. Thunderstruck, I looked and listened, but neither saw nor heard anyone; nor were there any other footprints. I fled in terror to my fort, wondering whether I should fear savage cannibals or the devil himself.

For the next few years, I kept fearful watch and made sure my guns were always loaded, but I saw no other signs of a visitor to the island. Then, early one morning in my twenty-third year of residence, I spied a campfire on the shore. I approached cautiously and, peeping from the trees, perceived with horror that some savage cannibals had come to my island, bringing their captured enemies and evidently intending to kill and eat them here on the shore. There were at least twenty of them. As I watched, they dragged two miserable wretches from their boats, one of whom they immediately struck down with a club. Suddenly the other captive broke and ran, heading straight toward me. Two of his enemies pursued him, but he easily outstripped them and, as I saw him approach, it occurred to me that he might become the companion and servant I had long wished for. So I came to the rescue, knocking down one pursuer with the butt of my gun and shooting the other as he raised his bow and arrow to shoot me.

When the savages left, the rescued man threw himself down before me and made gestures of thanks. I named my new companion Friday, for I calculated it was on that day that I rescued him.

Friday was strong and well-formed, handsome of feature, and quick to learn. I soon taught him to assist me in my work and to speak some English. I taught him to say master and let him know that was to be my name. I also taught him to say yes and no and to know the meaning of them. I likewise taught him to shoot, though not without some difficulties, for he could not at first understand how the gun worked and was astonished and not a little frightened by the noise it made. His astonishment did not wear off for a long time, and I believe, if I had let him, he would have worshiped me and my gun. For some time he would not touch the weapon, and once I found him speaking softly to it, imploring it not to kill him. With my guidance, however, he soon learned to use it skillfully.

Friday's lessons in shooting proved valuable, for one day, after we had lived together pleasantly for several years, our island was once again visited by canni-

bals bringing bound captives upon whom they planned to feast. I saw with horror that one of their prisoners was wearing European clothes—perhaps one of my own countrymen. "Friday," I said, "we must resolve to fight them; can you fight?"

Friday said he could fight, but added, in his broken English, "There come many great number."

"No matter for that," I said, "our guns will frighten those we do not kill."

We rushed from the woods and fired upon the cannibals, killing or wounding many of them. The survivors fled to their canoes and paddled away, leaving the European alive. We untied him and gave him food and drink, for which he thanked us in Spanish. Then, hearing a groaning noise, we looked and found an old man who lay bound in the bottom of one of the canoes. When Friday heard him speak and looked in his face, his reaction was wonderful. He kissed the man, hugged him, cried, laughed, jumped about, danced, sang, and then cried again. When at last he came to his senses, he told me that it was his father, who had also been taken by the savages.

The Spaniard and Friday and I began to think about how we might escape, but only a few days later we were surprised by the arrival of an English ship. And so I left the island, the nineteenth of December, as I found by the ship's account, in the year 1686, after I had been upon it twenty-eight years, two months, and nineteen days. I returned with Friday to England to find that the investments I had made many years before had fared well in the hands of honest friends and that I was a prosperous man.

Gulliver's Travels

(Adapted from the novel by Jonathan Swift)

After the appearance of **Robinson Crusoe** *in 1719, stories about voyages, shipwrecks, and distant islands became popular. Jonathan Swift's* Gulliver's Travels *(1726) benefited from this popularity, but Swift's book was unlike any other travel book ever written. In the book Gulliver describes his fantastic experiences in Lilliput, where the people stand only six inches tall, and in Brobdingnag, where the people are thirty-six feet tall and the cats are as large as oxen. As the excerpt below begins, Gulliver has been shipwrecked and washed up on an unknown shore, where he has taken a nap to recover his strength.*

When I awoke, it was just daylight. I attempted to rise, but was not able to stir,

for I found my arms and legs were strongly fastened to the ground and my hair tied down in the same manner. I likewise felt several slender cords across my body, from my armpits to my thighs. I could only look upward. The sun began to grow hot, and the light bothered my eyes.

In a little time I felt something moving on my left leg, advancing over my breast, and coming almost to my chin. Bending my eyes downward as much as I could, I perceived it to be a human creature not six inches high, with a bow and arrow in his hands. In the meantime, I felt at least forty more of the same kind following the first. I was in the utmost astonishment and roared so loudly that they all ran back in fright, but they soon returned, crying out in shrill voices, "Hekinah Degul!"

Struggling to get free, I managed to break the strings and wrench out the pegs that held my left arm to the ground, but the creatures ran off again before I could seize them. I heard one of them cry, "Togol phonic!" and instantly felt a hundred arrows discharged upon my left hand, which pricked me like so many needles. I now thought it prudent to lie still, and when the people observed I was quiet, they discharged no more arrows.

About four yards from me, near my right ear, I heard a knocking noise, like people at work. Turning my head that way, as far as the pegs and strings would permit me, I saw a stage erected about a foot and a half above the ground. It was capable of holding four of the inhabitants, with two or three ladders to mount it. From there, one of them, who seemed to be an important person, made a long speech, of which I understood not one syllable.

Before he began, he cried out, "Langro Dehul san!" Immediately fifty of the inhabitants came and cut the strings that fastened the left side of my head, which gave me the liberty of turning it to the right and seeing the person speaking and his gestures. He made a great speech in which I could observe many gestures of threats and others of promises, pity, and kindness.

I answered in few words, but in the most humble manner. I was almost famished with hunger, having not eaten a morsel for several hours. I put my finger on my mouth several times to show that I wanted food. The important person understood me very well and commanded that several ladders should be placed against my sides, on which more than a hundred of the inhabitants mounted and walked towards my mouth, carrying baskets full of meat. I observed the flesh of several animals, but could not distinguish them by the taste. There were shoulders, legs, and loins shaped like those of mutton, but smaller than the wings of a lark. I ate them two or three at a mouthful and took three loaves of bread at a time, each about the size of a musket ball. They supplied me as fast as they could, showing a thousand marks of wonder and astonishment at my bulk and appetite.

I then made another sign that I wanted drink. They flung up one of their largest barrels, rolled it toward my free hand, and knocked out the lid. I drank it off in a single gulp, which was easy enough, for it hardly held half a pint. They brought me a second barrel, which I drank in the same manner, and made signs for more, but they had no more to give me. When I had performed these wonders, they shouted for joy and danced upon my breast, crying, "Hekinah Degul!"

They daubed an ointment upon my hands and face, which, along with a sleeping potion they had placed in my wine, soothed me into a deep slumber. When I awoke, I found myself on a large cart, being carried toward Lilliput, the capital city of my captors, who I later learned were called Lilliputians. Fifteen hundred of their largest horses, each about four and a half inches high, were employed to draw me toward the metropolis. When we arrived, the emperor of Lilliput and his court rode forth to greet me, and I was taken to an empty temple outside the city where I was to lodge.

The great gate to the temple was about four feet high and almost two feet wide. The emperor's blacksmith brought ninety chains, like those that hang from a lady's watch in Europe, and almost as large, which were locked to my left leg with thirty-six padlocks. When the workmen found it was impossible for me to break loose, they cut all the strings that bound me and allowed me to stand up.

The noise and astonishment of the people at seeing me stand up are not to be expressed. When I got to my feet, I looked about me, and must confess I never beheld a more entertaining prospect. The country round appeared like a continued garden, and the enclosed fields, which were generally forty feet square, resembled so many beds of flowers. These fields were intermingled with woods, in which the tallest trees appeared to be seven feet high. I viewed the town on my left hand, which looked like the painted scene of a city in a theater.

That night I got into my house, with some difficulty. At first I slept on the ground. Later the emperor ordered a bed to be made. Six hundred beds of their ordinary size were brought in and sewn together.

The emperor held frequent councils to debate what course should be taken with me. They feared my breaking loose or causing a famine due to my huge diet. Some suggested starving me or shooting me with poison arrows, but were unsure how to dispose of me safely once I was dead. When the emperor saw how gently I treated his people, however, he decided to provide me with sufficient food and to grant me certain liberties, provided I would swear a peace with him and his empire. When I agreed, I was granted my freedom.

Treasure Island

(Retold with excerpts from the novel by Robert Louis Stevenson)

Robert Louis Stevenson published Treasure Island *in 1883, but the story takes place in the 1700s, not long after the events of* Robinson Crusoe *and* Gulliver's Travels. *The story is told by a boy named Jim Hawkins. One day Jim meets an old sea captain who tells him to keep an eye out for a "seafaring man with one leg." After the captain dies suddenly, Jim discovers a treasure map among the dead man's belongings. Jim shares his discovery with three adults—Captain Smollett, Squire Trelawney, and Dr. Livesay. They arrange for a ship so that they can set sail for Treasure Island, with Jim as cabin boy.*

Several weeks later our ship, the *Hispaniola*, was ready. The squire had hired as the ship's cook a one-legged pub owner named Long John Silver, who carried a parrot on his shoulder. From time to time the parrot would call out, "Pieces of eight! Pieces of eight!" Silver explained that he had lost his other leg while serving in the Royal Navy. At first I feared that Long John might be the one-legged sailor of whom the captain had spoken, but I soon changed my mind. Long John seemed to me the best possible shipmate, for as we walked along the docks together, he explained what the sailors were about, told me stories of ships and seamen, and repeated nautical terms until I had learned them perfectly, telling me I was "smart as paint."

Our captain was Mr. Smollett and at first all went well. Then one night I chanced to overhear Long John whispering with another crew member, telling him that if he would "join up," he could "end the cruise a wealthy man." As I listened, I realized, to my horror, that Silver and several of the other crew members were pirates who had sailed with the old captain who had stayed at our inn. They were planning to mutiny and take the treasure for themselves. After some discussion, the other man agreed to join Silver and the other pirates, saying, "There's my hand on it."

"You're a brave lad, and smart as paint," replied Silver. When I heard him address the man in the same words of flattery he had used on me, I wanted to kill him. But I kept hidden and listened as Silver continued: "Just speak soft and keep sober till I give the word. We'll wait,

> **Talk and Think**
> Ask your child why he thinks Jim Hawkins is hurt when he hears Long John Silver call another person "smart as paint."

but when the time is right, let 'er rip! I claim Trelawney. I'll wring his neck with these hands!"

I told the squire, the doctor, and the captain what I had heard. They were shocked to learn about Silver, but vowed to be on guard and to strike first.

The next day we reached the island, and I went ashore with some others. I hid among the trees and spied on Silver as he tried to recruit more men for his plot. When one man refused to join him, Silver knocked him down with his crutch and buried his knife up to the hilt in the sailor's back. Afraid he might kill me, too, I turned and ran into the forest. I had not gone far when I came upon a sunburned man with long hair, ragged clothing, and a scruffy beard. He ran toward me, calling out in a voice that sounded like a rusty lock. He said his name was Ben Gunn. He had been marooned on the island by some angry shipmates after leading them on an unsuccessful quest for pirates' gold. He was rich, he confided (which made me doubt his sanity), but he had lived off wild goats' flesh and coconuts all this time. I decided to tell him our story, and he promised to help us if we would help him escape the island. He told me where I might find his little homemade boat, hidden in a cove.

Suddenly I heard the sound of cannons and realized that the fight between my friends and the pirates had already begun. I took leave of Ben Gunn and ran back toward the boat, till I saw the English flag flying about the trees. I ran toward it and found a stockade I had seen marked on the map, which was being stoutly defended by my friends. They had fled there with arms and provisions, and now the pirates were approaching. I scaled the wall to welcoming cries and went to work keeping the guns loaded, while my friends fired continually, killing a number of the rogues who rushed upon the fortress. At last the pirates retreated, leaving many of their own dead, and several of ours.

I told my friends about my meeting with Ben Gunn. The squire, the doctor, and the captain had a conference, after which the doctor took a musket and set off briskly through the trees. I guessed he was going to see Ben Gunn. It was stiflingly hot in the stockade, and blood and dead bodies lay all around. I envied the doctor, walking in the cool shadow of the woods with the birds about him, and a mischievous idea entered my head: suppose I went looking for Ben Gunn's boat? But I was only a boy, and I knew they would never let me go alone, so I filled both pockets of my coat with biscuits, grabbed two pistols, and snuck away.

Once I found the little boat, I had another mischievous idea. When night fell, I rowed quietly out to the *Hispaniola*. There were only two pirates on board, and they were engaged in a drunken argument, unaware of me. When the argument ended, one pirate lay dead, and the other, the coxswain Israel Hands, nursed a knife wound in the leg. At this point I made my appearance, waving my pistols and announcing that I was taking command of the ship. Hands seemed to give in, apparently too badly injured to resist. I lowered the hateful Jolly Roger, hurled it overboard, and raised the British flag. Then I did my best to steer the boat to a cove on the other side of the island. Just as we reached the cove, Hands came lurching toward me with a dagger. I drew my pistols and pointed them squarely at him. Hands made as if he would surrender, but then, in an instant, back went his right hand over his shoulder. He hurled a knife, which sang through the air like an arrow, pinning my sleeve to the mast. Without knowing what I was doing, I fired both pistols, and, with a choked cry, the pirate plummeted into the water.

I assumed that my friends still held the stockade, and, as I made my way back in the darkness, there was no way to tell otherwise. But when I entered, I was greeted by Silver's parrot screeching, "Pieces of eight! Pieces of eight!" I was taken prisoner by the pirates, who told me that my friends had abandoned the stockade and the map in exchange for their freedom and had now retreated to another part of the island. My heart sank when I heard this, and I was not a little astonished, for I could not imagine why my friends would give Silver the map. But I had problems of a more pressing nature, for the buccaneers wanted to kill me on the spot. But Silver cried out, "Avast there!" He had decided to keep me alive, just in case he should need a hostage.

The next morning Silver led us off to seek the treasure. He was armed to the teeth, with his parrot perched upon his shoulder gabbling. He tied one end of a line about his waist and the other around mine, and, as he hobbled along, I followed obediently behind him, led like a dancing bear. Even with the map, we had trouble finding the spot. As we approached the tall tree near which it was supposed to lie, we came upon a human skeleton, its bony hand seeming to point the way to the treasure. In another moment we came to the spot. There on the ground was a deep ditch and the remains of a huge chest, split open and emptied of its contents. The treasure had been taken!

The pirates turned upon Silver for leading them on a fool's errand. They drew their pistols, vowing to kill both him and me, but just then shots rang out from the other direction. I turned and saw my friends coming, led by Ben Gunn. Some of the buccaneers fell, and the rest quickly surrendered.

Dr. Livesay and the others led me and the captive pirates to Ben's cave, where the treasure lay safely stowed, as it had been ever since Gunn found it. They chided me for sneaking away from the stockade but allowed me to rejoin their party. We loaded the treasure aboard the *Hispaniola* and headed for home, leaving all the pirates save Long John Silver to survive as Ben had done, with the help of some arms and provisions. It was our intent to see Silver brought to justice, but one evening when we stopped in a port, he jumped ship with a sack of gold coins and got away. All of us had an ample share of the treasure and used it wisely or foolishly, according to our natures. It is said there is more treasure buried on the island, but nothing would bring me back there again. The worst dreams I ever have are when I hear the surf booming about its coasts or when I start upright in bed, with the voice of Silver's parrot ringing in my ears: "Pieces of eight! Pieces of eight!"

Rip Van Winkle

(Condensed from the story by Washington Irving)

In a village in the Catskill Mountains, there lived a simple, good-natured fellow by the name of Rip Van Winkle. He was a kind neighbor, and the children would shout with joy whenever he approached. Rip Van Winkle was a lovable soul who was ready to attend to anybody's business but his own. But as to keeping his own farm in order, he found it impossible, and his children were as ragged as if they belonged to nobody.

Rip was one of those happy fools who take the world easy, eat white bread or brown, whichever can be got with least thought or trouble, and would rather starve on a penny than work for a pound. If left to himself, he would have whistled his life away in perfect contentment, but his wife was continually dinning in his ears about his idleness, his carelessness, and the ruin he was bringing on his family. Rip would shrug his shoulders, shake his head, cast up his eyes, but say nothing. This always provoked a fresh volley from his wife, so that he left the house to go outside—the only side that belongs to a henpecked husband.

Rip used to console himself, when driven from home, with the company of a group of sages and fellow idlers who convened on a bench in front of an inn. Sitting beneath a portrait of His Majesty King George the Third (New York in those days was still a province of England), they talked over village gossip and told stories. If by chance an old newspaper should fall into their hands from some passing traveler, they would listen as Van Bummel, the schoolmaster, read them its contents, and it would have been worth any statesman's money to hear the discussions that followed. Nicholas Vedder, a patriarch of the village, made his opinions known by the manner in which he smoked his pipe. Short puffs indicated anger; when he was pleased, he would inhale the smoke slowly and emit it in light and delicate clouds.

One day, seeking to escape the labor of the farm and the clamor of his wife, Rip shouldered his gun and walked high into the Catskills to hunt for squirrels.

Take a Look
Turn to the map of the United States on page 99. Point out New York State and explain that this is where the Catskill Mountains are.

All day the mountains echoed and re-echoed with the reports of his gun. Finally he threw himself on a green knoll that looked down into a deep glen, wild and lonely. Rip lay musing on the scene as evening gradually advanced, and sighed as he thought of going home.

As he was about to descend, he heard a voice calling, "Rip Van Winkle! Rip Van Winkle!" He perceived a strange figure toiling up the rocks and bending under the weight of something on his back. He was surprised to see any human being in this lonely place, but supposing it to be one of his neighbors in need of assistance, he hastened down to help. The stranger was a short old fellow with a grizzled beard. His dress was of the antique Dutch fashion and he bore a stout keg that Rip supposed was full of liquor. He made signs for Rip to assist him, and together they clambered up a narrow gully. Every now and then long rolling peals like thunder seemed to issue out of a deep ravine. Passing through this ravine, they came to a hollow that looked like a small amphitheater.

In the center was a company of odd-looking persons playing at ninepins. The thunderous noise Rip had heard from afar was the sound of the ball rolling toward the pins. Like Rip's guide, they were dressed in an outlandish fashion, with enormous breeches. What seemed particularly odd to Rip was that these folks maintained the gravest faces, the most mysterious silence, and were, in fact, the most melancholy party he had ever witnessed. They stared at Rip in such a way that his heart turned within him and his knees banged together for fear.

Rip's guide emptied the keg into large flagons. The company quaffed the liquor in profound silence and then returned to their game. As Rip's apprehension subsided, he ventured to taste the beverage. One taste provoked another, and at length his senses were overpowered and he fell into a deep sleep.

Upon waking, he found himself on the green knoll whence he had first seen the old man. It was a bright sunny morning. "Surely," thought Rip, "I have not slept here all night." He recalled the strange men. "Oh! That wicked flagon! What excuse shall I make to Dame Van Winkle?" He looked around for his gun, but found only an old firelock encrusted with rust. Suspecting he had been robbed, he determined to revisit the scene of the previous evening to demand his gun. As he rose to walk, he found himself stiff in the joints. With some difficulty, he found the gully up which he and his companion had ascended, but could find no traces of the ravine that had led to the amphitheater. He shouldered the rusty firelock and with a heart full of trouble turned his steps homeward.

As he approached the village he met a number of people, but none whom he knew, which somewhat surprised him for he had thought himself acquainted with everyone in the country round. Their dress, too, was of a different fashion. They all stared at him with surprise and stroked their chins. When Rip did the same, he found to his astonishment that his beard had grown a foot long! A troop of children ran at his heels, hooting after him and pointing at his gray beard. There were houses in the village that he had never seen before, with unfamiliar names inscribed over the doors. He began to wonder whether both he and the world around him were bewitched.

With some difficulty he found his own house. The roof had fallen in and the door was off its hinges. He entered and called for his wife and children, but all was silent. He spotted a dog that looked like his own and called out to him, but the dog snarled and showed his teeth. "My own dog has forgotten me," sighed poor Rip.

He hastened to the village inn. Before it there now hung a flag adorned with stars and stripes. He recognized the face of King George on the sign, but now his

Make a Connection

The flag with the stars and stripes and the portrait of King George turned into George Washington are hints that the Revolutionary War has taken place. Turn to page 163 to find more information about the war.

red coat was blue, his head wore a cocked hat, and underneath the figure was printed GENERAL WASHINGTON. There was a crowd of people around the door, but none that Rip knew. He inquired, "Where's Nicholas Vedder?"

There was silence, then an old man replied, "Nicholas Vedder! Why, he is dead and gone these eighteen years!"

"Where's Van Bummel, the schoolmaster?"

"He went off to war and is now in Congress."

Rip's heart sank at hearing of these sad changes. He said in despair, "I'm not myself. I was myself last night, but I fell asleep on the mountain, and everything's changed, and I can't tell who I am!"

The bystanders looked at each other in puzzlement. Then a comely woman pressed through the throng. She had a child in her arms, which, frightened by the gray-bearded man's looks, began to cry. "Hush, Rip," cried she, "the old man won't hurt you." The name of the child and the air of the mother awakened a train of recollection in his mind. He caught the mother and child in his arms and said to the woman, "I am your father— young Rip Van Winkle once—old Rip Van Winkle now! Does nobody know poor Rip Van Winkle?"

Talk and Think

As you read the story with your child, ask her to consider what may have caused all these changes.

All stood amazed, until an old woman, peering into his face for a moment, exclaimed, "Sure enough! It is Rip Van Winkle! Welcome home again, old neighbor. Why, where have you been these twenty years?"

Rip's story was soon told, for the whole twenty years had been to him but as one night. Many were skeptical, but an old man who was well versed in the local traditions corroborated his story in the most satisfactory manner. He assured the company that the Catskill Mountains had always been haunted by strange beings; that the great discoverer Hendrick Hudson kept a vigil there with his crew of the *Half Moon*; that his father had once seen them in their old Dutch clothing playing at ninepins in the hollow of the mountain.

Rip's daughter took him home to live with her, her mother having died some years before after breaking a blood vessel in a fit of passion. Having arrived at that happy age when a man can be idle with impunity, Rip took his place once more on the bench at the inn door and was reverenced as one of the patriarchs of the village. He used to tell his story to every stranger that arrived. Some doubted the truth of it, but the old Dutch villagers almost universally gave Rip full credit. Even to this day, whenever a thunderstorm comes up on a summer afternoon, they say that Hendrick Hudson and his crew are at their game of ninepins; and it is a common wish of all henpecked husbands in the neighborhood, when life hangs heavy on their hands, that they might have a quieting draft out of Rip Van Winkle's flagon.

The Legend of Sleepy Hollow

(Condensed from the story by Washington Irving)

Not far from the eastern shore of the Hudson River is a little valley known as Sleepy Hollow. A drowsy, dreamy atmosphere seems to hang over the land, as if it were under the sway of some witching power. The whole neighborhood abounds with local tales, haunted spots, and twilight superstitions, but the dominant spirit that haunts this region is the apparition of a figure on horseback without a head. It is said to be the ghost of a Hessian trooper whose head was carried away by a cannonball during the Revolutionary War. The ghost rides forth nightly to the scene of battle in search of his head, and he travels with great speed to get back to the churchyard before daybreak.

In this out-of-the-way place there lived a worthy fellow by the name of Ichabod Crane who instructed the children of the vicinity. The name Crane was well suited to him. He was tall and exceedingly lank, with narrow shoulders, long arms and legs, and hands that dangled a mile out of his sleeves. He had huge ears, large green eyes, and a long nose. To see him striding along on a windy day, with his clothes fluttering about him, one might have mistaken him for a scarecrow escaped from a cornfield.

From his schoolhouse could usually be heard the voices of his pupils, reciting their lessons, interrupted now and then by the voice of the master or by the sound of his birch switch as he urged some unfortunate along the path of knowledge.

According to custom, Ichabod Crane was boarded and lodged at the houses of the farmers whose children he instructed. With these he lived a week at a time, thus making the rounds of the neighborhood. His appearance at a home was apt to occasion a stir, for the ladies thought his taste and accomplishments vastly superior to those of the rough country farmers. He had read several books quite through and was a perfect master of Cotton Mather's *History of New England Witchcraft*, in which he most firmly believed. It was often his delight, after school was dismissed, to study old Mather's direful tales until dusk. Then, as he wended his way home, every sound of nature fluttered his overexcited imagination: the moan of the whippoorwill, the cry of the tree toad, or the dreary hooting of the screech owl.

He loved to pass long winter evenings with the old Dutch wives as they sat spinning by the fire and listened with interest to their tales of ghosts and goblins—in particular, the legend of the headless horseman. But the pleasure in all this was dearly purchased by the terrors of his subsequent walk homeward. What fearful shapes and shadows beset his path! How often did he dread to look over his shoulder, lest he should behold some uncouth being close behind him!

In addition to his other vocation, Ichabod Crane was the singing master of the neighborhood. Among his musical disciples was Katrina Van Tassel, the only child of a substantial Dutch farmer. She was a blooming lass of eighteen, ripe and rosy-cheeked as one of her father's peaches. She soon found favor in Ichabod's eyes, not merely for her beauty but for her vast inheritance. Old Van Tassel was a thriving, liberal-hearted farmer and a doting father. Every window and crevice of his vast barn was full to bursting with the treasures of the farm. Sleek porkers grunted in their pens and regiments of turkeys went gobbling through the farmyard. The **pedagogue's** mouth watered as he pictured every pig roasted with an apple in its mouth and every turkey daintily trussed up with a necklace of savory sausages. As he rolled his eyes over the fat meadowlands and the orchards burdened with ruddy fruit, his heart yearned after the damsel who was to inherit them, and he determined to gain her affections.

He was to encounter, however, a host of fearful adversaries: Katrina's numerous rustic admirers. The most formidable of these was burly Brom Van Brunt, a local hero of some renown. His Herculean frame had earned him the nickname of "Brom Bones." Brom Bones was famous for his horsemanship and always ready for either a fight or a frolic, though he had more mischief than ill will in him. With all his roughness, there was a strong dash of good humor at bottom. Whenever a madcap prank occurred in the neighborhood, people whispered that Brom Bones must be at the bottom of it.

When Brom Bones began wooing Katrina, most other suitors gave up the chase, not wanting to cross the lion in his affections. But Ichabod Crane persevered in his quest. He was therefore delighted when, one fine autumn morning, a farmhand came to the school door with an invitation for Ichabod to attend a merrymaking at Van Tassel's. He turned his students loose an hour before the usual time, yelping in joy, brushed his only suit of rusty black, and fussed over his appearance before a broken looking glass. He borrowed a horse so that he could arrive gallantly mounted. The horse was gaunt and swaybacked; his rusty mane and tail were knotted with burrs; one eye had lost its pupil and was glaring and spectral and the other had the gleam of the devil in it. He must have had fire and mettle in his day, for he bore the name of Gunpowder. Ichabod was a suitable figure for such a steed; his elbows stuck out like a grasshopper's, and as he rode, the motion of his arms was not unlike the flapping of a pair of wings.

The castle of Van Tassel was thronged with the flowering beauties of the adjacent country. It was not the charms of the buxom lasses that caught our hero's gaze as he entered the parlor, however, but those of a Dutch country table piled high with autumn food. There was the doughty doughnut, the crisp cruller, and a whole family of cakes. And then there were apple and peach and pumpkin pies, beside ham and smoked beef, dishes of preserved plums, peaches, pears, and quinces; not to mention roasted chickens, and bowls of milk and cream. As Ichabod sampled every dainty, he chuckled to think that he might one day be lord of all this splendor.

Ichabod danced proudly with the lady of his heart, his loosely hung frame clattering about the room, while Brom Bones sat brooding by himself in the corner. When the revel began to break up, Ichabod lingered behind to have a little talk with the heiress Katrina, fully convinced that he was now on the high road to success. Something, however, must have gone wrong at the interview, for he soon sallied forth from the mansion with an air quite desolate. He went straight to the stable and with several hearty kicks roused his steed.

It was the witching time of night when Ichabod traveled homeward. All the ghost stories that he had heard over the years now came crowding upon his recollection. The night grew darker; the stars seemed to sink deeper in the sky. He had

never felt so lonely. A splash by the side of a bridge caught his ear. In the dark shadow, he beheld something huge, misshapen, black, and towering. The hair rose upon his head. He stammered, "Who are you?" He received no reply. The shadowy object put itself in motion and bounded into the middle of the road. It appeared to be a horseman of large dimensions, mounted on a black horse of powerful frame. Ichabod quickened his steed, in hopes of leaving the mysterious horseman behind. The stranger, however, quickened to an equal pace. The odd silence of Ichabod's companion was soon fearfully accounted for. For upon seeing his fellow traveler in relief against the sky, gigantic in height, and muffled in a cloak, Ichabod was horror-struck to perceive that he was headless and that he carried his head before him on his saddle. In desperation Ichabod rained kicks upon Gunpowder. The specter followed close behind. Away they dashed, stones flying.

An opening in the trees now cheered him with the hope that the church bridge was at hand, the place where, legend said, the horseman should stop. Ichabod cast a look behind to see if his pursuer would vanish. Instead, he saw the goblin rising up in his stirrups, in the very act of hurling his head at him. Ichabod tried to dodge the horrible missile, but too late. It encountered his cranium with a tremendous crash. He tumbled into the dust, and Gunpowder and the goblin rider passed by like a whirlwind.

The next morning the old horse was found quietly cropping grass at his master's gate. The students were assembled at the schoolhouse, but no schoolmaster arrived. The tracks of horses' hoofs were traced to the bridge. On the bank was found the hat of the unfortunate Ichabod and close beside it a shattered pumpkin.

There was much gossip and speculation about the disappearance of Ichabod Crane. Some said he had been carried off by the headless horseman; others reported that he had simply left town in humiliation at having been dismissed by Katrina. Shortly after his rival's disappearance, Brom Bones conducted Katrina in triumph to the altar. Whenever the story of Ichabod was related, Bones looked exceedingly knowing and always burst into hearty laughter at the mention of the pumpkin. The old country wives, however, maintain to this day that Ichabod was spirited away, and it is said that one may still hear his voice, chanting a melancholy psalm tune among the solitudes of Sleepy Hollow.

> **Talk and Think**
>
> Ask your child what is implied by Brom Bones's suspicious behavior at the end of the story.

Learning About Language

Parts of Speech

Have you ever thought of the role each word in a sentence plays? In every sentence, each word has a job. Some words explain an action. Other words tell what something looks like, feels like, or sounds like. Still other words explain who or what is the focus of the sentence. In English, there are eight parts of speech, which means there are eight possible jobs a word can have in a sentence. Here are seven of these parts of speech and examples of how each one can be used in sentences:

Parts of Speech	Examples of Use
Noun: a word that names a person, place, animal, thing, or idea	I love **pizza** and **lemonade**. **Measles** is a terrible **disease**.
Adjective: a word that modifies, intensifies, or tells about a noun	It was a **dark** and **stormy** night. She is one **smart** girl.
Pronoun: a word that takes the place of a noun	**She** loved to play hide and seek, but **they** did not.
Verb: a word that describes an action or a state of being	We **caught** and **released** seventeen fish. I **am** an insomniac.

Parts of Speech	Examples of Use
Adverb: a word that adds to the meaning of a verb by telling how, or in what manner, the action occurred	She reads **well**. We ran **quickly** and **joyfully** to the porch.
Conjunction: a word that joins words, ideas, or phrases in a sentence	I bought bread **and** olives. Since they pulled my teeth, I can **neither** eat **nor** sleep.
Interjection: a word thrown into a sentence for emphasis	I like it, but, **good grief**, it sure is expensive! **Wow**! Your hair is green.

Do It Yourself

Ask your child to take any sentence from the book, write it on a sheet of paper, and then use different colored pencils to identify the various parts of speech in the sentence. He might underline nouns in red, circle verbs in green, or trace conjunctions in blue.

Words have jobs, just like people. And they can change jobs just as we do. For example, you might think that the word **run** is always a verb because it describes an action. But look at the way it is used in each of the following sentences.

I **run** two miles a day.
Here, **run** is a **verb**; it describes an action.

My **run** lasts about twenty minutes.
Here, **run** is a **noun**; it names a thing.

To really understand a sentence, you have to recognize the words and also understand what job each word is doing in the sentence.

Sentences

Complete Sentences

A complete sentence includes a subject and a predicate. The subject tells what or whom the sentence is about. The predicate tells what the subject is or does. In the sentences below, the subjects are in bold and the predicates are underlined.

> **I** like soccer.
> **Robert Louis Stevenson** wrote a famous book.
> **Harry Potter** defeated his greatest enemy with the help of his friends.

The subject is usually a noun or a pronoun, and it usually comes at the beginning of the sentence.

The predicate must always include a verb and may also include adverbs and other parts of speech. It usually comes after the subject, as it does in the sentences printed above.

If you leave out either the subject or the predicate, you won't have a complete sentence. You'll have a fragment. Here are two fragments:

> Visited the land of Lilliput.
> Robinson Crusoe.

To fix the first fragment, you need to add a subject. Ask yourself who visited the land of Lilliput, and then complete the sentence:

> **Gulliver** visited the land of Lilliput.

To fix the second fragment, you need to add a verb, so your sentence will have a predicate. Ask yourself what Robinson Crusoe did, and then rewrite:

> **Robinson Crusoe** survived on a deserted island.

Subject-Verb Agreement

Read this sentence: *She play with her friends after school.* Is this sentence written correctly? It has both a subject and a predicate, so it is a complete sentence. However, if you said the sentence is not written correctly, you are right. Although the sentence is complete, the wrong form of the verb is used. Whenever you write sentences, you must make sure that your subject and your verb agree. We don't say "he run" or "they runs." We say "he runs" and "they run." A singular subject takes a singular verb, and a plural subject takes a plural verb. See if you can pick the right verb form for each of the following sentences:

Pizza **is/are** delicious.
My friends **live/lives** down the street.
A flock of seagulls **was flying/were flying** overhead.

The last sentence is a little tricky. It might seem like there are many seagulls, so the subject must be plural. But really the subject of the sentence is "flock," and there's only one flock. That's why we say "A flock of seagulls was flying overhead."

Run-on Sentences

Another problem you can run into in writing is when you try to put too much in one sentence, like this:

We read *Treasure Island* it is an exciting story.

This is called a run-on sentence. One way to fix a run-on sentence is by dividing it into two separate sentences:

We read *Treasure Island*. It is an exciting story.

Kinds of Sentences

There are different kinds of sentences. A declarative sentence makes a statement and usually ends with a period.

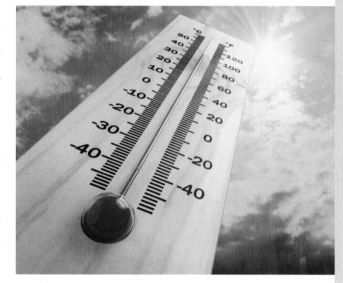

It's hot today.
The man began to sweat in the
    bright sunlight.

An interrogative sentence asks a question and ends with a question mark.

Did you ask Mom?

An imperative sentence is an order or a command. Imperative sentences are sometimes written with a period and sometimes, when they are said with great emotion, with an exclamation point.

Read Chapter 2.
Go to your room!

Exclamatory sentences are sentences that are exclaimed or shouted out, like "Go to your room!" or "That's gross!" Both of these are complete sentences, but sometimes when we are very excited, we don't speak in complete sentences. Then we might make exclamatory *statements* like these:

Gross!
Yippee! We won the game!

Punctuation

Commas

Commas tell readers when to pause within a sentence and which groups of words to read together. Here are some situations in which we use commas:

between the day and the year in dates	October 18, 2000
between the city and the state in an address	Charlottesville, VA
between items in a series	That man is mad, bad, and dangerous to know.
after the words "yes" and "no"	No, you may not stay up all night.
before conjunctions that combine parts of sentences	Sticks and stones may break my bones, but names can never harm me.
inside quotation marks when writing dialogue	"I'm so glad to see you," Sun said.

Apostrophes

Apostrophes are used to show possession. Singular nouns with a few exceptions show possession by adding 's.

My **uncle's** putt stopped just short of the hole.

Many plural nouns already have an "s" at the end; these words show possession by just adding an apostrophe.

The **sisters'** house was a mess.

There are some exceptions, though:

The **men's** room is bigger than the **women's** room.

Apostrophes are also used in contractions to show that some letters have been omitted. The contraction "that's" is short for "that is." The apostrophe tells you the letter "i" has been left out. Similarly, the contraction "we're" is short for "we are."

Quotation Marks

Use quotation marks when you want to distinguish somebody else's words from your own words. For instance, if you were writing a story about a fortune-teller, you might use quotation marks like this:

"I see good things in your future," said the mysterious woman, staring into her crystal ball.

Quotation marks are also used for titles of poems, songs, short stories, and magazine articles.

We read "Dreams," a poem by Langston Hughes.

Synonyms and Antonyms

A synonym is a word that means the same thing, or almost the same thing, as another word. "Quick" and "fast" are synonyms, and so are "costly" and "expensive." See if you can match the italicized words on the left with the synonyms on the right.

bad	buccaneer
friends	evil
pirate	buddies
try	spotless
clean	attempt

Do It Yourself
Think of a few words that are familiar to your child. Then ask your child to come up with her own synonyms and antonyms for them.

Antonyms are words that are opposites. "Soft" and "hard" are antonyms. So are "good" and "evil." See if you can match the italicized words on the left with their antonyms on the right.

advance	expensive
true	fail
succeed	shy
cheap	retreat
bold	false

Homophones

Homophones are words that sound the same but have different meanings. It's important to choose the right word when you're writing.

There are twenty rocks in my collection.
The fans cheered for **their** team.
They're from Florida.

I've got **your** book.
You're my best friend.

It's cold!
The bird built **its** nest in our yard.

Did you **hear** that?
Come over **here**.

Let's go **to** the mall.
I have **two** pairs of shoes.
You come, **too**.

Prefixes and Suffixes

Prefixes

Prefixes are groups of letters that are added to the front of words to make new words with different meanings.

"Im-" and "in-" mean "not." So something that's impossible is not possible, and someone who's inconsistent is not consistent.

"Non-" also means "not." A nonfiction book is not fictional—that is, it's a true story. A nonviolent protest is not violent.

"Mis-" means "wrong, bad, or badly." If you misspell a word, you spell it wrong. And if you misbehave, you behave badly.

"En-" means "in or into." To endanger someone is to put that person in danger. And to entrap someone is to draw the person into a trap.

"Pre-" means "before or earlier." A pregame show takes place before the game, and a prehistoric event took place before people began recording history.

Suffixes

Suffixes are a lot like prefixes, but they are added to the *end* of a word.

"-y" is a suffix that can be used to make adjectives. Does anyone you know display greed? Then that person is greedy. Are you ready to go to sleep? Then you must be sleepy.

"-ly" and "-ily" are suffixes that are often used to make adverbs. Take the adjective "quick," add "-ly," and you get the adverb "quickly." In the same way, "easy" becomes "easily."

"-ful" is a suffix meaning "full of." A thoughtful person is full of thoughts, and a playful baby is full of play.

"-able" and "-ible" are suffixes that mean "capable of or worthy of a specific action." If a shirt is capable of being washed, we say it is washable. If you can bend and flex your arms and legs well, we say you are flexible.

"-ment" is a suffix used to make verbs into nouns. If everybody in the room agrees (verb), you have achieved agreement (noun). If you are amazed (verb), you are in a state of amazement (noun).

Writing and Research

Once you've learned how to write sentences, you can practice putting sentences together into paragraphs and longer works. Here are some things you might try writing:

1. An email to a friend or family member
2. A short story
3. A summary of what you did today
4. A description of an object or of a person
5. A poem
6. A report

To write a report, first choose a topic you'd like to learn more about. Then go to your school library or public library and ask the librarian to help you find information on your topic. (You can also find information by searching the Internet. Be sure to have an adult help you with your search.) As you learn interesting facts or read quotations that you think you might want to use in your report, write down what you found and also where you found these things. Whenever you find something in a book, write down the title of the book, the author, and where, by whom, and when the book was published. Most of this information can be found in the first few pages of a book.

When you write your report, think of it as a set of paragraphs, each of which should have its own purpose. Before you start writing, you should have a good idea about the goal of each paragraph in your essay. For instance, if you were writing a report on Babe Ruth, you might have a paragraph telling when Ruth lived and which baseball teams he played for, another on his achievements as a hitter, and a third on his record as a pitcher. Your last paragraph should be your conclusion, in which you restate your point and finish up your report.

> **Do It Yourself**
> Ask your child to create an example citation for this book, using what she just learned!

At the end of your report, you'll want to include a bibliography. A bibliography is a list of books and articles you used to write your report. Here's what some entries from a bibliography for a report on Babe Ruth might look like:

Creamer, Robert. *Babe: The Legend Comes to Life*. New York: Simon & Schuster, 2005.

Holub, Joan. *Who Was Babe Ruth?* New York: Grosset & Dunlap, 2012.

Smelser, Marshall. *The Life That Ruth Built: A Biography*. Lincoln, Nebraska: University of Nebraska Press, 1993.

Thomson, Charles. "Why the Babe Was the Greatest." *Sports Illustrated*, January 17, 1976, pages 23–32.

Notice that the entries in the bibliography are listed alphabetically by the author's last name.

Writing a report isn't easy, but, like other things in life, you can become good at it by practicing.

Familiar Sayings and Phrases

PARENTS: Every culture has some sayings and phrases that make no sense when carried over literally into another culture. To say, for example, that someone has "let the cat out of the bag" has nothing to do with setting free a trapped kitty. Nor—thank goodness—does it ever "rain cats and dogs"!

In this section, we introduce a handful of common American English sayings and phrases and give examples of how they are used. The sayings and phrases in this section may be familiar to many children, who hear them at home. But the inclusion of these saying and phrases in the *Core Knowledge Sequence* has been singled out for gratitude by many parents and by teachers who work with children from home cultures that are different from the culture of literate American English.

As the crow flies

When a bird flies from place to place, it flies through the air and takes the most direct route. But when people drive, they have to follow roads and often have to go farther. When people give a distance "as the crow flies," they mean the shortest distance between the two points, not the distance you would have to travel if you followed roads.

As Dan and his mom drove along the river, they could see the beach on the opposite side. Dan asked, "How far is it to the beach?"

"It's only about a quarter of a mile as the crow flies," his mother said. "But we have to drive three miles north to the bridge and then three miles south once we cross the bridge."

Beauty is only skin deep.

People use this saying to mean that you can't judge what a person is like on the inside by how good he or she looks on the outside.

"That new girl sure is pretty," Kim said.

"Yeah, but I wonder if she's nice, too," Carol said. "After all, beauty is only skin deep."

The bigger they are, the harder they fall.

When a huge oak falls in the forest, it makes a tremendous crash. When a small sapling falls, you can barely hear it. When people use this saying, they mean that the larger or more powerful something is (it could be a person, a team, a country, or something else), the bigger the shock will be when a setback occurs.

"But, Coach," Sam said, "we'll never be able to beat Central. They're the defending state champions and haven't lost a game yet this season!"

"Never mind that," the coach said. "If we play our best game, we can beat them—and the bigger they are, the harder they fall!"

Birds of a feather flock together.

We use this saying to mean that similar people, or people who have similar interests, like to be with each other.

"Those guys always eat lunch together," Jenny said, nodding toward a group of boys in the cafeteria.

"Yeah," said June. "They're on the same baseball team and they love to talk about mitts and bats and home runs."

Jenny nodded. "Birds of a feather flock together!"

Blow hot and cold

This phrase comes from one of Aesop's fables, in which a man blows on his fingers to warm them up and then blows on his soup to cool it down. In both cases, the man is opening his mouth, but what comes out is very different. If a person says one thing and later says the opposite, we say that the person is blowing hot and cold.

"Is Felicia going to try out for the soccer team this year?" Stacy asked.

"I don't know," Tricia replied. "Last week she was saying yes, but this week she's saying no. She's really blowing hot and cold."

Break the ice

Before ice-breaking ships were invented, sailors who wanted to sail during the winter had to walk out onto frozen water and break up the ice before the boat could move forward. Nowadays people use the saying "break the ice" to refer to ending an awkward silence by beginning a conversation.

It was the first day of summer camp. The four girls began to unpack their clothes and make their beds in silence. None of the girls knew each other, and no one knew what to say. Finally, one of them broke the ice by saying, "Hey, where's everybody from?"

Bull in a china shop

If a person is clumsy in a place where things can be upset or broken, or handles a delicate situation badly, we say the person is acting like a bull in a china shop.

Leroy slammed the door behind him. A painting fell off the wall, and his mother's crystal vase wobbled on the dining room table. "I'm home!" he yelled, then tripped on the doormat and fell onto the floor.

"Honestly, Leroy," his mother said as she helped him up, "sometimes you're just like a bull in a china shop!"

Bury the hatchet

This phrase comes from Iroquois culture. When two nations declared war on each other, they were said to take up the hatchet. When they agreed to end their war, they were said to bury the hatchet. To bury the hatchet is to stop holding a grudge and make peace with someone else, to let bygones be bygones and forgive and forget.

Colin could not forgive his sister for breaking his tennis racquet. He kept up a sulky silence when he was around her. Finally, his sister said, "Oh, Colin, can't we bury the hatchet? I hate it when you are mad at me!"

Can't hold a candle to

Before electricity, servants had to hold candles for their masters so the masters could see. When we say one person or thing can't hold a candle to another person or thing, we mean that the first is not nearly as good as the second.

"How's the frozen pizza?" the girls' mother asked.

"It's okay," Isabel said. "But it can't hold a candle to your homemade pizza!"

> **What About You?**
> Ask your child, "Has there ever been a time when you've found an imitation of something that is not as good as the real thing?" Ask him to use the phrase "can't hold a candle to" to describe his own personal preference.

Don't count your chickens before they hatch.

Because not every egg in a nest hatches into a baby chicken, people use this saying to mean that you may be disappointed if you count on having something before it is really yours.

"I can't wait to use this gift card my grandma just sent me to buy apps on the tablet I'm getting for my birthday!" Nathan said.

"But how do you know you're going to get a tablet for your birthday?" Annie asked. "Don't count your chickens before they hatch!"

Don't put all your eggs in one basket.

Once upon a time a girl went to her family's henhouse to gather eggs for breakfast. Instead of taking only a few eggs, she packed all the eggs into her basket. On the way back to the house, she tripped and broke the eggs. Then there was nothing left for her family to eat. She wished she had not put all her eggs in one basket. If someone tells you not to put all your eggs in one basket, the person is reminding you of what can happen when you rely too heavily on one plan and don't think about what could go wrong.

"Dan's older brother wants to go to Harvard. He says he won't even apply to any other colleges."

"But what will he do if he doesn't get into Harvard? Maybe he shouldn't put all his eggs in one basket."

Etc.

"Etc." is an abbreviation of et cetera [et SET-er-uh], a Latin phrase meaning "and the rest." It can also mean "and so forth, and so on," or "and other things like the ones I've just mentioned."

I like large dogs: St. Bernards, Irish wolfhounds, Great Danes, etc.

Go to pot

This phrase was originally used in the kitchen. All of the leftover scraps that weren't good for anything else went to pot. That is, they were thrown into a big pot to make a stew. Eventually, the meaning changed. Now when we say something has gone to pot, we mean it has not been taken care of and has gone bad or been ruined.

"Have you checked the garden recently?" Dan asked.

"No," Pete replied, "not for a week or so."

"You'd better get out there, or the weeds will take over and the whole thing will go to pot."

Half a loaf is better than none.

This means that having something is better than having nothing, even if it's not exactly what you want.

When Theo's father gave him $5, he complained that he wasn't given $10. "Theo," his mother said, "there are many people who don't have a penny. You need to learn that half a loaf is better than none."

Haste makes waste.

This saying means that when you rush you don't do as good a job as when you are careful and take your time.

It was Sammy's night to do the dishes. He quickly rinsed all of the dinner plates, and then ran the silverware under the faucet.

"What's your hurry?" his father asked.

"I told Karl I'd meet him at the park!"

"If you aren't more careful cleaning these dishes," his father said, picking up a plate with a spot of spaghetti sauce on the rim, "you'll have to do them over again. Then you'll really be late. Haste makes waste!"

Laugh, and the world laughs with you; weep, and you weep alone.

This saying means that when you are happy, people want to share your happiness, but when you are sad, people don't want to be with you.

"Come on, Tom, cheer up!" Kimiko shook Tom's shoulder. "Why are you in such a bad mood?"

"Oh, I don't know," Tom said. "Nobody likes me."

"Well, what do you expect, with that big frown across your face?" Kimiko said with a smile. "Laugh, and the world laughs with you; weep, and you weep alone!"

Lightning never strikes twice in the same place.

We use this expression to mean that if something unfortunate has happened, the chances are that it probably won't happen again in exactly the same way.

"Hey, Kareem, don't stand there! Remember last month when a lightbulb fell and hit Mr. Vasquez right on the head?"

"Yeah, I remember. But what are the chances of that happening again? Lightning never strikes twice in the same place."

Live and let live.

This saying means mind your own business and let other people live as they wish to live.

"You need a haircut, Daryl." Kenya put her hands on her hips. "And look at those ugly shoes! You need to buy some new ones."

"Listen, Kenya. I like the way my hair looks, and I think these are cool shoes," Daryl said. "I'm going to keep dressing the way I want to dress. As for you, you'd better learn to live and let live."

Make ends meet

When someone is having trouble making enough money to pay the bills, we say the person is struggling to make ends meet.

"Where's your dad?" Sarah asked.

Elizabeth explained, "He's at work. He has to work overtime every night to pay the bills, and on weekends, too. He says it's what he has to do to make ends meet."

Make hay while the sun shines.

Farmers need dry weather to make hay, so they take advantage of sunny weather when it comes. This saying means that you should take advantage of good times when you have them, because they may not last forever.

Jason and Frank were watching television. They watched a commercial in which a famous basketball player flew through the air and made an amazing dunk.

"Why does he even bother making commercials?" Jason asked. "He makes millions just playing basketball."

"Go easy on the man," Frank said. "He's just trying to make hay while the sun shines. You think he'll be able to dunk like that in ten years?"

Money burning a hole in your pocket

Sometimes money gets spent so quickly that it almost seems like it's burning a hole in your pocket.

"A lot of people gave me tips after I shoveled their sidewalks over the winter," Luke said. "I'm rich!"

"So why don't you open a savings account and start putting your money in the bank?" Luke's big sister asked. "Otherwise, that money is just going to burn a hole in your pocket!"

On the warpath

When a group of Native Americans traveled to engage in battle, they were said to be on the warpath. Nowadays we use the phrase to describe anyone who is angry, in a bad mood, or eager to get in a fight.

"Just because Paul lost his camera doesn't mean he can go around yelling at everybody," Roger said.

"I know," Celia replied. "But he thinks someone stole it, and he's going to be on the warpath until that camera shows up!"

Once in a blue moon

A blue moon is the second full moon in a calendar month. Blue moons are rare. So something that happens only once in a blue moon happens rarely.

"Sarah," Rebecca said excitedly, "remember that skirt I liked? I just found it at the mall. It was on sale for 75 percent off!"

"Wow! How often does that happen?" Sarah replied.

"Once in a blue moon!" Rebecca cried.

One picture is worth a thousand words.

Often a picture can explain something better than words.

"Here's a picture of Rick after he won his diving medal." Sonia showed Mrs. Smith the photograph.

"Goodness!" Mrs. Smith said. "Doesn't he look proud!"

"Yes, he does," Sonia said. "Just look at his face. A picture is worth a thousand words!"

An ounce of prevention is worth a pound of cure.

People use this saying to mean that it's better to anticipate a problem and try to prevent it than to wait until it gets really bad later on.

"If you don't brush your teeth more often, you'll get cavities," Al's sister said. "And then you'll have to get fillings when you go to the dentist."

"Yikes, I don't want that to happen!" Al said. "I suppose you're right: an ounce of prevention is worth a pound of cure."

RSVP

When "RSVP" is written on an invitation, it means that the people who are inviting you would like you to tell them whether or not you will be able to come. "RSVP" is an abbreviation of the French phrase **r***épondez* **s***'il* **v***ous* **p***laît, which means "please reply."*

Helen was excited about receiving an invitation to Laura's birthday party. When she saw "RSVP" written on the invitation, she rushed to the phone. "Hello, Laura? It's Helen. I just called to RSVP. I would never miss your birthday party!"

Run-of-the-mill

We use this saying to describe anything that is very ordinary.

"How was your day, Carmen?" Mrs. Morello asked.

"It was pretty run-of-the-mill," Carmen replied. "But I'm really looking forward to our field trip to the museum tomorrow."

Seeing is believing.

This saying means that you can't necessarily believe something exists or is true unless you see the evidence for yourself.

"You should have seen the fish I caught," Eddie said. "It was this big!" He spread his arms as wide apart as he could.

"Yeah, right," said Daniel, shaking his head. He knew Eddie liked to exaggerate.

"I'm not kidding!" Eddie exclaimed. He ran into the house, and then staggered out holding a gigantic fish.

"Wow!" Daniel said. "Seeing is believing."

> **Make a Connection**
>
> Ask your child to think of examples from the stories she read in the Literature section that express some of the phrases she has just learned the meanings of. For example, "seeing is believing" could be applied to the story "The Fire on the Mountain" on page 24.

Shipshape

When a ship is ready to sail, with all its decks cleaned and equipment in good order, it is shipshape. We use this saying to describe anything that is in perfect order.

Mrs. Walters waved her hand around the messy classroom. The desks were littered with sheets of colored paper, pots of paint, pans of water, and paintbrushes. "Listen up!" she called out. "Nobody goes to lunch until this room is shipshape."

Through thick and thin

If you're riding a horse in the forest, it's harder to ride through thick woods than it is to ride through thin woods. But a determined rider will ride through thick and thin to get to his destination. We use this expression to describe someone who persists through good times and bad.

"Maleek and I are best friends," Dwayne explained. "He's stuck with me through thick and thin."

Timbuktu

Timbuktu is a famous town in Africa. When people use the term, however, they usually mean a place that seems exotic or very far away.

When the factory closed, Susan asked her mother, "Does this mean that Dad is going to be transferred to a new location?"

Susan's mother replied, "It looks that way. Let's just hope they don't send him to Timbuktu."

Two wrongs don't make a right.

We use this saying to remind each other that you can't correct a wrong action by doing something else that's wrong.

"Carl hit me, so I hit him back!" Bill said.

"What's the point of that?" Bill's big brother asked. "It didn't make anything better, did it? Two wrongs don't make a right, you know."

When it rains, it pours.

When people say this, they mean that something that starts out bad can turn into a disaster.

Kelli limped into the kitchen and collapsed on a chair.

"What happened to you?" her brother asked.

Kelli grimaced. "What a rotten day! First, I missed the bus and had to walk to school. When I got there, I got in trouble for being late. Then, I messed up on my math test, realized I left my lunch at home this morning, and turned my ankle in gym class. And now I think I'm getting a cold. I'll tell you, when it rains, it pours!"

You can lead a horse to water, but you can't make it drink.

This saying means that you can show people what you want them to do, but you cannot force them to do it.

Vera disliked bowling. All of her friends insisted that she come with them to the bowling alley, though, because they needed an extra person on their team.

"Who cares whether or not you hit a bunch of pins with a stupid ball?" Vera thought. When it was her turn to play, she crossed her arms over her chest and refused. She explained, "Just because you got me to come with you doesn't mean I'm going to play. You can lead a horse to water, but you can't make it drink!"

Suggested Resources

Poetry

A Child's Garden of Verses, by Robert Louis Stevenson (Sterling, 2007)

The Random House Book of Poetry for Children, by Jack Prelutsky and Arnold Lobel (Random House, 1983)

The Twentieth Century Children's Poetry Treasury, by Jack Prelutsky (Knopf Books for Young Readers, 1999)

Stories and Myths

Chinese Fairy Tales, by Frederick H. Martens (Dover Publications, 2012)

Chinese Fairy Tales and Fantasies, by Moss Roberts (Pantheon, 2007)

Favorite Children's Stories from China and Tibet, by Lotta Carswell-Hume (Tuttle Publishing, 2012)

Native American Tales and Legends, by Allan A. Macfarlan (Dover Publications, 2012)

When the World Began: Stories Collected in Ethiopia, by Elizabeth Laird (Oxford University Press, 2000)

The Core Knowledge Language Arts program for grade 4 is available for purchase through Amplify Education. Select units are available for free download from www.coreknowledge.org/ckla-files. These materials are designed to teach basic spelling, vocabulary development, reading comprehension, grammar, and writing skills.

II
Geography
and History

Introduction

So what does your child need to know about geography and history? In this chapter, we'll review the basics of geography, world history, and early American history. Geography is the study of what's where, why it's there, and why we should care. It analyzes how humans are challenged by, adapt to, use, and change their natural environments. By fourth grade, students should know the rudiments of world and North American geography. They should be able to read and color maps—and make simple maps of their own. They should be shown maps of their own town and state, be invited to study maps during field trips and family vacations, and, as their skills develop, be allowed to navigate on trips. Children can learn more about geography from atlases, books on foreign lands, subscriptions to geography magazines such as *National Geographic Kids*, and online interactive maps such as Google Earth.

In both world and American history, we have tried to emphasize the *story* in history, without overly emphasizing dates. Some crucial dates—such as 1066, 1492, and 1776—should be memorized. Most others serve a useful purpose without being committed to memory, because they help reinforce the child's sense of chronology and historical context. And they establish a foundation for more sophisticated understanding in years to come.

The world history topics for fourth grade build on the topics introduced in third grade. In third grade, students studied ancient Rome. In fourth grade, they learn about the cultures that developed in Europe when the Western Roman Empire collapsed. They also learn about other civilizations that flourished in this era, including China, several African kingdoms, and an Islamic empire.

In American history, children build on their knowledge of the colonial period from third grade as they learn about the Revolutionary War, the Declaration of Independence, the Constitution, the first presidents, and some early American reformers. The ideas and events discussed are central to our national identity and to our understanding of what it means to be a citizen of the United States.

Several of the readings in the Language and Literature section can be connected with topics in this chapter: the Ethiopian folktale with ancient African kingdoms; the Chinese folktale with ancient China; King Arthur and Robin Hood with the Middle Ages; and the poems by Longfellow, Emerson, and the Benéts with the American Revolution.

Parents and teachers are encouraged to build on the foundation provided here by discussing what fascinates children about history and seeking out additional books on topics of interest. At the end of this chapter, you will find a list of high-quality books on various topics that will help you do just that.

World Geography

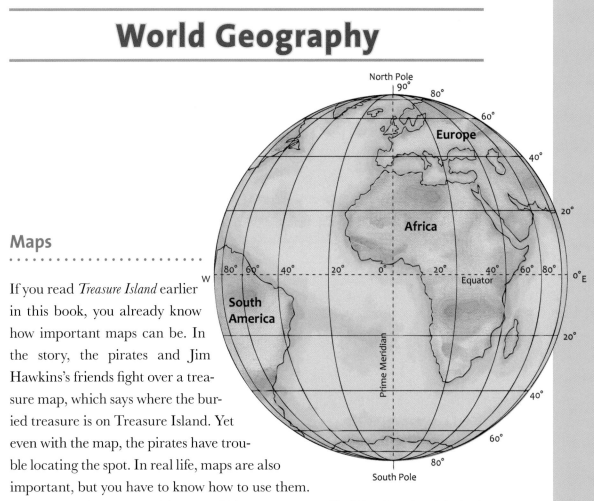

Maps

If you read *Treasure Island* earlier in this book, you already know how important maps can be. In the story, the pirates and Jim Hawkins's friends fight over a treasure map, which says where the buried treasure is on Treasure Island. Yet even with the map, the pirates have trouble locating the spot. In real life, maps are also important, but you have to know how to use them.

Look at the map on this page. This map shows half of Earth as it might look from a spaceship in orbit. You may already know that the imaginary line that divides the globe around the middle is called the equator. But what about all those other lines parallel to the equator? And what about the lines that run north and south? What are they for?

Mapmakers draw imaginary lines and divide the world into sections in order to locate places accurately. The lines running parallel to the equator are called parallels; they measure degrees of latitude north and south of the equator. The lines that run from pole to pole are called meridians; they measure degrees of longitude east and west of the prime meridian. You can remember the difference

All Together

To help your child remember the difference between parallels and meridians, repeat this mnemonic aloud with him several times: parallels are parallel, and meridians meet.

between meridians and parallels by remembering that parallels are parallel and **m**eridians **m**eet at the poles.

Can you see how the parallels and meridians intersect? They form a grid on which you can pinpoint any location. Each point of intersection is a coordinate. Looking at the map, you can also see that each parallel and each meridian has its own number. We will learn more about these numbers and about coordinates.

But first, how does the map below differ from the first map you looked at? The first map looks almost like a picture of a globe. But this map looks more like a globe cut open along a north-to-south seam through the Pacific Ocean and stretched flat. Mapmakers do this to show the whole world on one map.

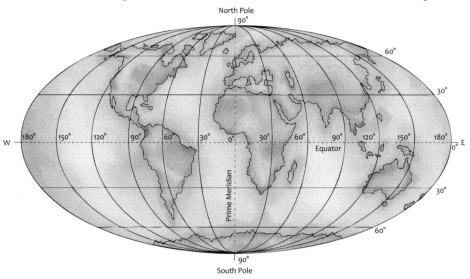

Hemispheres

Mapmakers and people who use maps sometimes divide Earth into large sections shaped like half a grapefruit. These sections are called hemispheres. "Hemisphere" is a Greek word meaning "half a sphere." On the stretched-out map above, you can see that the equator divides the globe into two hemispheres. Everything north of the equator is in the Northern Hemisphere; everything south of the equator is in the Southern Hemisphere.

Earth can also be divided into Eastern and Western Hemispheres. The meridian that divides these two hemispheres runs through Greenwich [GREN-itch], England. Many years ago, when our system of longitude and latitude was created, Greenwich was the home of a famous observatory, where astronomers studied the stars. Mapmakers agreed to use this location for an imaginary line just as important as the equator but running from the North Pole to the South Pole. This line is called the prime meridian.

Can you find the prime meridian on the map? Look for the meridian that runs north and south through England and is marked 0°. The small superscript circle after the zero is a symbol that stands for "degree." Degrees are the units we use to measure longitude and latitude. Everything to the west of the prime meridian on the stretched-out map is in the Western Hemisphere, and everything to the east is in the Eastern Hemisphere. Find the Eastern and Western Hemispheres on the map on page 96 and then, if possible, on a globe.

Follow Your Finger

To look at the hemispheres in more detail, you'll need a globe. First, find the prime meridian. With your finger, trace this line to the equator. Do you see that the prime meridian is marked 0°?

Next, trace your finger along the equator moving west from the prime meridian. See how the degree numbers on the meridians go up as you go west? When you reach the 180th meridian (180°), you've gone exactly halfway around the world. The 180th meridian is the continuation of the prime meridian on the other side of the globe. The 180° line and the prime meridian (0°) divide the globe into the Eastern and Western Hemispheres.

Continue tracing your finger along the equator to the west. What hemisphere are you crossing now? What happens to the longitude degree marks as you move back toward the prime meridian? Do the numbers keep getting larger or do they get smaller?

Coordinates

Now that you know about the prime meridian and the equator, you can find the coordinates for any place in the world. Let's find the coordinates for the country of Greece to see how this is done.

To begin with, you'll need to find Greece on the map on page 95 by looking for the Mediterranean Sea. Can you find Italy's boot? Greece is the peninsula that extends into the Mediterranean just east of Italy. You can see that a parallel and meridian intersect over Greece. The parallel is marked 40°, and the meridian is marked 20°.

So the coordinates of Greece are 40° and 20°, but how do we write these coordinates? To show the exact location in the Eastern Hemisphere, we write 40°N, 20°E, because Greece is 40° north of the equator and 20° east of the prime meridian. 40°N tells you the latitude of Greece, and 20°E tells you its longitude. Put the two together and you've got its location.

Can you find 20°S, 20°E on the same map? What continent is this spot in? How about 20°S, 40°W?

> **Do It Yourself**
>
> Now that you've identified several locations, ask your child to find the coordinates of her own state or hometown. You may need to do this using a map of the Western Hemisphere with more detailed lines of latitude and longitude.

Map Scale

Take a look at the three maps that follow. Notice how each map focuses on a smaller area and shows more detail about the rivers or roads in that area. The map of the United States shows forty-eight states, while the state map shows just one state, Virginia, and the city map shows only one city in that state, Richmond. The full map of the United States shows much more of the world's surface than the state map, and the state map shows much more than the city map.

Each of these three maps is drawn to a different scale. Scale is the proportion between the distance on the map and the actual distance on Earth's surface. For

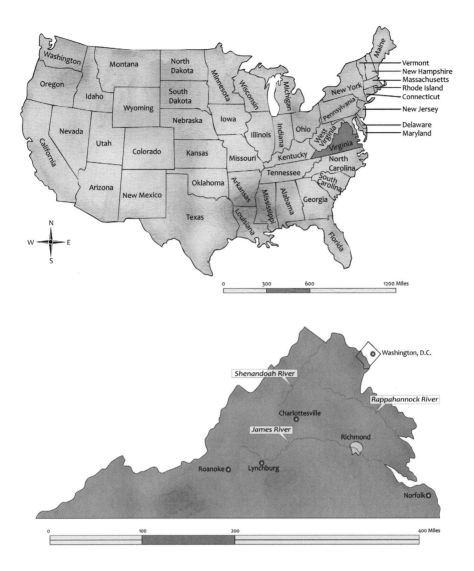

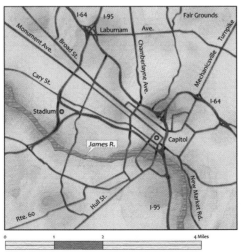

instance, a distance of one inch on one map might represent one real mile; on another map, one inch might represent one hundred miles.

To figure out how much real distance is represented on a map, you'll need to use the map scale. The map scale looks like a ruler and is often located at the bottom of a map or in a corner. On the national map, the scale is in the lower right. It tells you that the distance to the first mark represents three hundred miles in real life. On the state map, the distance to the first mark represents one hundred miles, but on the city map, the distance to the first mark represents only one mile.

You will use the scale to measure distances from place to place. Find a ruler or a piece of string and use it to measure the distance from the stadium to the capitol on the city map. It should be about one inch. Then, place the ruler or string next to the scale for the city map to find out how much real distance one inch on the map represents: two miles. So the distance between the stadium and the capitol—as the crow flies—is about two miles. If you were touring Richmond, you could probably walk or bike between these two places.

Now look back at the state map and measure the distance from Lynchburg to Charlottesville. You should find that this distance is less than one inch. Does that mean it would be easier to travel from Lynchburg to Charlottesville than it was to travel from the stadium to the capitol? Not so fast! First, figure out what real distance that one inch represents on *this* map. If you place your ruler next to the scale, you'll see that one inch on this map represents one hundred miles, so the distance from Lynchburg to Charlottesville is less than one hundred miles— perhaps about 75 miles. If you were touring the cities of Virginia, you would probably want to drive! However, you couldn't actually travel as the crow flies; you would need to travel as the wolf runs by staying on roads.

What a Relief!

The map of the United States on page 99 is a political map. It shows human-made boundaries, such as the boundaries between the states. But it does not tell you about the physical features of the land. You can't tell from this map whether

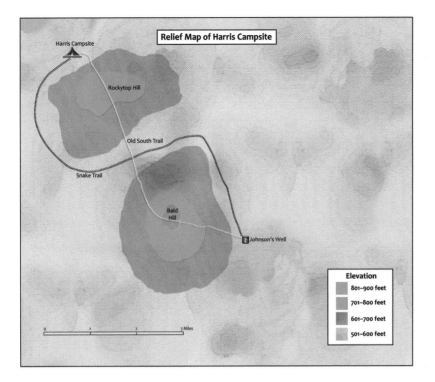

Relief Map of Harris Campsite

Harris Campsite

Rockytop Hill

Old South Trail

Snake Trail

Bald Hill

Johnson's Well

0   1   2   3 Miles

Elevation
801–900 feet
701–800 feet
601–700 feet
501–600 feet

Kansas is peaked with mountains or flat as a board. If you want to learn how flat or hilly a particular area is, you need to consult a special kind of map called a relief map.

Take a look at the relief map of the Harris campsite. It shows two hills—Rockytop Hill and Bald Hill. Can you use the key in the lower right to figure out which hill is higher? The top of Bald Hill is shaded orange. This color shows that the spot is between 801 and 900 feet above sea level. The highest part of Rockytop Hill is shaded green, which means it is between 701 and 800 feet above sea level. By comparing the colors using the map key, you can figure out the answer: Bald Hill is higher.

What if you wanted to hike from the Harris Campsite to Johnson's Well? There are two paths you could take: Snake Trail or Old South Trail. Which path is more direct? Which path is hillier? About how far would you walk if you followed Old South Trail? How about Snake Trail? (Hint: You may want to use a piece of string, instead of just a ruler, to measure the twisty paths.)

Mountains of the World

One piece of information a relief map can give you is where the tallest mountains are located. Look at the map below. It shows some of the major mountain ranges of the world and some of the tallest peaks. Let's learn a little about these ranges and peaks. As we do, look back at this map to find the ranges and peaks you learn about.

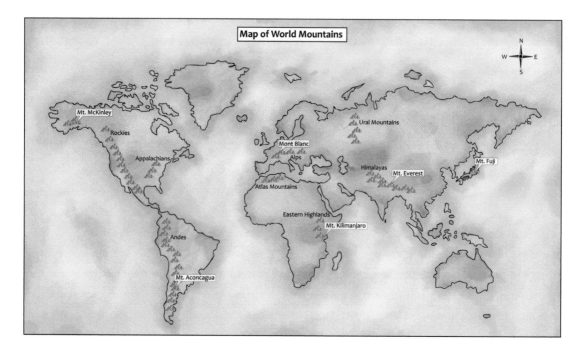

Map of World Mountains

Andes Mountains

The Andes [AN-deez] in South America stretch nearly 5,500 miles from the southern tip of the continent to the Caribbean coast. The highest mountain in the Andes, Mount Aconcagua, rises 22,831 feet above sea level.

The Andes Mountains and the surrounding territory were the home of the ancient Inca civilization. The Inca built a famous city, Machu Picchu, on a mountain ridge in the Andes.

Appalachian Mountains

The worn peaks of the Appalachians

The Appalachian Mountains extend nearly two thousand miles from Alabama to the Gulf of Saint Lawrence in Canada. They include the White Mountains of New Hampshire, the Allegheny Mountains of New York, Pennsylvania, and West Virginia, the Blue Ridge Mountains stretching from Georgia to Pennsylvania, and the Great Smoky Mountains of North Carolina and Tennessee.

The Appalachians have played an important role in the settlement of the United States. During the early years of colonial America, most settlers stayed east of the Appalachians, along the coast of the Atlantic Ocean. Eventually, Daniel Boone and other pioneers found passes that led through the Appalachians. These mountain passes opened the way for settlement in the Midwest and the Great Plains during the 1800s.

The Rockies

West of the Appalachians and beyond the Great Plains lie the Rocky Mountains. The Rockies stretch more than three thousand miles from New Mexico through the United States and Canada and north to Alaska. Denali (Mount McKinley) in Alaska is the highest mountain in North America at 20,237 feet above sea level.

The jagged peaks of the Rocky Mountains in Colorado have snow on them. The higher the altitude gets, the colder the temperature becomes, so even though there is no snow on the ground in the valley pictured here, there is snow on the mountains!

The Rockies are much taller than the Appalachians—so much taller that the Appalachians look like rolling hills in comparison. Because of their high elevations, the Rockies were an even bigger barrier to settlers. Eventually, pioneers blazed paths to the West such as the Mormon Trail and the Oregon Trail, and thousands of settlers followed these trails across the Rockies to Washington, Oregon, and California.

Why a Tall Mountain Is a Young Mountain

Geographers have discovered a general rule about the age of mountains—young mountains tend to be tall, while old mountains tend to be shorter. The Rockies and Appalachians are good examples of this rule. Scientists tell us the Rockies are about 70 million years old and the Appalachians are about 280 million years old.

Because the Appalachians are so old, their peaks have been worn down by weathering and erosion over millions of years. These natural processes explain why the Appalachians have a rounded look and seldom rise above six thousand feet. The Rockies, by contrast, are younger, and so they have not been worn down as much. Many peaks are pointed and jagged, and dozens rise more than fourteen thousand feet above sea level.

The High Peaks of the Himalayas

Although the Rockies are tall, they are not nearly as tall as the Himalayas in Asia, where many peaks reach more than twenty-five thousand feet. This range includes the world's tallest mountain, Mount Everest, which rises 29,035 feet above sea level.

The peak of Mount Everest

Until 1953, no person had ever climbed to the top of Mount Everest. Freezing temperatures, ferocious winds, avalanches, and blizzards stopped everyone who tried. Another obstacle was thin air. Humans breathe oxygen to survive, but not all of the air in our atmosphere contains the same amount of oxygen. As you climb farther above sea level, the amount of oxygen in the air decreases—the air gets thinner. On top of Mount Everest, the air is so thin that even the slightest physical actions can leave you gasping for breath.

Talk and Think

Several unsuccessful expeditions to reach the summit of Mount Everest (and return safely) occurred before Hillary and Norgay. Why do you think people attempted to climb such a dangerous mountain as Mount Everest?

The first people to overcome all these obstacles and reach the peak were New Zealand beekeeper Edmund Hillary and his Tibetan guide, Tenzing Norgay, in May 1953. Although they spent only fifteen minutes at the peak, Hillary and Norgay were regarded as international heroes for their successful climb and descent, paving the way for future expeditions.

Tenzing Norgay and Edmund Hillary being honored after becoming the first people to climb to the peak of Mount Everest

Ural Mountains

The Ural Mountains, as you can see on the map on page 102, run right between Asia and Europe. In fact, the eastern side of the mountain range is considered a traditional boundary marker between the two continents. The Urals extend about 1,550 miles roughly north to south. These mountains are very old and, therefore, are shorter than some of the other mountains about which you are reading. The highest peak, Mount Narodnaya, is little more than 6,200 feet tall. The Urals are thought to be 250 million to 300 million years old, and scientists consider even their relatively small height to be tall for such old mountains.

African Mountains

The Atlas Mountains stretch for about 1,200 miles along the northwest coast of Africa. These mountains are named for the Greek god Atlas, who supported the sky on his shoulders. With an average height of eleven thousand feet above sea level, the Atlas Mountains are tall enough to keep coastal rains from moving inland and watering the Sahara Desert.

Mount Kilimanjaro and its icy peak

The tallest mountain in Africa is Mount Kilimanjaro, at 19,340 feet above sea level. This beautiful, towering peak is actually the remains of three ancient volcanoes. Even though it is close to the equator, where temperatures are continually hot, Kilimanjaro has such a high elevation that it wears a cap of ice throughout the year.

The Alps

The Alps cover much of Switzerland and Austria as well as parts of France and Italy. The highest peak in the Alps is 15,771-foot Mont Blanc. "Mont Blanc" means "white mountain" in French. Why might it be named this, based on your understanding of tall mountains?

In 1991, two hikers in the Alps came across a human body frozen in the snow. Tests revealed that the body was roughly 5,300 years old. Freezing temperatures had preserved the man's body so well that it was like an ice mummy. Scientists were able to determine how old the man was when he died, what he was wearing, and even what he ate for his last meal. The iceman—nicknamed "Ötzi"—was between twenty-five and thirty-five years old when he died. He stood about five feet tall, wore a fur cap and leather shoes, and carried an ax, bow, and arrows. The iceman of the Alps has given scientists valuable new information about how people lived in prehistoric times.

This is what Ötzi, the Iceman of the Alps, might have looked like when he was alive about five thousand years ago.

World History

Europe in the Middle Ages

A world of kings and queens, knights and castles may sound like a page from a fantasy book, but these are not make-believe stories. History is full of tales of legendary heroes, and our study of world history begins here. Welcome to the Middle Ages!

"Middle of what?" you might ask. The phrase "Middle Ages" and the adjective "medieval" refer to the period of European history between ancient and modern times. Some historians say the Middle Ages span from 476 to 1453 CE. Others might not use exact dates, but generally they agree with this time span.

> **Talk and Think**
>
> Take a moment to review the two traditional systems of calendar eras. BC (Before Christ) and AD (*Anno Domini* or "In the Year of Our Lord") were typically used before the secular system, BCE (Before Common Era) and CE (Common Era), became popular. The two systems are equivalent (i.e., "476 CE" corresponds to "AD 476").

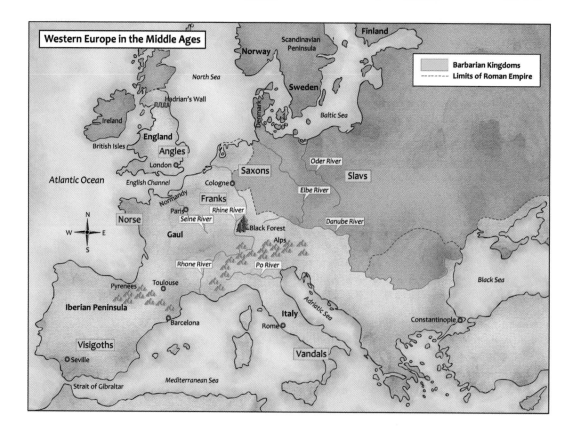

Map: Western Europe in the Middle Ages

Barbarian Kingdoms
Limits of Roman Empire

Map labels: Finland, Norway, Scandinavian Peninsula, North Sea, Sweden, Denmark, Baltic Sea, Hadrian's Wall, Ireland, England, British Isles, Angles, London, Oder River, Slavs, Atlantic Ocean, English Channel, Cologne, Saxons, Elbe River, Normandy, Franks, Rhine River, Paris, Seine River, Danube River, Norse, Black Forest, Gaul, Alps, Rhone River, Po River, Pyrenees, Toulouse, Black Sea, Iberian Peninsula, Italy, Adriatic Sea, Barcelona, Rome, Constantinople, Visigoths, Seville, Vandals, Strait of Gibraltar, Mediterranean Sea

After Rome

The Middle Ages began when the vast Roman Empire collapsed. The Romans had controlled all the lands along the coast of the Mediterranean Sea, including Greece, Turkey, Egypt, and North Africa. Julius Caesar had conquered what is now France, and other Roman generals had crossed the Pyrenees and gained control of the Iberian Peninsula, including modern-day Spain and Portugal. The Romans had even crossed the English Channel and colonized England, Wales, and part of Scotland. The only parts of Europe that remained free from Roman control were Ireland, northern Scotland, Scandinavia, and the lands east of the Danube and Rhine Rivers.

By the 300s and 400s, the Roman Empire had grown too big with too many distinct territories for one person to rule. The Roman emperor Diocletian's solution was to split the empire in two. The western emperor, based in Rome, ruled Italy, France, Spain, England, and other western lands. The eastern emperor based his capital in Constantinople (now called Istanbul) and ruled Greece, Turkey, the Balkan Peninsula, and the Middle East. Diocletian maintained control of the eastern half of the empire because it had greater wealth and access to trade routes. Diocletian appointed a military officer named Maximian to rule the western half.

As early as the year 200, new people started entering Roman territory. They were experienced warriors, and eventually they learned to outfight the Roman armies. By 476, these people had overthrown the last western Roman emperor and set up barbarian kingdoms. Some of these kingdoms eventually became modern countries like France and England. But in the East, the other Roman emperor kept on ruling. The Eastern Roman Empire (also known as the Byzantine Empire) lasted until 1453.

What Does That Mean?

The ancient Greeks and Romans called foreigners *barbarians* because they did not understand their languages. When the foreigners spoke, the Greeks heard only "bar . . . bar . . . bar."

The Barbarians

The fiercest barbarians, the Huns, originally lived north of China. The Huns tried to invade China for many centuries, but the Great Wall of China prevented them from entering China. Then, in the mid-400s, their invasions turned westward and extended all the way to Europe under the leadership of their king, Attila [ah-TILL-ah]. Everywhere the Huns went they caused terrible destruction. They became famous for their wild and savage ways.

Other tribes also succeeded in taking over Roman territories. The Visigoths sacked the city of Rome in 410 and eventually settled in Spain. The Vandals looted Italy so badly that the word "vandalism" is still used to describe destruction of other people's property. The Franks were Germanic

Take a Look
Ask your child to look at the borders of the Roman Empire on the map. Discuss how these borders changed as a result of invasion from barbarian kingdoms, especially the Visigoths on the Iberian Peninsula, the Vandals on the Italian Peninsula, the Franks in northern Gaul, and the Angles and Saxons on the British Isles.

tribes that settled in modern France, which is named for them. The Angles took over Britain and gave their name to England ("Angle-land"). At the same time, the Saxons also invaded Britain. The languages of the Angles and Saxons eventually blended together to form Anglo-Saxon, or Old English. Old English is the earliest form of the English language, spoken a thousand years ago. Many of our most common words can be traced back to Anglo-Saxon, such as "man," "house," and "dog."

Were the Dark Ages Really So Dark?

You may have heard the Middle Ages called the Dark Ages. This name is sometimes applied to the first three hundred years or so after the fall of Rome, and sometimes to the whole medieval period. The Italian poet Petrarch coined the phrase. Petrarch, who lived much later, in the 1300s, praised the culture of the ancient Greeks and Romans, feeling that nothing positive had happened after the fall of Rome. He saw the Middle Ages as a time of violence, poverty, and ignorance. To Petrarch, the Dark Ages were a period of "darkness" after the classical period of Roman greatness.

Today, we know that Petrarch was unfair to the Middle Ages. The Middle Ages had their fair share of poverty and warfare, and only a few people could read and write. But all of these problems were common before and after the Middle Ages, and now we understand that it is inaccurate to describe the whole period as an age of darkness. As you will see, medieval times included great achievements in government, religion, and art.

The Rise of the Christian Church

For the Christian Church, the early Middle Ages were a time of growth. Christianity expanded across the Roman Empire under the rule of Emperor Constantine and became the empire's official religion under Emperor Theodosius I in 380 CE. The religion continued to prosper even after the Western Roman Empire collapsed.

The early Christians referred to barbarians and other non-Christians as heathens [HEE-thens], and they felt it was their duty to convert these heathens to

Christianity. Most of the invading tribes eventually did accept Christianity as their main religion.

The leader of the western Christian Church, the bishop of Rome, was called the pope. The pope claimed to be Jesus Christ's (or God's) representative on Earth. During the Middle Ages, popes formed partnerships with kings and nobles throughout Western Europe, a move that helped the popes become increasingly powerful figures.

As time went on, conflicts developed between the eastern followers of the church, who spoke Greek, and the western followers, who spoke Latin. In 1054 CE, the two sides split in a quarrel over what were true Christian beliefs and practices. As a result, they formed separate churches during the Great Schism [SKI-zum]. The eastern church became known as Orthodox, because it claimed its beliefs were orthodox (or "correct"). The western church called itself Catholic, because it claimed

Pope Gregory VII, head of the Roman Catholic Church 1073–1085

to be universal, which is what the word "catholic" means. Today, there are still two churches—Orthodox and Roman Catholic—that were formed by that split in the Middle Ages.

Over time, the western church grew wealthy and powerful. Kings and nobles donated land and gold in exchange for political favors, and as a result, the Roman Catholic Church became richer than any king in Europe.

Make a Connection

Look at page 225 to see an example of an illuminated manuscript created by monks.

Monks—men who chose to devote their lives to the Roman Catholic Church—were usually the best-educated people in medieval Europe. Some monks lived alone and separate from society, although many lived with other monks in close-knit communities called monasteries. Monks spent their entire lives in monasteries, performing chores and praying. Women who devoted their lives to the church and lived together were called nuns. During the Middle Ages, monks and nuns studied the writings of ancient Greeks and Romans. They took special

A monk copying a manuscript

care of the original documents and copied the text by hand. Thanks to their efforts, we can read ancient history and philosophy, which might have been destroyed otherwise.

Beginning around 800 CE, church leaders and monasteries started schools for children. About three hundred years later, the church established the first universities. In these schools, students learned to read, write, and speak Latin. They also studied astronomy, mathematics, medicine, and literature. But books were expensive, because they were copied by hand, so many students learned primarily from their teacher's lectures.

Charlemagne

Remember the Franks who invaded northern Europe? In 771, a mighty ruler took control of the Frankish land. His name was Charlemagne [SHAR-luh-main], which means "Charles the Great." Charlemagne reigned for more than forty-five years. He conquered other lands to increase the size of his empire. Ultimately, Charlemagne unified most of the western lands of the old Roman Empire. The pope recognized Charlemagne's considerable power and crowned him "Emperor of the Romans." In return, Charlemagne's military protected the pope.

Charlemagne had a great interest in education and culture. He invited scholars from all over Europe to his court. He encouraged a rebirth in the arts and rewarded men who were loyal to him. Those who worked for him in the military or the government received land as payment.

When Charlemagne died in 814, his empire disintegrated. More barbarians (such as the Norse Vikings) overran Europe. But Charlemagne had a lasting influence on European history. His practice of rewarding men with land spread throughout Western Europe and became the basis for a way of life called feudalism or the feudal system.

Feudalism

The phrase "feudal system" is almost as controversial today as "Dark Ages." It was never used in the Middle Ages. The phrase was invented later, and historians disagree over whether it is an appropriate term. Still, the term has stuck in many people's minds to the point where it's difficult to talk about the Middle Ages without using the term.

When we talk about feudalism, we mean a social system in which land was exchanged for service. The person who received the land was called the vassal. He promised to serve the original landowner, who was called the lord. The land grant that the lord made was called a fief [feef].

Some vassals served a king. Others served a rich and powerful lord in their region. Vassals were supposed to keep the fief only as long as they served their king or lord faithfully. Vassals, lords, and kings swore oaths to observe these rules, and the church taught that breaking these oaths was a terrible sin.

The lord's power was based on the number of vassals who swore loyalty to him. The more vassals he had, the more powerful he was. A woman might become a lord if her husband died and she had no son or other male relative, but in general, men dominated medieval government and society.

Lords were responsible to their king. A king expected that his lords would supply fighters when he needed them. These fighters were called knights. During battles, they wore metal armor designed to protect their bodies from heavy swords and other weapons. They often fought on horseback. Knights swore loyalty to their lord and their king. They received their pay in land or in money from those they conquered.

Although kings and lords were the most powerful people during the Middle Ages, peasants, or serfs, who worked on the lord's manors, or farms, did most of

Medieval knights riding into battle

the work. Serfs could not move away from the village without the lord's permission. They grew food, tended animals, and wove cloth. Serfdom was a hard life, but serfs were not enslaved; the lord could not sell them or members of their families. The king was supposed to protect the serfs and respect their rights.

In general, medieval society was like a pyramid, with the king and lords on top, knights below, and serfs on the bottom.

Consider the advantages and disadvantages of living in a feudal society. Who benefits the most? What problems and difficulties does it create?

Lords and Castles

Many times, the lord controlled a whole village and the surrounding land. The lord interpreted the laws and enforced them. He made money by collecting taxes and dues from his serfs and by making them share their crops or livestock. Sometimes he ran a mill or brewery, making them pay to grind their grain into flour or ferment it into beer.

At the same time, the serfs knew the lord would offer them protection in his castle in case of war or a raid from attackers. Protection was important because medieval life could be violent. There was not a large police force to prevent crime. Nobles feuded among themselves and often raided each other's lands. Kings fought wars against neighboring kings, while also facing rebellions from their lords. To defend themselves, nobles built castles in which they lived and stored weapons. Early medieval castles were simple wooden forts. Later, kings built stronger castles out of stone. Castle walls sometimes enclosed a series of small buildings, creating a little town. The castle needed a water supply within the walls, and food was stored so that people could withstand a siege [seej], or a prolonged external attack.

Life in a Castle

Castles were designed for protection, not comfort. Life in a castle was not pleasant. Most castles had only a few rooms: a great hall, a kitchen, and possibly a private chamber for the lord and his wife. The great hall was usually where everyone gathered together. People slept, ate, played, and worked in the great hall. Heat came from smoky buckets of coals or from fireplaces. The windows were small, and candles provided dim light. The stone walls and floors were cold and uncomfortable. The bathrooms were outhouses in the castle walls, with straw instead of toilet paper!

Noble fathers and mothers did not spend much time with their children. Nursemaids tended the young children. Books were extremely rare, but children of the Middle Ages did play with toys and listen to stories. Traveling storytellers and musicians (called minstrels), clowns (called jesters), and troupes of actors

often visited a castle to provide entertainment. From paintings, we can tell that people sometimes gathered to dance and to play outdoor sports. Our games of tennis, croquet, and bowling all began as lawn games during the Middle Ages.

Tutors sometimes taught young noble boys. At seven years of age, many of these boys were sent away to be educated, typically at the castle of a relative. There, they would serve as pages. Pages worked for knights and nobles, performing simple tasks such as running messages or serving food. After seven years of service, a page could rise to the next level and become a squire. Squires were still servants, but they began to train for military service and could accompany knights to battle.

The lines below are from a famous collection called *The Canterbury Tales*, written during the Middle Ages by the English poet Geoffrey Chaucer. In these tales, a group of English men and women ride together on a pilgrimage, or religious journey, to the cathedral at Canterbury. The lines describe one of the pilgrims, a squire. First, notice the old-fashioned kind of English it uses—maybe you can guess the meaning of some words. Then, read what it says in modern English.

> **All Together**
> Read the Middle English text aloud with your child. Some words may sound silly or different, but some sound the same!

Short was his gowne, with sleves longe and wyde.
Wel koude he sitte on hors and faire ryde.
He koude songes make and wel endite,
Juste and eek daunce, and weel purtreye and write.
So hoote he lovede that by nyghtertale
He sleep namoore than dooth a nyghtyngale.
Curteis he was, lowely and servysáble,
And carf biforn his fader at the table.

His gown was short, with sleeves long and wide.
He could sit well on a horse and ride well.
He could make songs and compose well,
Joust and also dance, and draw and write well.

He loved so hotly that at night
He slept no more than a nightingale does.
He was courteous, humble, and willing to
    serve,
And carved in front of his father at the table.

Chaucer's squire

Squires who succeeded in their years of training became knights. Noble birth was not required for a boy to become a knight. However, a knight's horse, armor, and weapons were very expensive, so most knights came from wealthy families. Knights were exclusively male. Noble girls were brought up to be ladies— they were taught sewing, embroidery, weaving, singing, and how to use herbs for healing. A few girls learned to ride horses (sidesaddle, with their long skirts draped over one side).

The Life of a Knight

Young men eager to become knights could prove their strength and abilities by taking part in tournaments. Tournaments, or jousting matches, were fake battles staged for practice, fun, and fame. Here is an announcement of a jousting match from around 1400 CE:

> *Six gentlemen this 3rd day of May next, shall come before the high and mighty re-doubted ladies and gentlemen to appear at just before noon, to joust with all comers on said day until six that afternoon.*
>
> *And the said ladies and gentlewomen shall give unto the best jouster of all a costly diamond. Unto the next best a ruby worth half as much. And to the third a sapphire worth half of that. And on the said day there should be officers or arms to measure that the spears are of the same length.*

Chivalry

During the Middle Ages, noblemen and noblewomen developed their own customs and rules for good behavior. This set of rules is called the code of chivalry [SHIV-al-ree], after the French word *chevalier* [she-val-YAY], which means "horseman" or "knight." According to the code of chivalry, knights were supposed to guard women, help the poor, serve the church, and treat fellow knights as brothers. Knights were expected to be brave in war and gentle toward women. They treated knights captured in war as honored guests until a ransom, or reward money, was received and the captured knight was free to return home.

Medieval Towns

By the 1200s and 1300s, many people were moving from country villages to larger towns and cities, where they found jobs. Lords tried to keep serfs at home by treating them better. They gave them more freedom and offered lower taxes and rents. But still, many serfs left for the better opportunities in towns. By 1300, there were few serfs left in Western Europe, although serfdom did continue in Eastern Europe (where it had previously been less common).

In the 1300s, the largest cities, such as Florence, Italy, and Paris, France, had fewer than a hundred thousand people. Yet they were still crowded with street vendors, shopkeepers, and traders selling objects from distant regions. Most towns held markets two or three times a week, where local farmers sold produce and craftsmen and traders sold everything from candles to clothes. In a typical town, up to half the adult males were craftsmen making tools, furniture, and other important items by hand.

Learning Your Trade

Medieval craftsmen and merchants formed associations called guilds. A town might have a carpenters' guild, a butchers' guild, a shoemakers' guild, and a cloth merchants' guild, among others. The vast majority of guild members were men, but women were allowed to join in some instances. Guilds set down strict rules about how, when, and where people could trade. Only guild members could do business in certain towns, and prices were fixed by the guild. If a member made something that did not meet the guild's standards for workmanship, he might have to pay a fine or could be kicked out of the guild.

Medieval children began training for a craft or trade between the ages of seven and nine. The father paid a master craftsman or merchant to train his son as an apprentice. Apprentices lived in the home of the master who taught them. They worked for that master for seven years. Eventually, the apprentice became a journeyman, who traveled around to learn more from other masters. If he was smart and lucky, a journeyman might finally become a master, join a guild, set up a shop, get married, and start a family—and then one day teach his trade to a new apprentice.

Charters and Churches

As medieval towns grew, kings and nobles granted townspeople the right to govern themselves through a mayor and town council. They spelled out these rights in town charters. Medieval towns were not very democratic because only a few of the richest merchants and craftsmen held almost all the power. Still, it was during the Middle Ages that the idea emerged that people had rights and liberties and could govern themselves.

Making Connections

Turn to page 221 to learn more about the building of cathedrals in the Middle Ages.

Medieval people took religion and its message of helping the poor very seriously. They built hospitals and other institutions to help people in need. They believed helping those in need allowed them to express their love for God. They also built large, beautiful churches and cathedrals that expressed God's greatness and people's pride in their city. Sometimes, it would take more than a hundred years to complete a great medieval church, and the people who started building it died long before its completion. Today, several medieval churches are considered to be examples of the world's finest architecture.

However, the deep religious feelings that medieval society held caused problems for dissenters. Some people expressed ideas that were different from what the pope and other church leaders said. Church leaders referred to these contradictory opinions as "heresy" and the people who held them as "heretics." Often, these heretics were treated cruelly. Some Christians also mistreated the Jewish people who lived in medieval cities. At times, conflicts over what were the true beliefs of a religion sparked violence.

England: The Rise of a Medieval Kingdom

Remember how England was conquered by the barbarian Angles and Saxons after the fall of Rome? After many years of fighting among themselves, the Anglo-Saxon people came together under a single king and converted to Christianity around 600 CE.

One of the most important Anglo-Saxon kings was called Edward the Confessor. Edward the Confessor got his name because he was a deeply religious man, always eager to confess his sins to God and follow the rules of the Church of England. He died in 1066, leaving no children as heirs to the throne. An important nobleman, Harold Godwinson, was chosen as the next king. But across the English Channel in a part of France called Normandy, a duke named William had another plan.

William the Conqueror

Normandy got its name from the Norsemen (or Vikings) who had settled in northern France 150 years earlier. The Normans had become so powerful that their duke was wealthier than the king of France. Norman armies were the best in Europe. But Duke William wanted more than just to control Normandy.

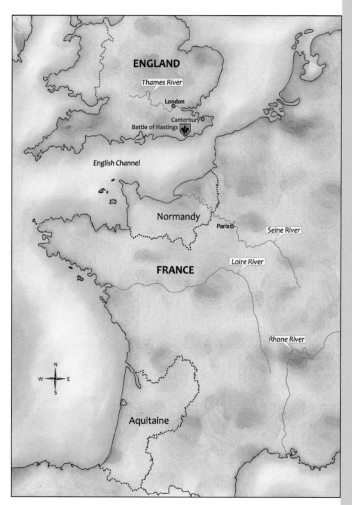

Claiming to be the true king of England, he sailed across the English Channel in September 1066 along with seven hundred ships carrying seven thousand knights. The armies of King Harold of England and Duke William of Normandy met in October 1066 at the Battle of Hastings. After a bloody battle in which Harold was killed, the Normans defeated the Anglo-Saxon army. Duke William was crowned King William I. He also became known as William the Conqueror.

The Anglo-Saxons hated William. They didn't want to be ruled by a foreigner. William made his Norman knights English noblemen and gave them titles and property in England.

Despite the hatred he aroused, William the Conqueror made his mark on English history. He organized a national government and sent sheriffs throughout the land to collect taxes from the people. He built castles all over England, stationing soldiers to put down rebellions. He also hired people to make a list of all the property and landowners. These people put together a book called the *Domesday Book*. It was the first time records were kept about who had a right to what land—and this written record made it easier for William and the kings who came after him to collect taxes.

King Henry II

Henry II

After William the Conqueror died in 1087, England had other kings—some strong and others weak. One of the most notable was Henry II, who became king of England in 1154.

King Henry demanded all kinds of taxes from the nobles. To collect these taxes, he sent soldiers, sheriffs, and judges across his kingdom. He also set up a new system of law that is the basis of today's courts in England and the United States. For the first time, a jury (a group of citizens) listened to a case to determine if someone was guilty of a crime. People could also appeal a verdict. If a person did not agree with the decision made in his local lord's court, he could ask the king for another trial in the royal court.

Murder in the Cathedral

For the first few years of Henry II's reign, his main assistant was Thomas Becket. Becket helped Henry create a powerful government through tax collections. The king trusted Becket, appointing him Lord Chancellor, and Becket was almost as wealthy and powerful as the king himself.

Then, Henry made a mistake. In an attempt to gain control over the Church of England, he appointed Becket as Archbishop of Canterbury, the most powerful church leader in England. Henry figured that his best friend would run the Church of England the way he wanted, but things didn't work out that way. As soon as Becket became Archbishop of Canterbury, he drastically changed his outlook and way of life. Becket became more religiously devout than ever before and started taking his role in the Church of England very seriously. When Henry and the church disagreed, Becket sided with the church rather than the royal government.

Furious, Henry ordered Becket arrested, but Becket escaped to France. Pope Alexander III threatened to kick Henry out of the Church of England (which meant that his subjects did not have to obey him) unless he allowed Becket to return as archbishop. Finally, Henry gave in and Becket returned to England, where he immediately began opposing the king again.

Henry was annoyed. During a royal dinner, with many nobles in attendance, he is said to have complained, "Will no one rid me of this troublesome priest?" Was Henry just sulking, or was he actually encouraging his knights to assassinate Becket? We will never know Henry's true intention. But either way, four knights heard King Henry's words as a command. They murdered the archbishop while he was kneeling in prayer in Canterbury Cathedral.

All Europe was struck with horror. The pope declared Becket a saint. Thousands of people came to Canterbury to pray at his tomb, and many claimed to experience miracles there. For instance, it was said that blind people who visited Becket's tomb suddenly regained their sight.

King Henry ruled for

The murder of Becket in Canterbury Cathedral

nearly twenty years after Becket's death, but he was overcome by guilt. He begged the pope for forgiveness and gave back everything he had ever taken from the church. Still, he could not forgive himself. To punish himself even more for Becket's death, he walked barefoot for three miles along the rocky road to Canterbury until his feet bled. Then, he prayed for forgiveness at Becket's tomb and allowed monks to whip him. Despite these attempts at humility, Henry remained unpopular with most of his subjects.

Meanwhile, Henry II's ambitious wife, Eleanor of Aquitaine [AH-qui-tain], plotted with their three sons to overthrow him. Henry banished Eleanor as a traitor. He had her locked up in a castle in France. His sons fled to France as well. When Henry died, he thought he had failed as king. But actually he had done something historic—he had made the king the supreme ruler over all the feudal lords of England.

From the Magna Carta to Parliament

Talk and Think
Explain to your child that common law is a set of laws that have been established by judges. Court decisions set a precedent. This means that if a judge makes a decision at a trial, that decision may be used in the future to decide how to handle similar cases. The decision may even help define rules that citizens are required to follow. Ask your child to consider why it is important for all citizens, even the king, to follow the same laws.

John, the youngest of Henry's sons, became king in 1199. He fought many expensive wars, wasting lots of money. He also lost most of England's land in France. The English lords became more and more disgusted by his recklessness. In 1215, following a major English defeat by the French, the lords forced King John to sign a charter limiting his authority. The proud lords called it the Magna Carta, which is Latin for "great charter."

The Magna Carta is one of the most important documents in English history. It sets forth the idea that all people must follow the common law—not just peasants but knights, nobles, and the king as well. The Magna Carta also states that the king must respect the rights of the other nobles and consult with them if he wants to make new laws.

Edward I, King John's grandson, wanted to strengthen the royal government. Edward I did not want to make decisions on his own. Instead, he looked to representatives from the kingdom to advise him as he made decisions. In 1295, he formed a Model Parliament [PAR-lah-ment]. This parliament was a group of knights, nobles, and clergy

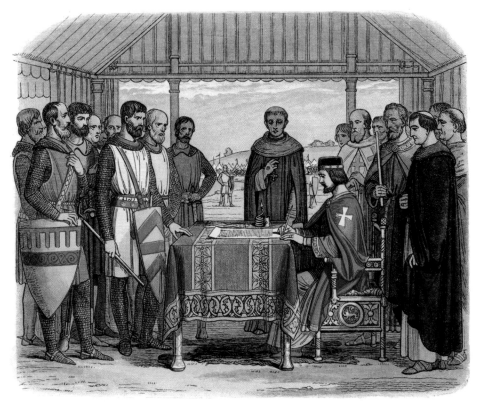

King John signing the Magna Carta

who approved the laws that the king proposed. Although England was still far from being a modern democracy, this assembly was the origin of the United Kingdom's parliamentary system.

The Black Death

A terrible disease swept through Europe during the late 1340s. Called the Black Death, the disease got its name from the black lumps it caused on a sick person's skin. The modern name for this disease is bubonic [byoo-BON-ick] plague. Infected fleas that rodents carried spread the bacteria that caused the bubonic plague to humans. With the high number of rodents in the crowded towns of medieval Europe, the disease spread quickly.

People who caught the Black Death first developed painful sores that oozed pus and blood. Fever and sometimes vomiting of blood followed these skin problems. Two-thirds of those who caught the disease died. So many people died so rapidly that the dead had to be stacked in mass graves. The Italian writer Boccaccio [bo-COTCH-chee-oh] said that the plague spread "like a fire through dry grass."

No one knew how to stop this horrible new disease. Most people were afraid even to visit the sick. They tried different treatments—wrapping patients with cold towels or encouraging them to sniff perfume, because many people believed the plague was caused by hot, stinky air. Many people, especially church leaders, thought God had sent the plague to punish people for their sins. Some people, called Flagellants, walked from town to town, whipping themselves as punishment for mankind's sins. They believed God might stop the Black Death if they performed extreme acts of repentance.

In just three years, one out of every three people in Europe died. Then, suddenly, around 1351, the plague seemed to disappear. But it did return—in 1361, again in 1369, and on many more occasions for the next three hundred years.

The Hundred Years' War

From 1337 to 1453, the armies of the kings of France and England fought each other during what is known as the Hundred Years' War. The battles took place almost entirely in France. Both armies raided French villages for food and money, causing widespread hunger and hardship. During long breaks in the fighting, soldiers without jobs wandered around Europe, at times demanding money in return for protecting people—and robbing them if they refused to pay.

Because of the plague and the Hundred Years' War, Western Europe suffered horribly. Many people died, and villages simply disappeared. Trade slowed down and even stopped in some areas. Desperate peasants rebelled, and soldiers crushed these rebellions.

Joan of Arc

One of the most remarkable figures to emerge during the Hundred Years' War was a French teenager known as Joan of Arc. Joan was born around 1412, when the war had already been raging for seventy-five years. As a young girl, she had mystical experiences and claimed that God wanted her to lead the French people in driving out the English invaders. France's young uncrowned king, called the dauphin [doe-FAN], allowed this peasant girl to command an army. Wearing knight's armor and riding at the head of a large body of soldiers, Joan defeated the English army and forced it out of the town of Orléans [or-lay-AWN] in 1429. Then, she helped the dauphin be crowned King Charles VII.

Joan of Arc

However, French leaders believed Joan had finished serving her purpose. In 1430, she was captured during battle, and King Charles made no effort to pay a ransom and save her. The English accused her of heresy, witchcraft, and wearing men's clothes. (A girl wearing pants was considered unnatural and improper—and, to the English, any girl who could beat their soldiers in battle must surely be a witch!) An English-controlled court found her guilty, and Joan of Arc was burned at the stake.

Joan was only nineteen years old when she died, but she achieved what the French kings and armies had not. Her victory at Orléans was a turning point in the Hundred Years' War. After that, the English began to lose the war, and France continued to regain its former territories. The inspired courage of a young French peasant girl had shaped history forever.

The End of the Middle Ages

Life was so miserable during the Hundred Years' War that many people thought it was the end of the world. We know it wasn't actually the end of the world, but some historians consider the year 1453, when the Hundred Years' War ended, to be the end of the Middle Ages. It was an important year in world history elsewhere, too. In 1453, Turkish invaders captured Constantinople, marking the end of the Eastern Roman Empire.

The Rise of Islam

The word "Islam" [IHS-lahm] means "submission" in Arabic, and for those who follow the religion of Islam, it means submission to one God. About 1.6 billion people around the world today practice Islam. More than five million of those people are in the United States. The people who practice this religion are called Muslims [MUZ-lims].

Muslims follow the teachings of Muhammad [moo-HAH-mahd], who lived on the Arabian Peninsula from 570 to 633 CE. Muslims believe that about 1,400 years ago, in the city of Mecca [MEK-kah], Muhammad received the word of God, whom they call Allah [ah-LAH], the Arabic word for God.

The Prophet Muhammad

Muhammad was born in Mecca, the location of a sacred temple called the Kaaba [KAH-bah]. In Muhammad's time, travelers came to Mecca to fill the Kaaba with idols, or statues of the many gods they worshiped. Local merchants wanted this practice to continue because every traveler bringing an idol to the Kaaba also spent money while visiting Mecca.

Muhammad was a trader himself. He loved his neighbors and his city, but he was uncomfortable with the way people were worshiping many gods and filling

Today, the Kaaba in Mecca is a holy site for Muslims.

the Kaaba with idols. To contemplate these problems, he left the city and went alone into the desert to meditate.

According to Islamic tradition, as Muhammad was meditating in a cave, the angel Jibrail [JIB-rill] appeared to him.

"Read!" Jibrail ordered.

"I cannot read," Muhammad answered. Few people in those days knew how to read.

Jibrail squeezed Muhammad tightly. "Read!" he said again. "Read in the name of your Lord, who created you from a drop of blood."

Muhammad told his wife he had received a message from God. For a long time, she was the only one who believed him.

Several years later, Muhammad is said to have undergone another miraculous experience. Muslims believe that Muhammad was taken up into the sky by angels. He traveled from Mecca to Jerusalem, where he prayed with earlier prophets, including Abraham and Jesus. As he stood on a rock in the city of Jerusalem, he ascended (or went up) into heaven and received God's instruction to tell people to pray five times a day. Muslims built the Dome of the Rock in Jerusalem to commemorate this great event (see page 228).

Trouble in Mecca

Muhammad began telling people in Mecca about his experiences and the ideas that were coming to him. At the time, the people of Mecca followed various religions. Jews and Christians believed in a single God, but there were many others who worshiped multiple gods. Muhammad insisted that there was only one God, which upset some of his neighbors, and so they tried to stop him from spreading his monotheistic message. But Muhammad continued sharing his beliefs. Gradually, more people came to believe that he was Allah's true prophet.

Muhammad taught that every action or thought should be guided by the will of Allah. He urged Muslims to see themselves as Allah's creatures, placed on Earth to serve Allah and humanity. He told his followers that Allah judges people's actions when they die. If they have done good, they will be rewarded; if they have done evil, they will be punished.

At first, Islam was just a local religion with a few followers, but as Islamic ideas spread, Muhammad and his followers came into conflict with the powerful traders in Mecca. To make a living, these traders welcomed visitors to Mecca and sold goods to them. They worried these visitors might not come to Mecca anymore if they heard that Muhammad was stirring up trouble. Finally, they forced Muhammad to leave the city. In 622, he and his followers moved north to a city that is now called Medina.

Muhammad's journey to Medina is called the Hijra [HEEZH-rah]. The year 622 CE is a very important event in the history of Islam—it is even the starting point for the Muslim calendar. Muslims date years in reference to the Hijra in the same way that Christians date years in reference to the birth of Jesus.

The Hijra also led to the construction of the first mosque [MOSK], or Muslim place of worship. The night Muhammad arrived in Medina, he began to build a rough structure, now considered the first mosque of Islam.

Islamic Rituals

There are mosques all over the world. Every mosque has minarets [min-ah-RETS], or towers from which a holy man calls the faithful to prayer five times a day. Before entering a mosque, Muslims remove their shoes and wash at a special fountain. They sit on rugs laid down on the mosque floor in a room designed to face toward Mecca. When the prayer leader arrives, the faithful stand, raise their hands together above their heads, and follow a series of prayer movements. They end by kneeling and lowering their heads to the ground.

The two minarets of the Grand Mosque in Mecca

Muhammad's Return

Muhammad expected all people in Medina, no matter what their religion, to live in peace and harmony. However, different religious groups continued to fight for power. Finally, in 630, Muhammad himself led an army in a raid on Mecca. His goal was to rid the city of polytheistic worshipers. Muhammad and his men took Mecca without much fighting. Muhammad removed all the idols from the Kaaba and dedicated the temple to the worship of the one God of Islam—Allah.

Two years after restoring the Kaaba to the worship of Allah, Muhammad delivered his last sermon. He asked his followers to obey Allah and treat each other with justice and kindness. Muhammad died not long after at the age of sixty-three and was buried in his house next to the mosque in Medina.

Girl studying the Qur'an

The Qur'an

While Muhammad was alive, many of his followers committed his teachings to memory. After Muhammad died, his followers wrote down the ideas he had taught them. Muhammad's words are read as holy verses today, written down in a book called the Qur'an [kohr-AN].

The Qur'an is the sacred scripture of the Islamic religion. Its title means "the recitation," and the book recalls the instruction to read given to Muhammad by the angel Jibrail. The Qur'an is written in Arabic. Muslims always study it in its original language, even if they do not speak Arabic. Muslims believe the Qur'an contains the actual words of God, so learning to read and recite those words is an act of worship.

Some of the important words of Islam can be spelled in different ways. "Qur'an" is sometimes spelled "Koran," "Mecca" is also spelled "Makkah," and "Kaaba" is sometimes written as "Ka'abah" or "Ka'ba."

The Five Pillars of Islam

Devout Muslims compare their religion to a building that is supported by five pillars. The Five Pillars of Islam are a set of five rules that form the central philosophy of the Islamic faith.

The First Pillar is called *shahada* [sha-HA-dah] in Arabic. As a statement of their faith, Muslims say, "There is no god but Allah and Muhammad is his messenger." This simple statement is the basis of all Muslim beliefs.

A child looks on as adult Muslims pray in the streets of India.

The Second Pillar is called *salat* [sah-LAHT] in Arabic. *Salat* means "prayer." Muslims recite prayers from the Qur'an five times per day—at dawn, midday, afternoon, evening, and night. At each of these times of day, they stop whatever they are doing to bow down in worship in the direction of Mecca.

The Third Pillar is called *sawm* in Arabic. *Sawm* means "fasting," or going without food and drink. Muslims fast during daylight hours throughout the holy month they call Ramadan [rah-mah-DAHN]. Muslims believe fasting brings spiritual rewards. When the fast is over at the end of Ramadan, they celebrate with a festival.

The Fourth Pillar is called *zakat* [ZACK-at] in Arabic. Through *zakat*, which means "giving to others," Muslims share their wealth and show kindness in practical ways to those less fortunate.

The Fifth Pillar is called *hajj* [hahzh] in Arabic. *Hajj* is a word for the pilgrimage to Mecca. All healthy Muslims are expected to make a pilgrimage to Mecca at least once in their lives. Today, more than three million Muslims go to Mecca every year to complete the *hajj*.

Spreading the Word of Islam

After Muhammad's death, Muslims began conquering other territories to govern them according to the rules of their religion. One by one, Muslims took over the great cities of the ancient Middle East—Damascus in Syria, Antioch in Turkey, Tyre in Lebanon, and finally Jerusalem in today's Israel. Islamic armies and settlers pushed east to India and China and west across North Africa. In 711, Muslims crossed the Mediterranean Sea and moved into nearby Spain. They began marching over the Pyrenees Mountains to France, but French soldiers stopped their advance.

Muslims lived in Spain for the next seven centuries. They built strong forts, beautiful mosques, and graceful palaces, like the Alhambra (see page 227). They developed irrigation systems to water their crops better and brought plants from all over the world to Spain, including cherries, apples, pears, almonds, sugarcane, and bananas.

Arabic Numerals

It's hard to imagine a world without the numerals 1, 2, or 3. But do you remember that the Romans used other numerals? They wrote I for 1, V for 5, and X for 10. In our daily life, we use Arabic numerals, developed by Muslim scholars from the Arab world, who may have borrowed them from scholars in India. Muslims introduced these symbols to Europeans. Nowadays, Arabic numerals are the most common symbols for numbers.

The angel Jibrail urged Muhammad to read, and as a result, literacy and education have been important in the Islamic religion ever since. The Spanish city of Córdoba [KOHR-do-vah] became a great center of Muslim learning and culture. Muslim scholars studied the Qur'an along with works of science and philosophy from other cultures, including ancient Greece. The Muslim philoso-

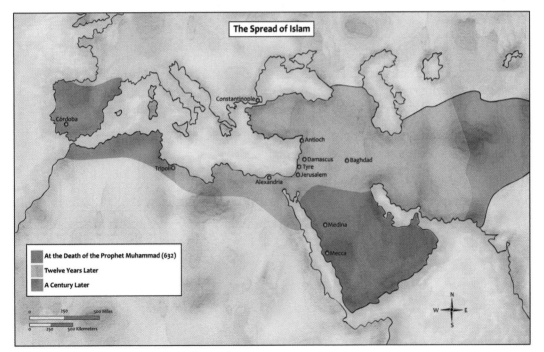

Islam spread rapidly across North Africa and into Spain.

pher Avicenna (or Ibn Sina in Arabic), who lived in the country of Persia (today's Iran) from 980 to 1037, wrote medical books that influenced doctors for generations.

The Crusades

Three different religions considered Palestine, the land that included Jerusalem, to be a holy land. It was the home of King David, an ancient leader of the Jewish people, and the place where King Solomon built his temple. Thus, the Jews considered Jerusalem to be a holy city. Because Christians believed that Jesus was crucified, buried, and resurrected in Jerusalem, they also considered it a holy city in their religion. Muhammad had visited the city, too, and according to Islamic belief, he rose into the heavens during that visit. Therefore, Muslims considered Jerusalem an important holy city in their religion, second in importance only to Mecca.

Muslims took over Jerusalem as early as the seventh century. There, they lived peacefully with those of other religions until about 1000 CE, when their leader encouraged his people to destroy the Holy Sepulcher [SEPP-uhl-ker], considered by Christians to be the tomb of Jesus. In 1095, the Roman Catholic pope Urban II declared that Christians should go to war to reclaim the city of Jerusalem and the important Christian monuments in it. He called for a crusade—a war to win the Holy Land for Christianity.

Christians from all over Europe responded to the pope's proclamation. They armed themselves and started on the long journey east. After successfully recapturing Jerusalem in 1099, Christian soldiers massacred nearly every Muslim and Jew they could find. Over the next two hundred years, many passionate Christians traveled to Jerusalem. Some entered the city peacefully on pilgrimages, but others attacked the city with trained armies of knights. This long series of conflicts over the Holy Land and the city of Jerusalem is called the Crusades.

The word "crusade" comes from the Latin word for "cross." The Christian soldiers fighting in these wars were called Crusaders. The Muslims called these wars the Frankish invasions. "Frankish" is another word for "French," but the Muslims used it to refer to all Western Europeans, whom they saw as invading their territory.

One of the most famous meetings during the Crusades took place in 1192, when King Richard I of England (also called Richard the Lion-Hearted) met Saladin of Egypt, a mighty Muslim leader. Richard won the name "lion-hearted" because of his bravery and eagerness to fight. He joined with the king of France to lead a Crusade to the Holy Land.

Saladin had become the most powerful Muslim of his time by conquering territory in North Africa. In 1187 CE, he captured Jerusalem. As Richard's small army approached the city, Saladin's troops surprised them outside the city gates. Even after his horse was killed, Richard kept fighting. Saladin, admiring Richard's courage, sent more horses for Richard's army. Saladin had such respect for Richard the Lion-Hearted that, even though the Muslims won the war, he agreed not to destroy the Christians' sacred objects and to let Christians make safe pilgrimages to Jerusalem.

Saladin

The Crusades involved long bloody battles that cost many lives, but they also opened up communication between Europe and the Middle East. Trade and travel increased between these two parts of the world, and the geography, culture, and learning of the Middle East and Asia became more widely known.

African Kingdoms

The Geography of Africa

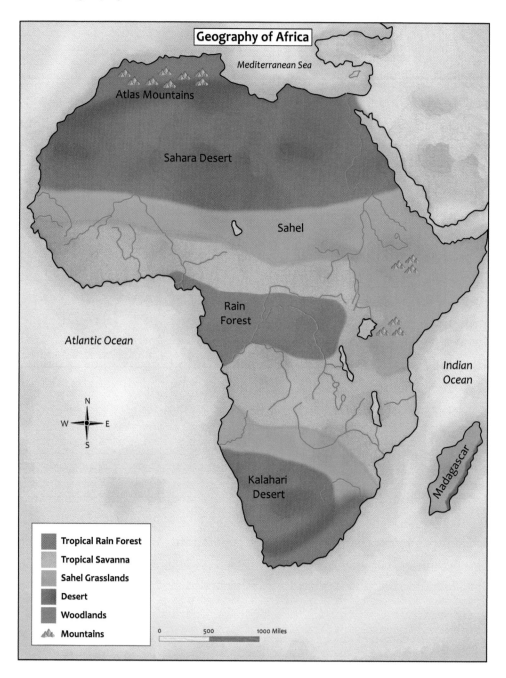

Geography of Africa

Mediterranean Sea

Atlas Mountains

Sahara Desert

Sahel

Rain Forest

Atlantic Ocean

Indian Ocean

Madagascar

Kalahari Desert

N
W E
S

Tropical Rain Forest
Tropical Savanna
Sahel Grasslands
Desert
Woodlands
Mountains

0   500   1000 Miles

The continent of Africa contains amazing geographical variety. One of the world's largest deserts, the Sahara, covers most of North Africa. But just north of the Western Sahara are the Atlas Mountains, whose peaks are covered with snow for much of the year. Just south of the Sahara is the Sahel, a broad band of short grassland and scrub vegetation that stretches from the Atlantic Ocean to the Indian Ocean. Farther south, more moisture helps create a savanna landscape of tall grasses and scattered trees. This is Africa's big-game country, home of lions, leopards, elephants, and rhinos. South of the savanna, the Congo River cuts through a lush tropical rain forest. South of the rain forests, the savanna resumes, eventually giving way to a southern desert, the Kalahari, which stretches nearly to the southern tip of the continent. Deserts, grasslands, rain forests, mountains, rivers, and abundant wildlife—you name it, Africa has it all!

Do It Yourself

Using the map of Africa and its scale, measure the length of the Sahara Desert in miles. How large is it?

Egypt and Kush

Africa has a rich history full of mighty rulers and massive kingdoms. You may already know about the ancient Egyptians, who lived and farmed along the Nile River, and whose rulers, the pharaohs, built massive pyramids in ancient times.

The Egyptian civilization clustered at the northern (or downriver) portion of the river, where it empties into the Mediterranean Sea (see the map on page 142). Farther south, a civilization called the Kingdom of Kush lasted for almost 1,500 years, from about 1000 BCE to 300 CE.

The people of Kush established a series of important trading cities. The first great city was Kerma, a walled city near the Nile. Trade with Central Africa and Egypt made Kerma rich—but Egypt wanted to control that trade. Around 1500 BCE, the Egyptians invaded Kerma and destroyed the city.

Hundreds of years later, around 1000 BCE, a second Kushite kingdom arose around the major city of Napata. This Kushite kingdom grew strong enough to conquer Egypt, and it lasted nearly twelve centuries. The Kushites of Napata built pyramids, the ruins of which still stand today.

The third great Kushite city, Meroë [mehr-OH-way], was famous for making and selling iron weapons. Kushites in Meroë developed a language of their own.

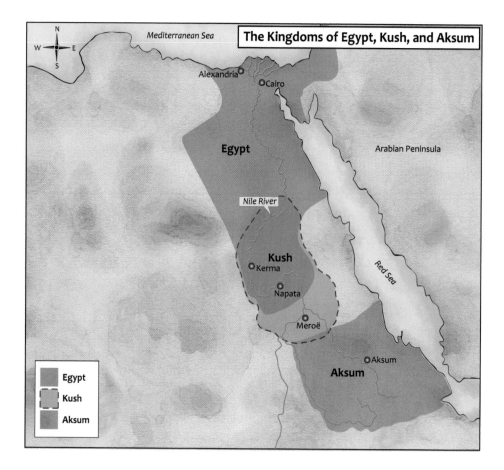

The Kingdoms of Egypt, Kush, and Aksum

They wrote inscriptions on temples and tombs. Yet even today, no one has cracked the code to read the ancient Kushite language. Because we can't read the inscriptions the Kushites left behind, we have to use other clues to learn how these people lived and what they believed. Pictures on Meroë's temple walls show the queens and kings who ruled Meroë. These pictures suggest that the powerful people in Kush considered chubbiness to be a sign of good health. Magnificent golden jewelry belonging to one Kushite queen has been found, showing the wealth and artistic skill that the later Kushites achieved.

Meroë stayed wealthy as long as trade continued with Egypt. When the Romans conquered Egypt, they sent their traders along the Red Sea coast instead of down the Nile River. As a result, trade slowed down, and the people of Meroë lost

The Kush also created pyramids, including these at Meroë.

their chief way of making money. Around 340 CE, another ancient African kingdom, Aksum, invaded Meroë. That invasion marked the decline of the kingdom of Kush.

Aksum

In the part of Africa that we now call Ethiopia, an ancient kingdom called Aksum emerged (see the map on page 142). The Kingdom of Aksum is also known as the Kingdom of Axum or the Axumite Empire. Inhabitants of the kingdom are called Axumites. Aksum was a major trading empire where traders brought iron, tortoise shells, animal hides, rhinoceros horn, gold, and enslaved people from the lands in the interior of Africa. These goods were traded for iron tools and weapons, copper implements, cloth, and wine.

Thanks to all this trade, the Kingdom of Aksum became wealthy and attracted people from Italy, Greece, Egypt, and Persia. Huge granite monuments still exist in this part of Africa, evidence that the Axumites were skilled architects and stonemasons. Archeologists have also found ancient coins made of bronze, silver, and gold.

The Kingdom of Aksum grew more powerful by gaining control of land in Africa and on the Arabian Peninsula. Ezana, a king of Aksum, converted to Christianity and made it the official religion of the kingdom during the 320s CE.

By 350, Aksum had conquered the city of Meroë and the Kingdom of Kush. For a while afterward, Aksum was the most powerful kingdom in East Africa. Then, in the late 500s, a severe drought made it impossible to grow enough food for the large population. At the same time, the Persians took over much of the trade between Africa and the Middle East. These factors contributed to the decline of the Kingdom of Aksum.

Trading Caravans

The Nile River and Red Sea are natural water routes for travelers to follow, but Africa presents challenging land features, such as the vast Sahara Desert. Nevertheless, trade across the Sahara has been happening for at least two thousand years. Around 400 CE, traders brought camels from Arabia. These sturdy animals made crossing the desert easier. Camels carry heavy loads, can go for days without water, and are able to cover ground rapidly. Even with camels as transportation, it took about three months for a caravan to cross the Sahara. The journey was long and difficult, but the rewards made it worth the effort.

So what did these camel caravans carry across the desert? One answer is salt. Because salt is so widely available and cheap today, it can be hard to imagine a time when salt was worth its weight in gold. However, in a world without refrigerators, salt was one of the best ways to preserve meat and fish. But salt is not easy to obtain. It must be harvested from salt water or dug from mines. For that rea-

son, the salt from the Sahara was valued highly in other parts of Africa and the Middle East.

Traders exchanged salt for the goods they wanted from other parts of Africa. People in West Africa had discovered how to separate gold nuggets from other stones in their rivers. People living farther south hunted wild elephants for their tusks. Tusks are made of ivory, which was highly prized for making carvings and jewelry. Traders brought gold and ivory from West Africa to trade for salt from the north. These caravans also carried enslaved human beings, who were sold at markets.

West African Kingdoms

· ·

Traders who crossed the Sahara came to know the people living in West Africa.

Ghana was the first of West Africa's great trading kingdoms. Ghana was most powerful from about 800 until 1100. Then another kingdom, called Mali [MAH-lee], gained in strength, especially from about 1235 to 1400. A third West African trading kingdom, Songhai [SONG-high], became the region's strongest power by 1450 and maintained its power until about 1600.

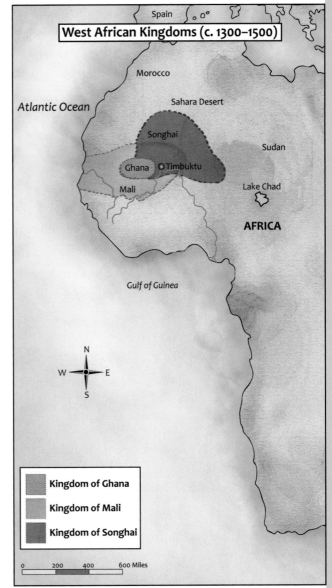

Ghana

One group, located amid the Sahel grasslands south of the Sahara, called their land Wagadu [wa-ga-DOO]. Outsiders called it Ghana [GAH-nah], the word people in Wagadu used to mean "warrior king."

Mali

Ancient Africans loved to listen to storytellers, whom they called griots [GREE-ohs]. Griots would play the drum, sing songs, and dance to tell stories about the ancestors of their people.

A modern-day griot

One griot's song tells of the great leader of Mali named Sundiata Keita [SUN-dee-ah-tah KAY-tah], known also as the "Lion King." Much of what we know about Sundiata Keita comes through legend and story, which tells us that he ruled Mali from 1230 to 1255 and helped his country gain wealth, land, and power. Sundiata's armies conquered gold mines in the south and captured what was left of Ghana's empire. Sundiata also built a new capital city, Niana, which became a rich trading center. Over time, Mali became one of the richest farming regions in West Africa. As he conquered more land, Sundiata brought many separate villages together into one country. The people respected Sundiata for his leadership and his religion.

Because many of the merchants and traders were Muslim, Sundiata learned about Muhammad and the Qur'an. During his lifetime, he followed Muslim practices, while keeping the support of non-Muslims. His devotion to Islam made an impression on his people, who mourned his death in 1255.

Mali's next great ruler, Mansa Musa, reigned from 1312 to 1336. The word "Mansa" means "king of kings" or "emperor." Like Sundiata, Mansa Musa was a devout Muslim. In 1324, he decided to fulfill the important responsibility of Muslims and make the *hajj*, or pilgrimage, to Mecca. It was no small feat to travel from Mali to Mecca. Mansa Musa had a three-thousand-mile journey to make across

Take a Look

If you look on a map of the world today, you will find countries in Africa called Ghana and Mali, but these countries are in different places from the ancient kingdoms of the same names.

the Sahara, and he did so in the grandest Malian style. Thousands of people—his wife, children, servants, cooks, and griots—all went with him. Eighty camels carried three hundred pounds of gold each. Wherever he stopped on Friday, Islam's holy day, he provided gold to the city in order to build a mosque there.

Mansa Musa's pilgrimage gained the attention of the Muslim world. It was not, however, the last of his efforts on behalf of Islam. Back home in Mali,

Take a Look

Ask your child to take a closer look at the map. What else does she notice?

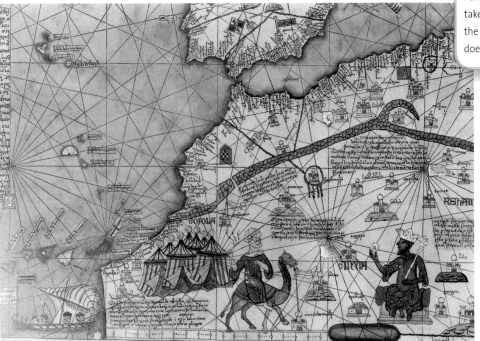

Mansa Musa and his wealth were so legendary that he was shown, seated and holding a nugget of gold, on the first European map of North Africa. The map was made about 1375 CE.

he built more mosques and Islamic schools. His armies conquered the small trading town of Timbuktu, which Mansa Musa helped transform into a great center of Islamic learning. He brought Muslim architects to the city to design magnificent buildings. He hired Muslim professors to teach in the new schools. Because of Mansa Musa and the many traders coming from the Middle East, Islam became an important religion in Africa.

Ibn Battuta: World Traveler

We know much about the kingdom of Mali thanks to a man from Morocco named Ibn Battuta [IB-un bah-TOOT-ah]. Ibn Battuta loved to travel and experience new places. A Muslim, he made his pilgrimage to Mecca in 1325, at the age of twenty-one. But he didn't return home afterward. He continued farther into Asia and also traveled around the Mediterranean Sea. He visited kings and governors, especially those in Muslim countries. He visited Timbuktu in 1352, fifteen years after the death of Mansa Musa. Later in his life, Ibn Battuta wrote

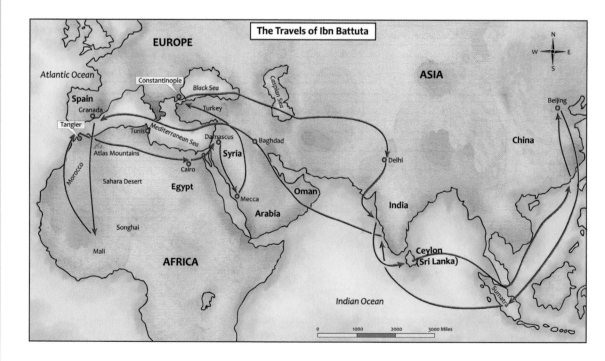

a book about his travels. In the next section you will hear the story of a young boy's discovery of Ibn Battuta's writings.

The Longest Pilgrimage

It was raining for the third day in a row, and Michael was even getting tired of watching television. With both of his parents at work, the only other person at home to talk to was his older sister, Laurie. Laurie was back from college on a break, but she spent most of her time in her room, working on some project. Michael looked out the window again and saw lightning flash over the high rooftops of the city. He sighed. It wasn't going to stop raining for hours.

Michael knocked on Laurie's door and poked his head into the room. His sister was hunched over a book, one of the many that she had brought home with her. Surprised, she turned around.

"Hey, Mike. Is everything okay?"

"Yeah, everything's fine. I'm just bored, and I can't go outside because of the rain."

"It's still raining?" Laurie, who had been too caught up in her work to notice the storm outside of her window, laughed. "I guess I should take a break."

"What is this all about, anyway?" Michael picked up one of the books that were lying all around the room. It was a library book with no illustration on the cover.

"Well," said Laurie, stretching her cramped limbs, "it's about an ancient explorer who traveled all across Asia and Africa and worked with a scribe to write a book about what he saw."

"Marco Polo?" asked Michael. He had learned about Marco Polo in school, and he knew he was a famous explorer from long ago.

"No, actually. The man I'm learning about went to different places from Marco Polo, and was one of the most impressive travelers of all time. His name is not as familiar, though. Have you ever heard of Ibn Battuta?"

Michael nodded. "Mr. Floros said on Friday that we would learn about Ibn Battuta when we came back on Monday!" he exclaimed.

Laurie smiled. "That is so exciting, Michael! Ibn Battuta was a really interesting man. He visited almost every part of the Muslim world, and Africa and China, too. His motto was 'Never travel the same road twice.' He met about sixty important leaders, like sultans and kings, and ended up helping some of them make decisions. And he started off on his own when he was twenty-one years old, without any guides or friends."

By now, Michael was sitting on the floor, flipping through the book he had picked up. He looked up and declared, "According to this, Ibn Battuta left Tangier, which is in North Africa, to make a pilgrimage, or *hajj*, to Mecca. He was from a Muslim family. Making pilgrimages to holy places is very important to the Muslim faith. So his journey wasn't that extraordinary at first." Michael found an old-fashioned map in the book and squinted at it. "But where is Mecca?" he mused.

Laurie came over and pointed to a spot down near the bottom of Saudi Arabia.

"That's where Mecca is. It's pretty far away from Tangier, isn't it? But once Ibn Battuta started to travel, he didn't want to stop. While he was on his way to Egypt, near Cairo," Laurie said, tapping the map near the top of the Nile River, "he visited a holy man who, it was said, could make whatever his guests wished appear. Of course, this wasn't true, but when Ibn Battuta was staying with this holy man in his home for the night, he had a dream that he would go all over the world."

"Is that true?" Michael asked.

"It might be a tall tale," Laurie said with a shrug. "He didn't write this all down while he was on his journey, anyway. A young poet named Ibn Juzayy wrote it all down for him thirty years later, when the sultan of Morocco demanded that these stories be put down in writing."

"Okay, but where did he go after he got to Mecca?" Michael asked.

"He got on a ship and sailed down the coast of East Africa," Laurie said. "He went all the way down to Kilwa, which is here"—Laurie tapped the map where Africa started to get narrow—"and met the sultan there. Almost everywhere he went, he met the sultan or the leader of the place he was visiting. His descriptions of these leaders, whether they were generous or unfair or even crazy, help us to know more about them."

Laurie moved her finger back up the coast of East Africa and all the way up to Constantinople.

"Next he went north," she said, "up through Turkey. He met a sultan who showed him the remnants of an **asteroid**, which was so big and heavy that four of the sultan's men couldn't break it with hammers. He met another leader, Uzbeg Khan, who took him up to Constantinople, a great city with a strong emperor. Ibn Battuta went east, to India, too. He even went to China, although it wasn't really a part of the Muslim world."

"Why did he go east?" asked Michael, whose head was already swimming with pictures of asteroids, ships, and sultans.

"Because he thought that he could be a successful scholar there. In fact, the sultan in Delhi liked him, but this sultan turned out to be an unpredictable man. Sometimes he was very nice, and sometimes he was too harsh. This sultan finally sent him to China as his ambassador. Ibn Battuta didn't like it there, though."

"Why didn't he like it?" asked Michael.

"It may have been the customs, or something about the people, but I think he was homesick, too. He went home again."

"Did he stop traveling?"

"Not yet," Laurie said, and tapped West Africa on the map. "He returned to Mecca several times. Also, he traveled south from Morocco, to see the great kingdoms of West Africa. Do you know why there were powerful kings in West Africa during medieval times?"

"I know that they had a lot of salt there," said Michael.

"And gold, too! So much gold that the *mansa*, or king, of Mali went on a long pilgrimage in 1324 and left gold everywhere he stopped on Fridays. By the time Ibn Battuta got there, though, there was a new king, and he wasn't as generous. Ibn Battuta had been expecting baskets of gold and cloaks and silk, but instead the king sent him bread and some other local foods. He did get to stay in Timbuktu and watch some of their most ancient festivals, like one where poets serenade the king with amazing songs."

"Where else did he go?"

> **New Word**
> Does your child know what an **asteroid** is? An asteroid, which is also called a minor planet, is a rocky body that orbits the sun along a belt between Mars and Jupiter.

Laurie laughed. "I can't tell you all of the places he went to. It would take hours!"

"At least tell me where he went next!"

"All right, fine. When he finished traveling through West Africa, he went back home to Morocco. By this time, he had traveled seventy-five thousand miles. That's more than Marco Polo, by the way. The sultan of Morocco ordered that all his stories be put down in writing so that they could be read throughout history and teach us more about the world at that time."

Laurie stretched again and stood up. "Well, Mike, I need to get back to work."

But Michael wanted to know more. "Can you tell me more about what he saw in India? Or Arabia? Did he go through the desert?"

"Several deserts," laughed Laurie. "Here," she said, handing him her book, "you can borrow my copy of his book for a little while."

"Hooray!" exclaimed Michael, and thanked his sister before slipping into a nearby chair, letting her get back to her research. The rain was still pouring down, but Michael didn't notice the dreary skies: he had a lot of exploring to do.

Songhai

Soon after the time of Ibn Battuta's visit to Timbuktu, the kingdom of Mali began to lose power. Local leaders began fighting among themselves and broke away from the larger kingdom. Foreign raiders captured and destroyed the great city of Timbuktu in 1468 CE.

> **Make a Connection**
> Look back at the section on medieval Europe and compare Askia Muhammad with Christian rulers and crusaders such as Richard the Lion-Hearted. How were their actions similar? How were they different?

As Mali declined, the power of nearby Songhai began to increase. Many of the people of Songhai had embraced Islam. In 1493 (a year after Christopher Columbus set sail on his voyage of discovery), they chose an army general who was a deeply religious Muslim as their leader. His name was Askia Muhammad. The first word in his name, "Askia" [AHS-kee-ah], means "general." The second word in his name indicates his faith in the Islamic prophet Muhammad. This combination of features—a religious warrior—sums up the character of Askia Muhammad and his rule, which lasted from 1493 to 1528. Askia Muhammad led a jihad, or religious war, against nearby people who did not believe in Islam. His efforts increased the power of the Songhai Empire and spread Islam throughout West Africa.

The Great Mosque of Djenné in modern-day Timbuktu was made from mud bricks baked by the sun.

Songhai's wealth and culture attracted many traders. In the early 1500s, one visitor wrote about what was traded in one of Songhai's markets: meat, bread, melons, cucumbers, pottery, and many fine items crafted of gold, leather, and iron. Traders from other lands brought items the Songhai people wanted, such as salt, horses, swords, and woven cloth. Enslaved Africans also were bought and sold at the markets.

In 1591, the kingdom of Songhai was attacked by Morocco, a country to the north. The Moroccans had muskets and cannons. Songhai's soldiers had only spears and swords. "Everything changed," wrote a historian of the time. "Danger took the place of security, poverty of wealth. Peace gave way to distress, disasters, and violence." Soon, Songhai disappeared, and with it went the golden days of West Africa.

China: Dynasties and Conquerors

Historians divide up time using various measurements. They might talk about centuries for an empire, the reign of a king for a kingdom, or the length of a presidency in the United States. Historians who study China divide its past into dynasties [DIE-nah-stees]. A dynasty is a family or group of people who governs a country through several generations.

In 221 BCE, a ruler from the Chinese region known as Qin [cheen] conquered all the surrounding regions and founded the Qin dynasty. He gave himself the title "Qin Shihuangdi" [cheen shih-hwahng-dee], which means "First Emperor of the Qin Dynasty." Today's name for China comes from the word "Qin."

Qin Shihuangdi

After he came to power in 221 BCE, Qin Shihuangdi created an empire. His deputies laid out provinces, set up a central government, formed an army, and improved the roads and irrigation systems. He made sure everyone used the same written language. He also forced people to work hard, pay taxes, and obey the laws of his government.

Qin Shihuangdi worried that his territory might be attacked by armies from the north. He commanded workers to connect old forts along the border of his

The Great Wall
of China today

empire into a massive wall. Almost a million people were put to work to build this wall. Later rulers added new sections to the wall and connected old sections. Today, this gigantic structure is known as the Great Wall of China.

The Chinese people paid taxes to fund the construction of the wall as well as a magnificent palace for Qin Shihuangdi. Many people were unhappy with the emperor's rule, especially his order to burn most of the books in China, and some even tried to kill him. To protect himself, Qin Shihuangdi built a series of secret underground passages and slept in a different palace every night.

Make a Connection

Ask your child to compare the Qin dynasty to the Roman Empire. How did Qin Shihuangdi establish an empire?

The Han Dynasty

After Qin Shihuangdi died, people wanted relief from his harsh rule. The next period of Chinese history, the Han dynasty, lasted four hundred years, from 206 BCE to 209 CE. During this time, the ideas of Confucius [con-FYOO-shus] became the official philosophy of the Chinese government.

Confucius was a philosopher and scholar who had lived many years earlier, around 500 BCE. Confucius taught many rules for good behavior, including a version of the Golden Rule: always treat others with the greatest respect. Confucius wanted this rule to guide the personal behavior of everyone in society, including the rulers. Although the ideas of Confucius were not widely accepted during his lifetime, they won official acceptance during the Han dynasty and have played an important part in Chinese culture ever since.

Confucius

Under the Han dynasty, education became more important than it was during the Qin dynasty, and a Confucian school opened in the capital city. The territory of China expanded in every direction. Trade routes connected China to India, the Middle East, and Rome.

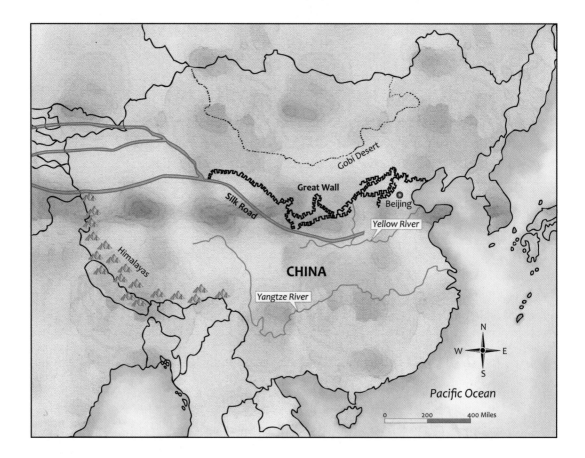

What sorts of items did people trade between China and the West? For starters, Chinese traders brought silk, a fabric that at the time was made only in China. Silk was such an important trade item that the network of trails that led from China to the Middle East and the Mediterranean came to be called the Silk Road.

Silk is made in a remarkable way. Caterpillars called silkworms spin cocoons. Then, people unwind their cocoons. With that thread, they weave silk cloth. For hundreds of years, only the Chinese knew how to raise silkworms and make silk.

The arts flourished during the Han dynasty. Artists made beautiful bronze and clay sculptures and painted scenes on silk cloth. Paper was invented in China during the Han dynasty, around 105 CE. At first, paper was made from silk rags, which were pounded into a pulp and moistened with water. Later, the Chinese used plant materials, like tree bark or bamboo stalks, to make pulp. It would be another thousand years before Europeans learned to make paper.

During the Han dynasty, many Chinese people began to follow an Indian religion called Buddhism [BOOD-izm]. Buddhism is a religion based upon the life and teachings of Siddhartha Gautama [sid-ARTH-a gow-TAH-ma], who lived around 500 BCE. Although he was born a prince, he gave up all his wealth and possessions. Instead of desiring material goods, he used meditation to become good in heart and pure in mind, and he persuaded his followers to do the same. Buddhism differs from Confucianism because Buddhists concentrate on inner enlightenment rather than rules for external behavior.

The Tang Dynasty

The Tang dynasty (618–906 CE) was a period of bustling trade. Chinese products, especially silk, were in great demand in Europe. Many caravans traveled the Silk Road, and many ships sailed in and out of China's southern ports, such as Canton.

This silk painting shows Chinese women playing a popular game called double-six, or backgammon, as we know it today.

During the Tang dynasty, the Chinese developed a system for printing books. Artists first carved images into blocks of wood. Then, the woodblocks were inked and pressed against paper. The world's first printed book, a sewn-together collection of woodblock-printed pages titled the *Diamond Sutra*, was made in China in the year 868 CE. It would be almost six hundred years before Europeans mastered the art of book printing.

During the Tang dynasty, Chinese merchants began using printed certificates to represent money when they were trading with people from far away, who might not have the goods they wanted. These certificates worked similarly to how our dollars represent money today.

Another important discovery changed warfare during the Tang dynasty. Chinese chemists discovered the formula for gunpowder: a combination of chemicals that explodes when lit. Consider for a moment how many things depend on the invention of gunpowder: guns and grenades, rockets and bombs—not to mention fireworks, which the Chinese enjoyed during the Tang dynasty just as much as we do today.

The Song Dynasty

Leaders during the Song dynasty, which lasted from 960 to 1279 CE, presided over another great age of artistic expression and scientific invention. The Chinese are thought to have invented the magnetic compass during this period. Thanks to inventions such as the iron plow, improved irrigation methods, and new types of seeds and fertilizers, farmers could grow more food. As a result of plentiful food and better living conditions, China's population grew to more than one million people.

More and more books were printed in China. People learned to carve individual words on small blocks and then combine these blocks to print a whole page of words. They could break up the blocks, rearrange them, and print another page—a process known as movable type. This huge step in printing technology meant the Chinese could print many more books, lowering the cost to buy them—which encouraged more Chinese people to read.

The Mongol Invasions

The land north of China, on the other side of the Great Wall, is called Mongolia. Mongolia is a cold, dry land that includes the massive Gobi Desert. From the first century CE on, fierce Mongol warriors had attacked China, trying to move south and take over its territory.

Around 1200, a mighty leader united the Mongol territories and created an army of soldiers so powerful that the Chinese could not keep them out. That leader was called Genghis Khan [JENG-giss KAHN]. His men attacked on horseback using arrows and fought ferociously. Around 1279, one of Genghis Khan's grandsons, Kublai [KOO-blye] Khan, attacked China. Kublai Khan defeated the emperor and became the new ruler of China. He chose the northern city of Beijing as his home. Beijing is still the capital of China to this day.

Eight other Mongol emperors succeeded Kublai Khan. Their combined reign is called the Yuan [ywahn] dynasty. The Yuan dynasty lasted from 1279 to 1368. During this period, the Mongol rulers opened China's borders to traders. Traders poured in by land and sea, eager to buy

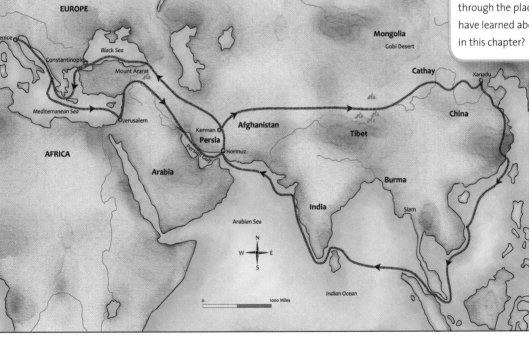

> **Talk and Think**
> Take a closer look at the routes that Marco Polo traveled. What might he have seen as he traveled through the places you have learned about earlier in this chapter?

China's silk, pearls, spices, gems, and fine porcelains. One of those traders was a fellow named Marco Polo.

Marco Polo

In the 1260s, Marco Polo and some of his relatives left the city of Venice, Italy. They wanted to make a fortune by traveling between Europe and China and trading valuables such as gold, jewels, and lamp oil. Marco Polo and his relatives crossed the Mediterranean Sea and landed in the Middle East. They rode camels past Mount Ararat, where people believed Noah's ark had landed after the flood. They traveled to the waters we now call the Persian Gulf, then through the steep, difficult terrain of modern-day Afghanistan, and on to the Gobi Desert. Altogether, it took the Polos three years to travel from Venice to Kublai Khan's palace in China.

And that was just the beginning of Marco Polo's travels! In all, Marco Polo spent twenty-four years traveling throughout China and other lands. If you read his book *The Travels of Marco Polo*, which was published in 1298, you may wonder (as people in his day did) how many of his stories are true and how many were products of his vivid imagination.

The Ming Dynasty

The Ming dynasty lasted three centuries, from 1368 to 1644. This dynasty began when Zhu, the orphaned son of peasants, proclaimed himself emperor and led an army against the Mongols, driving them out of China. Zhu and his descendants reaffirmed the native Chinese way of life, separate from years of Mongol influence, whom the Chinese considered foreigners. Many great works of art, especially fine porcelain pottery, date from the Ming dynasty. (You can see an example in the Visual Arts section of this book.)

In Beijing, the emperors built an elaborate imperial palace where they could live and govern without being disturbed. Known as the Forbidden City, it contains fantastic buildings, temples painted with dragons, and palaces ornamented with gold, all encircled by a wall. The Forbidden City still exists, but

The Forbidden City

it is not forbidden anymore, and you can visit the palace if you go to China today.

The Voyages of Zheng He

In the early 1400s, the Chinese launched a mighty fleet commanded by Admiral Zheng He [jung huh] to explore what the Chinese called the "Western Oceans." During his approximately twenty years of exploring, Zheng He sailed through the Indian Ocean, to Persia and Africa, and around the tip of Africa into the Atlantic Ocean. According to one estimate, his navy contained more than sixty treasure ships and about thirty thousand sailors. Zheng He's flagship was longer than a football field—more than four times as large as Columbus's flagship, the *Santa Maria*. Everywhere Zheng He went, his fleet amazed the foreign powers. They realized that China must be a mighty empire if it had such a navy.

There is no telling where the great Chinese navy might have sailed next and what they might have discovered if they had continued the voyages of Zheng He. Imagine if the Chinese navy had sailed across the Atlantic—the Americas might have been discovered by the Chinese instead of Europeans! But alas, it was not to be. Shortly after Zheng He's death in 1433, China's rulers decided to disband the fleet, and the nation entered a period of isolation.

American History and Geography

The American Revolutionary War

America in 1750

If you lived in the American colonies in 1750, you would have been a subject of the British king. You would have obeyed the laws of the British Parliament and shared some rights with British citizens. The American colonists and British citizens both gained from this peaceful partnership.

But this relationship was about to change completely. A war broke out in 1754, and the consequences of this war would convince the colonists to break away from Great Britain and form a new country: the United States of America.

The French and Indian War

In 1754, France and Britain went to war because each country claimed the same land in the Ohio Valley. France persuaded some of its Native American allies to take up arms against the British. Because the French and the Indians fought on the same side, this war is known as the French and Indian War.

The British government sent soldiers to defend its colonies, and American colonists fought side by side with them. Young George Washington acquired his first military experiences as a colonel during this war.

The French and Indian War lasted from 1754 until 1763. Many battles were fought, and many soldiers were killed on both sides. In 1759, the British launched a daring attack on the French city of Québec in Canada. The attack succeeded, and the Treaty of Paris, which ended the war, gave Britain almost all of France's territory in North America.

Taxation Without Representation

The French and Indian War cost a lot of money, and the British government was in serious debt. To raise the money they needed, King George III and his Parliament made the colonies pay more and higher taxes.

King George III

This decision angered the colonists. They protested against British businesses, held community meetings, and cried out in newspapers against what they saw as an injustice. They believed that no one should take their money unless they, or their elected representatives, agreed to it. But the British Parliament, which decreed that Americans would be taxed, was elected in Great Britain by British citizens. The American colonists had no say in who became members of Parliament. The Americans felt the lack of direct representation was unfair, illegal, and a denial of their rights as Englishmen. "No taxation without representation" became the colonists' rallying cry.

However, the British government did not listen to their pleas. In 1765, Parliament passed the Stamp Act, which required that all American newspapers, court documents, and other important papers had to be printed on special paper, marked with an official British stamp. Every time colonists used a sheet of stamped paper, they had to pay a tax. The colonies exploded with anger. Some Americans formed a secret society they called the Sons of Liberty to oppose the tax.

By the spring of 1766, Britain repealed the Stamp Act. The colonies thought their troubles were over. Yet in the very next year, Parliament passed a new set of tax laws called the Townshend Acts. These acts raised the prices of many goods that the colonists got from Britain, such as paper, paint, glass, and tea, making them even angrier than before. The Brit-

A Stamp Act stamp

ish government began to worry that the colonies might rebel, so Parliament sent an army to Boston, Massachusetts, in 1768 to maintain the peace.

A Massacre and a Tea Party in Boston

In March 1770, violence broke out on the streets of Boston. A small group of Americans had taunted and threatened some British troops. The British soldiers shot into the crowd, killing five colonists. News of the event spread throughout the colonies, and it became known as the Boston Massacre.

This famous but one-sided depiction of the Boston Massacre was made by the American patriot Paul Revere.

In 1773, the British Parliament made a new law saying that only one company, the British East India Company, could sell tea in America. The company planned to sell tea at a very high price. Boston's Sons of Liberty responded with what they called a tea party—but it

Take a Look
Examine the details of the picture with your child and ask her to identify details that support the caption's claim that it is a "one-sided" depiction of the event.

was not like any party you might have been to! The colonists dressed up like Native Americans and boarded the company's ships in the Boston Harbor. Then, they smashed open the crates of tea on board and dumped the tea into the water, leaving behind nothing for the East India Company to sell.

The Boston Tea Party made King George III and the British Parliament furious. Not only did the colonists disrespect the laws, but they destroyed about £18,000 worth of goods. (The pound was the unit of money used by Britain at this time—just as the dollar is used in the United States today.) Parliament passed more laws, limiting the rights and freedoms of the colonists. One law closed Boston Harbor until Americans paid for the destroyed tea, putting many in Boston out of work. Another law forced Americans to pay for housing for British troops. Colonists called the new laws the Intolerable Acts because they could not tolerate what they saw as British punishments any longer. In Great Britain, these laws

were called the Coercive Acts, because they were meant to coerce, or force, the colonists to obey.

The First Continental Congress

In 1774, men from twelve of the colonies met in Philadelphia, Pennsylvania, to decide how they could work together to oppose the harsh British laws. They called themselves the First Continental Congress because it was the first meeting, or congress, among representatives of the colonies. A delegate named Patrick Henry surprised everyone when he declared, "I am not a Virginian, but an American!" At the time, most Americans thought of themselves as being from a particular colony—from Massachusetts, New York, Virginia, and so on—but Henry's remark showed that a national identity was beginning to emerge.

The representatives to the First Continental Congress accomplished two important things. First, they advised their fellow colonists to form small volunteer armies, called militias. Second, they wrote a letter to King George, asking him to consider their complaints. However, the king did not respond, and the harsh laws remained in place.

The War of Words

At first, the colonists only waged a war of words against Parliament and King George. But gradually, an increasing number of colonists began to call for open rebellion against Britain. In 1775, Virginia's House of Burgesses held a secret meeting during which Patrick Henry challenged his fellow Virginians to join the people of Massachusetts and resist the British. Some members still hoped for peace, but Henry insisted that there were no grounds for hope. The British were already preparing for war by sending armies and fleets to America, and there had already been skirmishes in Massachusetts. He argued:

> *I have but one lamp by which my feet are guided, and that is the lamp of experience. I know of no way of judging of the future but by the past. And judging by the past,*

I wish to know what there has been in the conduct of the British ministry for the last ten years to justify those hopes [for peace]. . . .

Are fleets and armies necessary to a work of love and reconciliation? . . . Let us not deceive ourselves, sir. These are the implements of war. . . . Has Great Britain any enemy, in this quarter of the world, to call for all this accumulation of navies and armies? No, sir, she has none. They are meant for us: they can be meant for no other. They are sent over to bind and rivet upon us those chains which the British ministry have been so long forging. And what have we to oppose to them? Shall we try argument? Sir, we have been trying that for the last ten years. Have we anything new to offer upon the subject? Nothing. We have held the subject up in every light of which it is capable; but it has been all in vain. . . .

What About You?

Discuss the meaning of Henry's words "give me liberty or give me death!" Explain that Henry felt liberty, or freedom, was so important that it was worth fighting for, even to the death. What things do you and your child feel are worth fighting for?

Patrick Henry delivers his "give me liberty or give me death" speech.

Gentlemen may cry, Peace, Peace—but there is no peace. The war is actually begun! The next gale that sweeps from the north will bring to our ears the clash of resounding arms! Our brethren are already in the field! Why stand we here idle? What is it that gentlemen wish? What would they have? Is life so dear, or peace so sweet, as to be purchased at the price of chains and slavery? Forbid it, Almighty God! I know not what course others may take; but as for me, give me liberty or give me death!

While Patrick Henry's speech inspired the colonial leaders, Thomas Paine addressed everyone when, in 1776, he published a pamphlet called *Common Sense* urging the colonies to declare independence. More than seventy-five thousand copies of *Common Sense* were printed in a short time. People read the pamphlet and then passed it on to their friends. In a few months, most of the two and a half million colonists had read the words of Thomas Paine. He had convinced them they were ready for independence.

The Redcoats Are Coming!

In the New England colonies, people who desired independence began preparing for war. They gathered weapons and ammunition, storing them in secret locations. In Massachusetts, they hid guns and ammunition near the towns of Concord and Lexington, north of Boston. British spies soon learned of these stockpiles. The British planned to raid the towns and seize the weapons in April. But the Americans had spies in the British army, who learned—just in time—of the plans to raid.

Paul Revere, a silversmith in Boston, and his friend William Dawes learned that the British would soon be marching to Concord and Lexington. Revere and Dawes rode through the night, telling everyone, "The redcoats are coming! The redcoats are coming!" "Redcoat" was a common nickname for British troops, who wore bright red uniforms. A sixteen-year-old girl named Sybil Ludington also rode through the night in New York, waking up militiamen.

Paul Revere warns of the Redcoats' approach

Battles of Lexington and Concord

When the British arrived in Lexington, American militiamen were ready to meet them. These men called themselves minutemen because they could be ready for duty on a minute's notice. They were not trained soldiers like the British troops. They were volunteers with little or no military experience. They practiced drills occasionally and wore everyday clothing. But they were skilled marksmen, with much hunting experience in North American forests.

As the British drew near, somebody fired a shot. Nobody knows if it was a minuteman or a redcoat. But later, when the American Revolution became famous, this first shot became known as "the shot heard round the world." The phrase comes from a poem by Ralph Waldo Emerson, which you can read on page 21.

Later that day, in the nearby town of Concord, the British fought again, but the minutemen outdid them, continually firing at them as they retreated to Boston. In the end, the American militiamen had killed about three redcoats for every American lost. It was April 19, 1775, and the Americans had won their first victory!

Yankee Doodles Are Dandy!

In the first-grade book in this series, you learned the song "Yankee Doodle." As the redcoats marched toward Lexington, English army musicians played "Yankee Doodle" on their flutes. They meant to insult the Americans: "Yankee" was an offensive name for a man from New England, and a "doodle" was a fool. But after Lexington and Concord, the Americans wrote new words and sang the song you know, proudly calling themselves Yankee Doodles!

Battle of Bunker Hill

After the battles at Lexington and Concord, colonial militiamen stayed ready. They knew the British would strike back. On the night of June 16, 1775, more than one thousand Americans dug out a defensive position on Bunker and Breed's Hills, the best high ground in the town of Charlestown, across a narrow inlet from Boston. All night, they worked without food, drink, or sleep. By morning, they had a good start on forts, built of mud and rock, at the top of both hills. British troops fired cannons from ships in the harbor and from the ground below. By afternoon, barges brought even more British soldiers. They marched up Bunker Hill to fight the Americans.

The British failed in their first attempt to take Bunker Hill. Later in the day, they tried again and failed. Frustrated, Major General William Howe sent his troops up Bunker Hill one more time. The exhausted Americans did their best to hold out but eventually ran out of ammunition and had to retreat.

The British claimed the victory, but they had suffered more than twice as many casualties as the Americans. A British general remarked that another victory of this kind would ruin him. Many soldiers, both American and British, died at Bunker Hill, but something else had died there, too—Britain's confidence that it could easily defeat the Americans.

One of the heroes of the Battle of Bunker Hill was a freed slave named Peter Salem. At a crucial point in the battle, when the colonists were on the verge of defeat, Salem shot the British commander. This stunned the British and helped the colonists rally.

The Second Continental Congress

The Second Continental Congress had been meeting since May 1775. Delegates from all thirteen colonies attended. After the battles around Boston, the delegates had decided on new matters. They were now engaged in war. They needed to gather together an army to defend themselves, and they needed a general to take command.

They chose General George Washington, who had served during the French and Indian War. Washington had also served in the House of Burgesses in Virginia and was one of the most respected leaders in the colonies. In June 1775, he was appointed commander in chief of the Continental Army.

A British soldier (left) and an American soldier (right)

Who Had the Advantage?

George Washington was an experienced military leader, but the Continental Army was made up of ordinary citizens with few weapons. Commanding these inexperienced soldiers would be difficult—and fighting against Great Britain, the world's greatest military power, seemed like an almost impossible task. Washington worried that he and the Continental Army would be crushed right away.

On paper, the British had a great advantage. They had about thirty thousand professional soldiers, including hired soldiers from Germany. The Americans could only provide about fifteen thousand volunteers. The British soldiers were well armed, well trained, and well paid. By contrast, the Americans were short on ammunition and even shorter on money.

Most alarming of all was the imbalance between the two navies. The British had 270 mighty warships. The Americans had only eight small ships.

Although the British army and navy were bigger, richer, and more experienced, the Americans did have some advantages. The Americans knew the land where they were fighting, and British troops and supplies would have to cross the Atlantic Ocean on slow boats before they could be deployed.

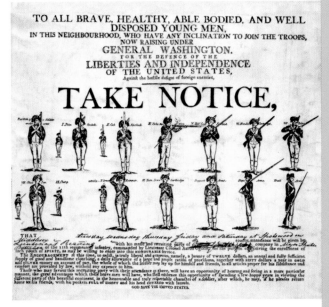

A recruiting poster for the Continental Army

The Americans were also motivated by powerful ideas—liberty and independence. One foreign observer described the American fighting spirit: "It is incredible that soldiers composed of men of every age, even of children of fifteen, of whites and blacks, almost naked, unpaid, and rather poorly fed, can march so well and withstand fire so steadfastly."

African Americans in the Revolution

About five thousand African Americans served in the Continental Army. Others joined the navy, and some did dangerous work as spies. About three hundred enslaved Africans joined the British, who promised to free them from slavery if they helped fight the Americans.

Breaking Ties: The Declaration of Independence

After appointing George Washington to head the Continental Army, the Second Continental Congress declared independence from Britain. The Congress appointed a committee to write the official letter that the colonies would send to King George. Thomas Jefferson of Virginia wrote the first draft of that letter, also called the Declaration of Independence. Benjamin Franklin and others changed certain words and sections. The Second Continental Congress approved

Signing the Declaration of Independence

the final document on July 4, 1776. Today, we still celebrate our independence on the Fourth of July.

The Words of the Declaration

The Declaration of Independence

Here is a famous section from the Declaration of Independence:

We hold these truths to be self-evident, that all men are created equal, that they are endowed by their Creator with certain unalienable Rights, that among these are Life, Liberty and the pursuit of Happiness.—That to secure these rights, Governments are instituted among Men, deriving their just powers from the consent of the governed,—That whenever any Form of Government becomes destructive of these ends, it is the Right of the People to alter or to abolish it.

The final phrase expresses one of the most radical ideas in the Declaration. It says not only that a government is based on the people's consent, but also that the people can change or replace the government when it does not work well anymore.

The Declaration goes on to list King George's actions that caused the Americans to break away from British rule, and then it boldly states that America will rule itself. It concludes with these stirring words:

We, therefore, the Representatives of the united States of America, in General Congress, Assembled, [do declare] That these United Colonies are, and of Right ought to be Free and Independent States; that they are Absolved from all Allegiance to the British Crown, and that all political connection between them and the State of Great Britain, is and ought to be totally dissolved; and that as Free and Independent States, they have full Power to levy War, conclude Peace, contract Alliances, establish Commerce, and to do all other Acts and Things which Independent States may of right do. And for the support of this Declaration, with a firm reliance on the protection of divine Providence, we mutually pledge to each other our Lives, our Fortunes and our sacred Honor.

In other words, the Declaration of Independence states that the united colonies are now a new country, free to make their own friends and enemies, wage war, and do business with other countries. The men who signed the Declaration promised to risk everything, including their lives and their honor, to start this new nation—the United States of America.

America's Most Famous Signature

John Hancock was president of the Second Continental Congress and added the first and most famous signature to the Declaration of Independence. Hancock's signature has become so famous that his name is a slang term for signature. When someone says, "Put your John Hancock here," it means you should sign your name.

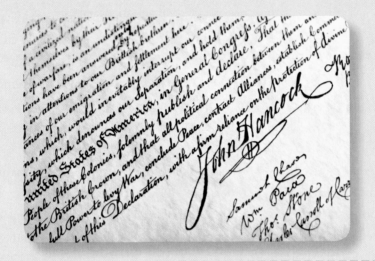

"The Times That Try Men's Souls"

The Americans had declared their independence, but because Britain wasn't willing to recognize this, they still had to fight for it. Unless they won the Revolutionary War, the Declaration of Independence would mean nothing.

The first months of war were difficult. Many American soldiers were killed, wounded, or captured in early battles. Others simply gave up and went home.

Some Americans began to wonder if they had made a mistake by declaring independence. But others kept up hope. Thomas Paine, author of *Common Sense*, wrote another pamphlet, called *The American Crisis*. "These are the times that

Thomas Paine

try men's souls," he wrote. By the word "try," Paine meant "test." He was saying that the Revolutionary War was testing the strength of the Americans' spirit. Did Americans have enough determination to keep going? Paine wrote, "The summer soldier and the sunshine patriot will, in this crisis, shrink from the service of his country, but he that stands it *now* deserves the love and thanks of man and woman."

By December 1776, General Washington's army had barely three thousand soldiers left. The British troops were right on their heels, forcing them to retreat from New York into New Jersey, and then farther south into Pennsylvania. It was a cold winter, and the soldiers felt weary and discouraged. On Christmas Eve, Washington gave the order to cross the icy Delaware River once again and march nine miles north to Trenton, New Jersey, under cover of darkness. There, they surprised a company of German soldiers fighting for the British and took one thousand prisoners.

Surprise victories such as this one encouraged the Americans, but Washington needed more soldiers. Congress offered twenty dollars and one hundred acres of free land in the West to each new volunteer. By the spring of 1777, Washington's army had nine thousand men. But the next major battles in Pennsylvania didn't go well for the American troops. The British army captured Philadelphia and chased the Continental Congress out of town.

Saratoga

Things changed for the better after the Battle of Saratoga in New York. The British planned to send thousands of troops, under the command of General John Burgoyne, down from Canada to capture territory in New England. While many American soldiers were ragged and half starved, General Burgoyne traveled with his personal supply of Champagne and silver cups with which to drink it! However, dragging heavy items such as these greatly slowed his advance.

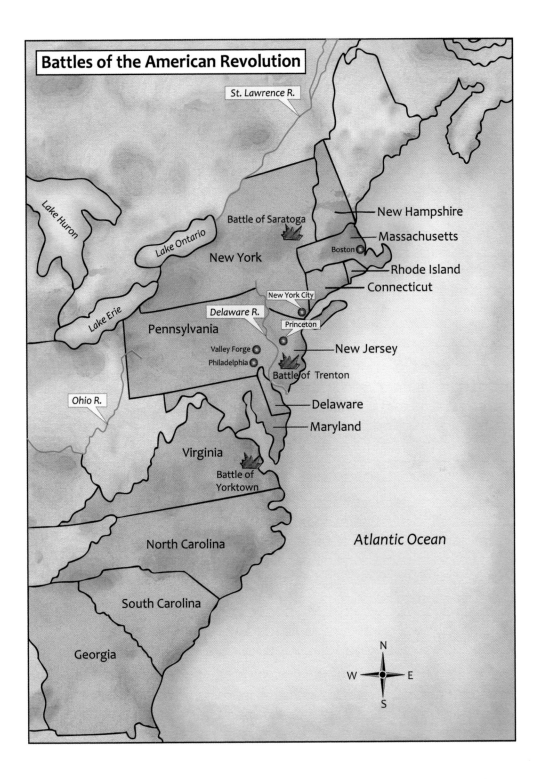

Battles of the American Revolution

St. Lawrence R.

Lake Huron

Lake Ontario

Battle of Saratoga

New York

New Hampshire

Massachusetts

Boston

Rhode Island

Connecticut

Lake Erie

New York City

Delaware R.

Pennsylvania

Princeton

Valley Forge

New Jersey

Philadelphia

Battle of Trenton

Ohio R.

Delaware

Maryland

Virginia

Battle of
Yorktown

North Carolina

Atlantic Ocean

South Carolina

N
W E
S

Georgia

The determined Americans made things difficult for Burgoyne in the wilderness. Sometimes, the British general found his way blocked by huge trees laid across the roads. His troops began to run out of food. They wrote to Britain for supplies and reinforcements, but help never arrived. As Burgoyne's troops grew weaker, the Continental Army grew stronger. In a series of battles, Burgoyne's forces were finally defeated at Saratoga in October 1777. The British general surrendered almost six thousand soldiers to the Americans.

Saratoga was more than just a major victory for the Americans. It was a turning point that made the world realize the young nation was capable of winning the Revolution. Using this British defeat, Benjamin Franklin persuaded the king of France and important French officials to help America. Soon, the French were shipping arms, ammunition, and troops to America. These additions shifted the tide of the war in America's favor.

Talk and Think

Think about what you've learned about the French and British in North America. Why might the French have been more likely to support the Americans over the British in the Revolutionary War?

The French Enter the War

To win the war, America needed to win battles on the sea. America had no actual navy, but the French navy came to America's aid starting in 1778.

Lafayette

The French sent several fleets to America, carrying guns, sailors, and troops to reinforce Washington's army. The French ships attacked British ships and set up a blockade that prevented British ships from delivering supplies and troops.

The French also sent generals to help with the war effort. The most famous of these military leaders was the Marquis de Lafayette. When he was only nineteen, Lafayette became inspired by the American cause. In 1777, a year before the French officially decided to support the Americans, Lafayette outfitted a ship at his own expense, planning to sail to America. French authorities tried to stop him, but he escaped and reached Philadelphia in the summer of 1777. He met George Washington, who was impressed by the brilliant young Lafayette. When Lafayette was wounded during his first battle at Brandywine, Washington sent his personal surgeon and told the doctors to treat him as if he were his own son.

More European Friends

The French were not the only Europeans who helped the American cause. Baron Friedrich von Steuben [STOO-ben] was a soldier from Prussia who could not speak a word of English when he volunteered to help the Americans. At first, he had to use an interpreter to communicate. Once Washington appointed him inspector general, he taught the inexperienced American soldiers military discipline and skills.

The Polish military engineer Thaddeus Kosciuszko [kosh-CHOO-shko] came to America in 1776, attracted by the ideal of freedom. He advised the Americans on battle plans and taught them how to build strong forts. His military knowledge also helped the Americans win the Battle of Saratoga.

Women in the Revolution

Many women helped in army camps and on the battlefields during the Revolution. They cooked for the soldiers in camp, tended the wounded, and carried pitchers of water to thirsty soldiers during battles. According to legend, one brave woman, nicknamed "Molly Pitcher," was married to an artilleryman. He was responsible for loading and

Molly Pitcher

firing a cannon. When he was wounded, Molly Pitcher stepped in and took his place at the cannon. The real woman behind this legend was Mary Ludwig Hays McCauly, who likely did serve directly at the Battle of Monmouth Court House.

Deborah Sampson was another female war hero. Sampson was so eager to fight for independence that she disguised herself as a man so she could join the Continental Army. When she was wounded, she tended her own wounds so no one would discover her secret. Eventually, she came down with a fever and had to go to the field hospital, where a surprised doctor discovered the truth. By that time, she had served in the army for three years!

Heroes and Villains

Nathan Hale just before his execution

The American Revolution produced famous heroes and notorious villains. One of the great heroes was Nathan Hale, a daring young American spy. In 1776, British soldiers captured Hale and gave orders for his execution. But Hale did not feel frightened. As he waited to be hanged, he calmly told those nearby, "I only regret that I have but one life to lose for my country."

Another brave hero was Scottish sea captain John Paul Jones. In 1779, Jones and his men attacked a British ship off the British coast. The Americans were outgunned and seemed to be losing the battle. The British captain called to Jones, asking if he was ready to surrender. Jones called back, "I have not yet begun to fight!" Then Jones pulled alongside the British ship and ordered his men to board it. The sailors fought by moonlight for two hours, with both ships in flames. At last, the British captain surrendered. Jones's brave and defiant words became a rallying cry for patriotic Americans.

John Paul Jones

For most of the Revolutionary War, Benedict Arnold was an important American leader. He helped the Americans win several battles, including the Battle of Saratoga. But Arnold, a proud man, felt unappreciated when he was passed over for a generalship. As a result, he secretly started working for the British. He tried to send the British advice on how to attack the important American fort at West Point. However, his plot was discovered and he fled to England. The phrase "Benedict Arnold" has been a synonym for "traitor" ever since.

Valley Forge

For the Americans, the low point of the Revolutionary War was the bitterly cold winter of 1777. While the British troops relaxed in Philadelphia, the Americans barely survived in tiny log huts at Valley Forge, twenty miles away. They were cold, hungry, and sick. They fought no battles that winter, but two thousand men died from sickness. One soldier wrote in his diary, "I am sick—discontented—and out of humor. Poor food—hard lodging—cold weather—fatigue—nasty clothes—nasty cookery—vomit half my time— smoked out of my senses."

However, that hard winter in Valley Forge made the Continental Army more disciplined and orderly, thanks to training from Baron von Steuben.

Under his expert guidance, the soldiers sharpened their fighting skills and renewed their confidence. After Valley Forge, the outlook of the war began to improve.

Washington and Lafayette inspect their shivering army at Valley Forge in 1777.

War's End: "The World Turned Upside Down"

In 1781, the British general Charles Cornwallis marched most of the British army to Yorktown, Virginia. George Washington knew this part of Virginia well, and he was aware that the British had camped at a spot where they could be surrounded. Washington sent a message to the leader of the French fleet, asking him to sail to Yorktown. Then Washington marched his army south from New Jersey. The Americans encircled the British army on land, while French ships sailed into the Chesapeake Bay, cutting off their chances to escape by sea.

American and French guns pounded away at Cornwallis's troops. Finally, on October 19, 1781, the British army surrendered. The redcoats marched in a long line, turning their weapons over to the Americans, while their band played a tune called "The World Turned Upside Down."

Certainly, the British must have felt that their world had been turned upside down on that day in history. A small and unprepared nation of ragtag colonies had beaten the mightiest military in the world!

Although the peace treaty between America and Britain was not signed until 1783, the Americans had proved that they could defend their independence by defeating General Cornwallis at the Battle of Yorktown.

Making a Constitutional Government

Starting Over

Now that the Americans had secured their independence, they had to develop their own form of government. The Declaration of Independence had laid down some ideas about government, such as the idea that a government should protect people's inalienable rights. But it did not explain how a government of "free and independent states" should be organized. To add to the problem, Americans from different states disagreed about how the national government would work.

During the Revolutionary War and early 1780s, most decisions about government were left up to the individual states. Each state created its own constitution, or written plan of government. Each had its own government officials, raised its own funds, and formed trade partnerships with foreign nations and neighboring states. Each state printed its own paper money, too.

The Articles of Confederation

The members of the Continental Congress thought the states should make their own arrangements, but they also saw the need for a central government to help states cooperate. After adopting the Declaration of Independence, the state delegates presented a written plan for a central government. This plan called for a strong central government, but many Americans worried that a powerful national government might boss them around the way the British king had.

First money coined by the United States

The Continental Congress debated the role of central government for a year and a half, until November 1777. In the end, they approved a document called the Articles of Confederation, which describes a loose union of states with a weak central government. There was no president and no court system. The central government could not force people to pay taxes or regulate trade among the states and foreign nations.

Getting the states to agree to the Articles of Confederation was even harder than writing this document. Each of the thirteen states had to ratify, or vote to approve, every one of the articles. This process took almost four years! At last, in 1781, all thirteen states agreed, and the Articles of Confederation became the first U.S. constitution.

Shays's Rebellion

As it turned out, the Articles of Confederation did not work as the congress had planned. The articles left too much power in the hands of the states and limited what the central government could do. One major event that revealed the weakness of the Articles of Confederation was Shays's Rebellion.

In 1786, farmers in Massachusetts were having a hard time paying their taxes. They tried to get financial help from the state. When their requests were denied, a farmer named Daniel Shays led an attack on a U.S. arsenal to seize its weapons. Congress lacked the funding for federal troops to defend the arsenal; instead, it had to rely on militiamen from Massachusetts to end the violence.

Shays's Rebellion showed many Americans that if a government was going to keep the country united, stable, and at peace, the national government needed more power. John Adams commented that the Articles of Confederation were like a "rope of sand" that barely held the states together.

During Shays's Rebellion, angry citizens took control of courthouses.

Drafting the Constitution

In February 1787, leaders of the Continental Congress asked representatives from every state to assemble in Philadelphia in May. The purpose of their meeting was to improve the Articles of Confederation. But that was not what happened.

The delegates from Virginia arrived ahead of everyone else and, meeting by themselves, decided what the Americans really needed was a new constitution, not just a revision of the Articles. They sat down and did the job on their own, before the other delegates arrived. The result was called the Virginia Plan. They presented it to the other state representatives when they arrived in Philadelphia, and many of its ideas eventually became part of the U.S. Constitution.

James Madison: Father of the Constitution

Before the convention in Philadelphia, a politician from Virginia named James Madison had begun to plan a new system of government for America. He started by studying histories of Greece and Rome, and he borrowed ideas about government from many civilizations, ancient and modern. He had read the writings of great philosophers about their ideal governments. When Madison had read all the books he could find in America, he wrote to his friends in Europe, asking them to send more books.

Madison wanted to create a government strong enough to put down rebellions and prevent states from ignoring federal laws. But he also wanted a government that would not interfere with people's basic rights. Madison's ideas became the basis for the Virginia Plan, which he wrote.

Madison is called the "Father of the Constitution" for many reasons:

James Madison

1. He researched and prepared a model government plan in advance of the Constitutional Convention.
2. He urged delegates to attend the convention and sent letters to leaders in all states.
3. He arrived early and prepared the Virginia Plan before other delegates arrived.

4. He was among the most vocal, hardworking, and influential of the debaters at the convention—he made more than 150 speeches!

5. He took down detailed notes, providing a thorough record of the debates at the convention.

6. He helped write a set of important newspaper articles, called the *Federalist Papers*, to promote adoption of the Constitution among the states.

7. He composed the first ten amendments to the Constitution, which are called the Bill of Rights.

Debates and Compromises: The Constitutional Convention of 1787

When most of the delegates finally arrived at the Constitutional Convention in May 1787, they began by talking about Madison's Virginia Plan. Much discussion and debate centered on Madison's plan to structure the government into three branches: executive, legislative, and judicial. Those three branches still form the basic structure of the U.S. government today.

The executive branch. Executives are the people who execute, or carry out, the laws of the country. The executive branch is in charge of running the daily duties of the national government. The president is the leader of the executive branch.

The legislative branch. To "legislate" means to "make laws." The legislative branch, also called Congress, is in charge of writing the laws that people must follow. Congress is made up of two houses, the Senate and the House of Representatives.

The judicial branch. Judicial comes from a Latin word for "judgment." The judicial branch includes the courts and judges, who interpret the laws and settle disagreements about those laws. The Supreme Court is the highest U.S. court.

Madison's plan caused disagreements between the large states and the small states. If the number of representatives each state sent to Congress were determined by the number of people who lived in that state, the larger states with more citizens would have an advantage. The smaller states with fewer people (such as Maryland, New Hampshire, and Delaware) feared that these states would have more power because they would have more representatives in the legislative branch. The states with larger populations (such as New York, Pennsylvania, and

Virginia) thought it unfair that a state with only five thousand people could have as much say in the government as a state with half a million.

A delegate from Connecticut came up with a solution. Every state, no matter the size, would have exactly two Senate representatives. But the number of elected officials sent by a state to the House of Representatives would be determined by that state's population. This idea, called the Connecticut Compromise, solved the problem and created a legislative structure that is still in place today. The Connecticut Compromise is sometimes referred to as the Great Compromise.

Executive Branch

Legislative Branch

Judicial Branch

The three branches of the government—the executive branch, legislative branch, and judicial branch—have checks on one another. This means that no one branch of the government can gain supreme power.

Slavery and the "Three-Fifths Compromise"

Delegates to the Constitutional Convention also argued about the issue of slavery. Wealthy southerners owned plantations on which enslaved Africans planted and harvested crops such as rice, tobacco, and cotton. In 1787, about 750,000 people with African roots lived in America. These African Americans made up about one-fifth of the population. Almost 90 percent of those African Americans were slaves.

Northerners did not generally grow their crops on large plantations, so slavery was rarer in the New England states. During the Revolution, two states—Pennsylvania and Massachusetts—even made slavery illegal. Some northern delegates came to the Constitutional Convention with the hope that slavery would be abolished, or outlawed, everywhere.

Many of the debates at the convention concerned the future of slavery in the United States. Although enslaved people could not vote, they did end up influencing the House of Representatives. Delegates argued whether the official U.S. population count should include the enslaved people. If it did, it would increase the number of representatives the southern states sent to Congress. Southern states wanted every enslaved person counted; northerners did not want them counted at all. Finally, the delegates came up with a "Three-Fifths Compromise," agreeing to count every five enslaved people as three people in a state's population.

The delegates wrote several clauses regarding slavery. Congress was not allowed to pass any laws to control or regulate the slave trade for twenty years. Northern delegates accepted another clause that allowed slave owners to recapture runaways and bring them back from other states. Southern delegates allowed Congress to collect tax money from plantation owners for every enslaved person they owned.

In the end, all delegates accepted these compromises, but many were unhappy with them. George Washington (who owned slaves in Virginia) wrote to Thomas Jefferson (who also owned slaves in Virginia) that it was his strong wish "to see some plan adopted by which slavery in this country might be abolished by law."

Enslaved people at work, with a plantation house in the background

The United States would eventually abolish slavery, but not for many years. All the states in the North had abolished slavery by the 1820s, but slavery was not prohibited in the South until after the Civil War, which ended in 1865.

What Does the Constitution Say and Do?

The Constitution that the Constitutional Convention drafted in 1787 is the same Constitution we use today. It has changed over the years only by the addition of amendments, or changes added to the end. The Constitution's words are the supreme law of the United States.

The Constitution begins with a short introduction, called the Preamble, which states the goals of the new U.S. government:

All Together
Read the Preamble to the Constitution aloud.

We the People of the United States, in Order to form a more perfect Union, establish Justice, insure domestic Tranquility, provide for the common defence, promote the general Welfare, and secure the Blessings of Liberty to ourselves and our Posterity, do ordain and establish this Constitution for the United States of America.

The U.S. Constitution is the oldest written national constitution in use.

Let's take a look at what this preamble means.

We the People . . . This famous opening phrase reminds us where the government's power comes from. This constitution was written and agreed to by U.S. citizens. It was not the act of a king handing down the law to everyone below him. Planning a government around the people was a new idea among the nations of the world in 1787, and so it was important for the Framers to announce this right away.

Also, by saying "we the people" instead of "we the states" or "we the representatives of New York, New Jersey, and so on," the Preamble makes the point that this constitution is a binding agreement among all individuals living in the country—not just among the leaders of the various states.

. . . *to form a more perfect Union* . . . The United States was already a confederation of states under the Articles of Confederation, but the Constitution's goal was an even better system of government.

. . . *establish Justice* . . . This phrase refers to the strong authority of the Constitution and the judicial branch of the newly created government. It is a clear reminder that federal law is the same law for all states.

. . . *insure domestic Tranquility* . . . The word "tranquility" means "peace." The word "domestic" means "at home." One of the purposes of the Constitution is to make sure peace at home is not disrupted, as it was during Shays's Rebellion.

. . . *provide for the common defence* . . . This phrase states that the government can create and maintain a national army to defend all the states, offering common defense, or protection for everyone.

. . . *promote the general welfare* . . . The Constitution guarantees that the central government will make decisions about trade and money issues for the benefit of all states and all people. No individual state will be allowed to let its interests harm the well-being of another state.

. . . *secure the Blessings of Liberty to ourselves and our Posterity* . . . This phrase recalls the fragile peace that existed in the years following the Revolution. When the Constitution was written, several foreign nations—including Britain and Spain—were in a position to attack the United States. Pirates raided American merchant vessels on the open seas, and American Indians were still allied with foreign nations. War was possible at any time. The freedom that had been won through the Revolution had to be secured, or kept safe, by the new government.

At the same time, freedom could be threatened when citizens or groups tried to take too much power. Enemies from within the nation could do as much damage as foreign enemies, and the Constitution was designed to protect against both. The word "posterity" refers to future generations of people, which include today's citizens and those who will be born after us. The Constitution is an attempt to guarantee liberty not only for those who wrote and approved it, but for all future U.S. citizens.

Checks and Balances

The Framers who wrote the Constitution wanted to make sure no single branch of government could take too much power for itself, so they devised a system of checks and balances. The checks are ways in which each branch prevents the other two branches from becoming too powerful. The balances are ways that each branch is equal to the others in power and responsibilities.

In this system, one branch has the authority to overrule certain decisions by the two other branches. For example, the president can veto, or reject, a bill passed by Congress, but Congress can override the president's veto with a two-thirds majority vote in each house and turn the bill into law. In another example, the president appoints justices to the Supreme Court, but the Senate must approve these appointments before they go into effect.

The Bill of Rights

Finally, the delegates came to agree on the rules describing the new government of the United States of America, and they were ready to share the document— the U.S. Constitution—with the people. But the states had to ratify, or approve, the Constitution before it became the supreme law of the land.

This process took three more years of debating, but finally the U.S. Constitution was ratified in 1790. Many states asked for certain changes, or amendments, that guaranteed the rights of individual citizens—rights such as the freedom to speak, the freedom to publish newspapers and books, the freedom to practice any religion, and the freedom to gather in a peaceful assembly. In 1791, ten amendments were added to the Constitution. Those first ten amendments are called the Bill of Rights. They promise important liberties to all American citizens.

For example, the First Amendment states that Americans can worship as they choose (this is called freedom of religion), speak freely as long as they are not unfairly harming others (freedom of speech), and publish opinions freely, again as long as they do not unfairly harm or lie about others (freedom of the press). The Fourth Amendment prohibits unreasonable search and seizure, promising that the armed services and police will treat Americans fairly. Other amendments guarantee that all Americans have the right to due process of law. When convicted of a crime, they will be judged through fair trials with decisions made by a jury of fellow citizens. And even if they are found guilty, the Bill of Rights protects Americans from cruel and unusual punishments.

National, State, and Local Governments

The Constitution outlines the national government. But states have their own constitutions, too. State governments, just like the national government, are divided into three branches—executive, legislative, and judicial—in a system of checks and balances. In the same way as the president leads the nation, a governor leads each state, helped by representatives in the state legislature. Most states are divided into cities and counties. However, there are a few exceptions. Louisiana, for example, is divided into parishes instead of counties. Alaska is divided into boroughs. Each division in a state has a local government as well. Most city governments are led by a mayor, elected by the people and helped by members of a city council.

In the United States, we believe in a government "of the people, by the people, and for the people," as President Abraham Lincoln said in 1863. But exactly how do Americans participate in their national, state, and local governments?

For one, they vote in elections to choose their government representatives. They volunteer or run for office themselves. They write letters to the editor of their local newspaper and to their representatives,

Do It Yourself
Encourage your child to write letters to local newspaper editors or government representatives on issues about which she feels strongly.

explaining what they think the government should do and why. They pay taxes, which help run governments and all that they make happen. Tax money helps build schools and auditoriums, parks and roads. Taxes pay to keep the streets clean and provide electricity to the streetlights. Taxes also provide the salaries of the armed forces, police officers, public school teachers, and librarians.

Early Presidents and Politics

Americans were pleased when George Washington took office as the first U.S. president in 1789. He had a hard job because he had no model to follow. The Constitution did not spell out the details of the president's job.

George Washington

Congress decided to create a cabinet, or group of advisors, to help the president make decisions. Washington's first job was to pick the best men he could find to fill these positions. The cabinet members were called secretaries, and each cabinet member oversaw one part of the government. The secretary of state worked on relationships with other countries. The secretary of the treasury worked on the nation's money. These positions and others like them still exist in the U.S. government today. Together, these people are called the president's administration.

Another significant member of Washington's administration was his vice president. In the country's first years, the presidential candidate who received the second-largest number of votes became vice president.

According to the Constitution, presidents were elected for four-year terms. Washington served as president for two terms, or eight years—and those eight years were not easy ones. In 1793, war broke out between France and Great Britain. Washington made sure the

Talk and Think

How might having the vice president be the presidential candidate with the second-largest number of votes make the relationship between the president and vice president different from what it is today?

young nation, still recovering from the Revolutionary War, stayed out of the war in Europe.

There were wars of words and ideas in the cabinet, though, especially between Thomas Jefferson, his secretary of state, and Alexander Hamilton, his secretary of the treasury. When Washington's second term ended, he had heard enough of their arguing. Besides, he felt that no president should serve for more than two terms. He feared that if he died while he was still president, it would set a trend and later presidents would serve for their entire lives, which would make them more like kings. Washington retired to his beloved home in Mount Vernon, Virginia, and lived only two more years.

The Beginning of Political Parties

When people run for president today, they run as a candidate from a political party. Today, the Democratic Party and the Republican Party are the two major political parties in the United States. People who belong to the same political party have similar views on many issues and disagree with other parties' views. Political parties are a way people with common beliefs can work together to achieve their goals.

But when Washington was elected, there were no political parties. Political parties as we know them began with those disagreements between Jefferson and Hamilton. These two men held very different beliefs about what the people wanted and what kind of government the United States should have.

Jefferson saw the United States as a nation of small farmers. He trusted the American people to make decisions by themselves and thought a strong central government might get in the way of freedom. He thought it was better for the state and local governments to have more power than the central government.

Hamilton thought it was a bad idea to give Americans that much freedom. While Jefferson championed the common people, Hamilton was suspicious of them. Hamilton is rumored to have once shouted at Jefferson: "Your people, sir—your people is a great beast!" Hamilton favored a strong central government and also tended to favor merchants and traders over farmers. He believed that if businesses worked closely with the government, that partnership would strengthen the nation overall. He argued that the United States should run a national bank that could help these businesses grow.

Jefferson opposed Hamilton's national bank. It would be dangerous, Jefferson argued, to have so much money under the control of one big bank. He feared that by following Hamilton's policies, a small number of Americans would become rich and powerful.

Jefferson's followers called themselves Republicans (though not the same Republicans as we have today), because they believed that in a republic the common man should play an important role in the government. Hamilton's followers called themselves Federalists, because they believed in

Thomas Jefferson

a strong federal (or national) government. Many politicians took sides, and soon the Republicans and the Federalists developed into the nation's first political parties.

At the time, most Americans did not predict that parties would become a permanent part of the U.S. political system. But, little by little, it became clear that parties were here to stay. Today, we realize that political parties are an important part of a democratic system. People will always disagree about what should be done, even though they all may sincerely want to do what is best for the country.

During U.S. elections, Democrats and Republicans run against one another; sometimes the candidate from one party wins, and sometimes the other one does. But the losing party keeps an eye on what the winning party does and tries to convince the voters next time that its candidate should win. Meanwhile, other people who hold beliefs different from those of the two main parties are called independents. Both parties try hard to get the independents' votes, which may swing toward Democrats on one issue and Republicans on the next. If both parties fail to satisfy voters, anyone who gets enough supporters can start a new party! That has happened several times in American history.

A New Capital City

For a while, New York City was the capital of the United States. But southern representatives had to travel very far from home to get there, so Congress decided to build another city, halfway between the North and the South. They founded the city we now call Washington, and they made sure that its land was not part of any state. They called the area the District of Columbia. Today, this capital city is called Washington, D.C.

The plan for the new capital was drawn up by a French mapmaker and artist named Pierre Charles L'Enfant [pee-AYR lahn-FAHN]. L'Enfant worked to-

The White House in 1817

gether with a talented African American surveyor named Benjamin Banneker to lay out the streets and buildings for the new city.

It took many years to finish constructing the new capital city. Workers had to build a house for the president and his family, now called the White House, and a new office building for Congress, called the Capitol. President John Adams, who was elected after Washington, was the first to live in the President's House, the original name for the White House. In 1800, when he and his wife, Abigail, moved in, the building had no stairs to the second floor and many of its walls were unfinished.

Our Second President: John Adams

John Adams was one of the hardest-working, most vocal, and most influential of all the Founders. He had taken part in almost every important action that helped form the new country. During the Revolutionary War, Adams served without pay as leader of the Continental Congress. Later, he served as the nation's first vice president under Washington.

When Washington stepped down, Adams ran against Thomas Jefferson for president. Adams just barely won the election, which meant that Jefferson became his vice president. Then, the arguments between Federalists and Republicans became

John Adams

even worse. Adams was a Federalist, which meant the Republicans did not agree with his views, but many people in his own party disagreed with his views, too.

Like Washington, Adams wanted to keep the United States out of European wars. But plenty of Americans wanted their country to join the war between the British and French, and they got angry at Adams. Tired of the criticism, Adams approved laws that placed a stiff penalty on anyone who criticized the government. These laws limited the rights of free speech and a free press promised in the Bill of Rights. A huge storm of protest developed. During his final years as president, Adams grew bitter. He once complained that he felt he lived in "an enemy's country."

Make a Connection

After reading the message that Abigail Adams sent to her husband, John Adams, reread the story of Joan of Arc on page 129. What does Abigail Adams's message seem to say about how the treatment of women changed between the time of Joan of Arc and the time of the Continental Congress?

Abigail Adams, the wife of John Adams, wrote letters to her husband when he was a delegate to the Continental Congress. She noted that some of the rights granted to men did not apply equally to women, and she tried to convince her husband to do something about this:

March 31, 1776. *I long to hear that you have declared an independency— and, by the way, in the new code of laws, which I suppose it will be necessary for you to make, I desire you would remember the ladies, and be more generous and favorable to them than [were] your ancestors.*

Best of Friends, Worst of Enemies

Adams and Jefferson started out as friends. They worked together on the Declaration of Independence. After the Revolution, Adams represented the United States in Great Britain while Jefferson represented it in France. They wrote letters to each other and shared many hopes for their new nation.

The troubles between these two great men began when Washington became president. Adams was vice president, and he leaned in favor of Hamilton's Federalist Party. Jefferson was secretary of state, and he was the leader of the Republican Party. The two men became fierce political enemies and ran against each other for president in 1796. When Adams became president, with Jefferson his vice president, their friendship broke down even more.

But this story has a happy ending. Both Adams and Jefferson lived long lives. Near the end of their lives, they became friends once again and started writing letters back and forth. As he lay dying, Adams thought of his friend Jefferson. Adams's last words were, "Thomas Jefferson still survives." It turns out that Adams's last words were wrong. On the very same day only hours beforehand, hundreds of miles away in Virginia, Jefferson had died, thinking of his friend Adams.

By a spooky twist of fate, both men died on July 4, 1826, the fiftieth anniversary of the signing of the Declaration of Independence!

Our Third President: Thomas Jefferson

Thomas Jefferson was one of the most extraordinary men living in an age full of great thinkers. Like George Washington, Jefferson was a Virginian plantation owner. But he was interested in many subjects besides farming. He studied literature, foreign languages, philosophy, politics, astronomy, geography, medicine, music, and architecture. He bought books wherever he traveled. His personal library grew and grew until he ran out of room. He contributed the books he owned to help start the Library of Congress, the official library of the United States. He wrote the words to the Declaration of Independence and designed many beautiful buildings, such as his home in Virginia, called Monticello.

Making Connections
Learn more about Jefferson's Monticello on page 239.

Mr. Jefferson's Big Purchase

Jefferson was a man with a vision. He imagined a future when the population of the United States would have grown so large that the country would need more territory. He also feared that if foreign powers controlled the surrounding regions of North America, they could make trade and travel difficult.

In those days, France owned most of the land west of the Mississippi River, from Canada to Mexico, and controlled all trade down the Mississippi through the port of New Orleans. This vast French territory was called Louisiana, after France's King Louis XIV. Jefferson sent James Monroe, his secretary of state, to France to ask the French leader, Napoleon, to sell the city of New Orleans. As it turned out, Napoleon offered to sell the entire territory of Louisiana!

In 1803, for $15 million, Jefferson bought the entire Louisiana Territory, an area of about 828,000 square miles, which now includes Iowa, Missouri, Arkansas, Nebraska, Kansas, Oklahoma, most of South Dakota, and parts of seven other states. Overnight, Jefferson doubled the size of the United States and gained control of the Mississippi River. The deal he struck came to be called the Louisiana Purchase.

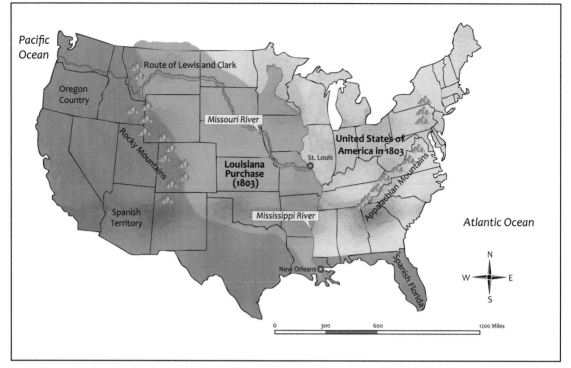

The Louisiana Purchase nearly doubled the size of the United States.

Lewis and Clark

Because he had the curiosity of a scientist, Jefferson wanted to learn all he could about these uncharted lands in the West. So in 1804, he sent an expedition to explore and map the land west of the Mississippi. During the years 1804 to 1806, a group of explorers led by two men, Meriwether Lewis and William Clark, walked and canoed all the way to the Pacific Ocean and then back to Virginia.

Lewis and Clark asked a young Shoshone woman, Sacagawea, to help them cross the plains and mountains and talk with the Native Americans they met. They made maps and wrote down their observations concerning weather patterns, rocks, soil, plants, and animals. They found the fossilized bones of prehistoric creatures. They recorded two hundred species of plants. They even brought back the skull of a mastodon, which Jefferson proudly displayed at Monticello. A mastodon is an extinct species of mammal related to elephants.

Sacagawea helped Lewis and Clark explore the Louisiana Purchase.

Our Fourth President: James Madison

James Madison was more of a scholar and a philosopher than he was a politician. Not as strong in his peacekeeping resolve as Jefferson and Adams had been, Madison allowed the United States to be drawn into the war in Europe.

There were good reasons why Americans would consider fighting. Both the United Kingdom and France were searching U.S. ships at sea. The British would kidnap American sailors and force them to fight against France.

The British were performing other actions that made Americans angry. Some U.K. officials and troops still lived in forts at the western edge of U.S. territory. They made friends with American Indians nearby and encouraged them to attack the American settlers.

Even so, Americans disagreed over which side the United States should support. Some wanted the United States to go to war with the United Kingdom;

some wanted to fight France; most did not want the United States to go to war at all. In 1812, those who supported a war with Britain were called "War Hawks." They convinced Madison to declare war on the United Kingdom.

The War of 1812

The United States returned to fighting the United Kingdom in a series of battles called the War of 1812. Afraid that the British would capture the capital city, President Madison left the capital and took command of a fort in Maryland.

The British sailed into the Chesapeake Bay. They did invade Washington but found the town deserted. All members of Congress, even the army, had fled. Dolley Madison, the wife of the president, stayed in Washington until the last minute, gathering up important valuables. Meanwhile, a servant and a slave removed and saved a famous painting of George Washington. The British started fires in the President's House, the Capitol, and other government buildings. They worried that the empty town was a trap, though, so they returned to their ships before they had completely destroyed the city. The President's House was later rebuilt, and—to cover up the fire damage—painted white. This is how it got its modern name, the White House.

The War of 1812 dragged on for two years. Finally the two tired countries signed a peace treaty on Christmas Eve in 1814. The War of 1812 was the last time the British and the Americans ever went to war against each other.

Oddly, the largest battle of the War of 1812 did not occur until after the peace treaty was signed. Word of the treaty had not yet reached the city of New Orleans. U.S. troops led by General Andrew Jackson took a well-protected position. The British troops attacked. The Americans fired their rifles, and the British, marching in the open, did not stand a chance. Many Americans died during the Battle of New Orleans, but the battle created a new national hero—Andrew Jackson.

Make a Connection
During the War of 1812, Francis Scott Key witnessed the British bombardment of Fort McHenry and wrote "The Star-Spangled Banner," which later became the national anthem.

Our Fifth President: James Monroe

James Monroe had joined George Washington's Continental Army at the age of eighteen. In one battle, a bullet became lodged in his shoulder, and it stayed there the rest of his life. He studied law with his friend Thomas Jefferson and represented the United States as an ambassador to France. He was elected governor of Virginia, and James Madison appointed him secretary of state. Monroe was elected president in 1816 and reelected by an overwhelming majority in 1820.

The Problem of Slavery

In 1820, Missouri was ready to become a state. Its status as a new state made some Americans worried. As the country expanded, the states argued more and more about slavery. The plantation owners in the South depended on the work done by enslaved people to make money. In the North, people made money on smaller farms and, more so, by working in factories. By 1820, almost no one in the North owned an enslaved African. In fact, a few people in the North had begun to speak out loudly against slavery.

Those who wanted to abolish slavery throughout the United States came to be called abolitionists. Abolitionists fought against slavery in many ways: by publishing books, delivering speeches, helping runaways escape, and convincing states to pass laws forbidding slavery.

Arguments about slavery occurred constantly in Congress. Since there were equal numbers of free states (in the North) and slave states (in the South), the arguments almost always ended in a draw. But if Missouri became a state—a slave state—it would tip the balance, and there would be more slave states than free ones.

The solution was a compromise. Missouri was admitted to the Union, but so was Maine. The addition of one slave state and one free state increased the number of states to twenty-four while also preserving the delicate balance. This decision was called the Missouri Compromise.

The Monroe Doctrine

During a presidential message in 1823, Monroe proclaimed what we now call the Monroe Doctrine. A doctrine is an official statement of policy. In this case, Monroe made an official statement about how the United States would interact with other nations. He was especially concerned about the way European nations continued to try to exert their power in North America, South America, and the Caribbean—in other words, the Western Hemisphere. One hundred years before, this territory had been called the New World and explored by people from many different European countries. Monroe wanted Europe to understand that the United States could take care of itself and its neighbors.

The new policy was essentially a warning to European powers. The United States would consider it a threat to its security if a nation from elsewhere in the world tried to establish a new colony or interfere with any government in the Western Hemisphere. Monroe stated that the United States had no plans to interfere in Europe or conquer any of its lands. In other words, he said to Europe, "You stay out of our affairs, and we'll stay out of yours."

Our Sixth President: John Quincy Adams

The son of John and Abigail Adams, John Quincy Adams was practically raised to be president. When he was ten, he accompanied his father on a diplomatic mission abroad. At fourteen, he became secretary to the U.S. ambassador to Russia. He studied at private schools in Europe and at Harvard University in Massachusetts.

John Quincy Adams became president in 1825, but he was never popular with the people. After one term in office, he was replaced by the much more popular Andrew Jackson. Later, Adams served in the House of Representatives, where he worked hard to abolish slavery.

Our Seventh President: Andrew Jackson

President Andrew Jackson, elected in 1828, was a different kind of president from those who came before him. He is sometimes called the "president of the common man." Born in the backwoods on the border between North and South Carolina, he was described by a neighbor as "the most roaring, rollicking, game-cocking, horse-racing, card-playing, mischievous fellow that ever lived in Salisbury."

Jackson had fought against the British during the Revolution and against the Native Americans siding with the British during the War of 1812. By leading the U.S. Army to victory, he became known as the "Hero of New Orleans." He was a man of the frontier and action, and a huge majority of voters elected him. People poured into Washington for his inauguration. Crowds

Andrew Jackson

swarmed through the White House, making a mess, standing on satin-covered chairs in their muddy boots, and knocking over punch bowls.

Jackson worked to make the United States more democratic than it had been before. At this time, only white men who owned a certain amount of property had the right to vote. Jackson supported the right of *all* white men to vote, regardless of their wealth, property, or education. He was a populist, which means he believed in the wisdom of the people. He was suspicious of rich people who tried to buy power in the government.

Before he became president, Jackson led troops in battles against American Indians. As president, Jackson continued his efforts to turn their native lands into U.S. territory. He urged Congress to pass the Indian Removal Act of 1830, which allowed the U.S. government to force American Indian tribes to move from their lands and homes, sometimes more than a thousand miles away.

Many were moved to what was called Indian Territory, now the state of Oklahoma.

As you read in the second-grade book in this series, one southeastern tribe, the Cherokee, refused to go, but U.S. soldiers forced them to walk eight hundred miles to Indian Territory. Many of them died along this "Trail of Tears."

Reformers

Making a More Perfect Nation

During the 1800s, daring men and women worked to make the United States a nation where all people had the liberties promised by the Declaration of Independence. These people were called reformers because they tried to reform, or change, society. Reformers started schools, organized meetings, gave speeches, and published articles to convince other people to believe in their causes. The abolitionists represented one of the biggest reform movements, but there were many others.

Dorothea Dix fought for the rights of the mentally ill. In the early 1800s, people with mental illnesses were imprisoned with people who had committed terrible crimes such as murder. Dix thought that people who were mentally ill needed special care in hospitals, not punishment in prisons. She encouraged state governments to run mental hospitals, helped improve conditions in those hospitals, and convinced doctors to treat mentally ill people with compassion.

Dorothea Dix worked for better treatment for the mentally ill.

Horace Mann pioneered the reform of U.S. education. During the 1800s, the few people who finished high school or college were the sons of rich families. Some schools stayed open for only a few months each year. Mann thought that everyone—men and women, rich and poor—deserved a good education. He worked to establish public schools run by state governments that provided education for most children at least half of the year.

Women's Rights

Lucretia Mott and Elizabeth Cady Stanton believed that the United States' promise of liberty would not be fulfilled until women had equal rights with men.

Example of bloomer dress

In July 1848, Mott and Stanton organized a meeting at Seneca Falls, New York, inviting people to discuss how to promote the cause of women's rights. One hundred people attended, and they shocked many Americans by demanding that women be given the right to vote. In a document called the Declaration of Rights and Sentiments, modeled after the Declaration of Independence, they wrote that men seemed to desire "an absolute tyranny" over women. But the women echoed the first words of the Declaration of Independence and countered, "We hold these truths to be self-evident: that all men and women are created equal."

Amelia Bloomer attended the convention at Seneca Falls. She was the editor of a magazine that supported equal rights for women. Bloomer also wanted to see reforms in the way women dressed. She thought women should be free to wear comfortable clothes that allowed them to live a more active life. Loose-fitting, comfortable pants worn under a short skirt are still called bloomers in her honor.

Sojourner Truth

Sojourner Truth was an African American woman born into slavery in New York in 1795. She gained her freedom in 1827, when New York freed its enslaved population. At that time, she stopped using her previous name and began calling herself Sojourner Truth. A sojourner is someone who visits a place for a while and then moves on. Truth saw herself as someone who traveled from place to place, helping people see the truth. She began to speak publicly in support of abolition and women's rights. Although she never learned to read or write, she was a powerful speaker.

In 1851, Truth attended a women's convention in Ohio. Many convention participants did not support her attendance. They were afraid that their cause, equal rights for women, would be damaged if it was linked with the rights of African Americans. During the meeting, a clergyman argued against women's rights. He said Jesus Christ was a man and described how Eve in the Bible had tempted Adam to disobey God's orders. He also argued that women were inferior in intellect, or brainpower, to men. The atmosphere of the convention became tense.

Then, Truth rose from her seat and approached the platform. Several women whispered, "For God's sake, don't let her speak!" But the president of the convention, Frances Gage, allowed Truth to speak and later wrote down her recollection of what she said:

Sojourner Truth

Talk and Think

Ask your child why he thinks that some members of the women's rights movement would not want their cause associated with the abolitionist movement.

Well, children, where there is so much racket there must be something out of kilter. I think that 'twixt the negroes of the South and the women of the North, all talking about rights, the white men will be in a fix pretty soon. But what's all this talking about?

That man over there says that women need to be helped into carriages, and lifted over ditches, and to have the best place everywhere. Nobody ever helps me into carriages, or over mud-puddles, or gives me any best place! And ain't I a woman?

Sojourner Truth pulled back her sleeve to show her right arm. Then, in a voice "like rolling thunder," she continued:

Look at me! Look at my arm! I have ploughed and planted, and gathered into barns, and no man could head me! And ain't I a woman? I could work as much and eat as much as a man—when I could get it—and bear the lash as well! And ain't I a woman? I have borne thirteen children, and seen them most all sold off to slavery, and when I cried out with my mother's grief, none but Jesus heard me! And ain't I a woman? Then they talk about this thing in my head; what's this they call it?

Someone in the audience whispered the word she was looking for—"intellect." And Truth continued:

That's it, honey. What's that got to do with women's rights or [African Americans'] rights? If my cup won't hold but a pint, and yours holds a quart, wouldn't you be mean not to let me have my little half-measure full?

The crowd cheered. Then, Truth pointed her finger and sent a sharp, fiery glance at the minister who had argued against women's rights:

Then that little man in black there, he says women can't have as much rights as men, because Christ wasn't a woman! Where did your Christ come from? From God and a woman! Man had nothing to do with Him!

If the first woman God ever made was strong enough to turn the world upside down all alone, these women together ought to be able to turn it back, and get it right side up again! And now that they is asking to do it, the men better let them.

By this point, the applause was so enthusiastic and loud that Truth had to pause before speaking her final words:

Obliged to you for hearing me, and now old Sojourner ain't got nothing more to say.

Sojourner Truth's speech had turned the tide in favor of women's rights and "turned the sneers and jeers of an excited crowd into notes of respect and admiration," as Gage described. Hundreds rushed up to shake hands with her and bid her good luck in continuing her quest to help the United States live up to its ideas of justice and equality.

Suggested Resources

World Geography

Mapping the World with Art, by Ellen Johnston McHenry (Ellen McHenry's Basement Workshop, 2013)

Ultimate Geography and Timeline Guide, 2nd Edition, by Maggie Hogan and Cindy Wiggers (STL Distributors, 2009)

Europe in the Middle Ages

Castles, by Philip Steele (Kingfisher, 1995)

Knights and Castles, by Philip Dixon (Simon & Schuster Books for Young Readers, 2007)

The Story of the World: History for the Classical Child: The Middle Ages: From the Fall of Rome to the Rise of the Renaissance, second revised edition, volume 2, by Susan Wise Bauer (Peace Hill Press, 2007)

The Rise of Islam

1001 Inventions and Awesome Facts from Muslim Civilization, by National Geographic Kids (National Geographic Children's Books, 2012)

Traveling Man: The Journey of Ibn Battuta 1325–1354, by James Rumford (HMH Books for Young Readers, 2004)

African Kingdoms

African Beginnings, by James Haskins (Amistad, 1998)

Mansa Musa: The Lion of Mali, by Khephra Burns (Gulliver Books, 2001)

The Royal Kingdoms of Ghana, Mali, and Songhay: Life in Medieval Africa, by Patricia and Fredrick McKissack (Square Fish, 1995)

China: Dynasties and Conquerors

Life in Ancient China, by Paul Challen (Crabtree Publishing, 2004)

The Silk Route: 7,000 Miles of History, by John S. Major (HarperCollins, 1996)

You Wouldn't Want to Work on the Great Wall of China! Defenses You'd Rather Not Build, by Jacqueline Morley (Children's Press, 2006)

The American Revolution

George vs. George: The American Revolution as Seen from Both Sides, by Rosalyn Schanzer (National Geographic Children's Books, 2007)

If You Lived at the Time of the American Revolution, by Kay Moore (Scholastic Paperbacks, 1998)

Let It Begin Here! Lexington and Concord: First Battles of the American Revolution, by Dennis Brindell Fradin (Walker Children's, 2009)

Paul Revere's Ride, by Henry Wadsworth Longfellow, illustrated by Ted Rand (Puffin, 1996)

Making a Constitutional Government

A Kids' Guide to America's Bill of Rights: Curfews, Censorship, and the 100-Pound Giant, by Kathleen Krull (HarperCollins, 1999)

A More Perfect Union: The Story of Our Constitution, by Betsy Maestro (HarperCollins, 2008)

If You Were There . . . When They Signed the Constitution, by Elizabeth Levy (Scholastic Paperbacks, 1992)

Early Presidents and Politics

. . . If You Grew Up with George Washington, by Ruth Belov Gross (Scholastic Paperbacks, 1993)

So You Want to Be President?, by Judith St. George (Philomel, 2004)

The Look-It-Up Book of Presidents, by Wyatt Blassingame (Random House Books for Young Readers, 1990)

Reformers

Breaking the Chains: The Crusade of Dorothea Lynde Dix, by Penny Colman (ASJA Press, 2007)

Sojourner Truth, by Kathleen V. Kudlinski and Lenny Wooden (Aladdin, 2003)

Sojourner Truth: Ain't I a Woman?, by Patricia C. McKissack and Fredrick McKissack (Scholastic Paperbacks, 1994)

You Want Women to Vote, Lizzie Stanton?, by Jean Fritz (Puffin, 1999)

III
Visual Arts

Introduction

This chapter discusses examples of Western European, Islamic, African, Chinese, and American art, which complement the concepts introduced in the chapters on world history and American history and geography. Parents and teachers can build on the brief treatment offered here by sharing with children additional books and pictures and by taking them to visit museums and interesting buildings. Although books are delightful and informative, there is no substitute for the experience of seeing works of art in person. Many museums make this experience possible for all by offering free admission once a week or more.

Children should experience art not only as viewers but also as creators. They should be encouraged to draw, cut, paste, and mold with clay, to imitate styles and artists they have encountered, and to develop a style of their own.

Art of Western Europe in the Middle Ages

Cathedrals

In the Middle Ages, a church was built in the center of almost every town in Europe, and magnificent Gothic cathedrals were created in the larger towns and cities.

These cathedrals were designed to suggest the majesty of God and to inspire prayer. Outside, towers and spires emphasize height and grandeur. Inside, tall ceilings create awe-inspiring spaces, sometimes one hundred feet high. Throughout the building, statues, paintings, and stained-glass windows depict stories from the Bible and the lives of saints.

Here are some stained-glass windows from the cathedral in Chartres, France. The circular window is called a rose window. It is high up in the cathedral and very big, so it casts colored light throughout the building.

This is Chartres Cathedral. Can you see the spiderlike stone supports sticking out the back of the cathedral? They help hold up the building.

One beautiful Gothic cathedral was built in Chartres [SHAR-truh], France. Walking into Chartres Cathedral is like walking inside a rainbow because it is filled with colorful light. Standing inside this enormous space, you feel very small, but the soft light and colorful windows make you feel warm and protected, too. Light filters through large stained-glass windows, casting colors on the floor.

Because Gothic cathedrals are so tall and have such large windows, stone braces called buttresses strengthen the walls. When they stick out beyond the wall, the way you see in the image above, they are called flying buttresses.

Often, Gothic cathedrals look symmetrical, with each side an exact reflection of the other. But in Chartres Cathedral, the two main towers look very different. This is because it took so long to build this cathedral. The south tower of the cathedral was built in the thirteenth century, around 1200. In comparison, the north tower wasn't finished until after 1400! Architectural styles had changed in those two hundred years. The designer of the north tower wanted to be modern more than he wanted matching towers!

In France's capital city of Paris, there is another great medieval cathedral called Notre Dame [NO-truh DAHM]. ("Notre Dame" is French for "Our Lady," which is another name for Mary, the mother of Jesus.) Notre Dame provides many examples of the Gothic arch, a curving shape with a point on top that makes doorways and windows look tall and elegant.

Take a Look

Show the photographs of cathedrals on page 222 and below to your child. Ask your child to describe the symmetry of each cathedral's design. Why might symmetry have been important to the designers of cathedrals?

This is the front of Paris's famous Gothic cathedral, Notre Dame. On the lowest level of the building, you can see the three Gothic arches that make up the main entrance. How many other Gothic arches can you find?

At the top of Notre Dame's two large stone towers sit statues of make-believe demons called gargoyles. People hoped these scary creatures would keep evil

Gargoyles, sculptures in the shape of imaginary creatures, peer down from the heights of Notre Dame Cathedral.

Talk and Think
Ask your child, "Why do you think these gargoyles are looking down?"

away from their church. Notre Dame's gargoyles had another job, too. These sculptures sit at the ends of drain spouts. When it rains, water runs through the roof gutters and drains out through the mouths of gargoyles.

Inside Notre Dame, the ceiling is made of tall pointed arches, crisscrossed by stone spines. Like the buttresses on the outside of a cathedral, these rib vaults were designed to help support the weight of all that stone in such a tall building. The rib vaults work like a skeleton, holding up the weight of the stone roof and ceiling.

The soaring interior of the Cathedral of Notre Dame, in Paris

Books of Silver and Gold

During the Middle Ages, books in Europe were not printed; they were copied by hand, often by monks. Few books existed, so they were highly valued. Some were heavily illustrated and were as much pieces of art as they were literature.

Some of the beautiful books created in the Middle Ages still exist today. These books are called illuminated manuscripts. A manuscript is a book written by hand. Many of the pages were illuminated, which means that color and shine were added to them with paint and bits of real gold and silver.

This page from *The Book of Kells* shows Mary, the mother of Jesus, with the baby Jesus. Angels surround Mary and Jesus. Can you see the bits of real gold or silver used on this page? © HIP/Art Resource, NY

Around 900 CE, monks in Great Britain created one of the most famous illuminated manuscripts in the world, *The Book of Kells*. *The Book of Kells* contains the four Gospels—the first four books in the New Testament—which tell the life of Jesus. *The Book of Kells* is written in a special ornate handwriting. Paintings decorate many of its pages, including the one shown on page 225.

The monks did not use paper for *The Book of Kells*. They used parchment, made from the skin of sheep or calves. Velvety smooth sheets of parchment were cut and stitched together to make a book. The monks used pens made of goose quills and paintbrushes made of animal fur to apply colored paint, gold, and silver to the parchment pages.

Medieval Tapestries

Churches and monasteries were not the only places where art was found in the Middle Ages. Kings and queens and lords and ladies wanted beautiful art objects around them. They enjoyed seeing pictures of their favorite stories woven into tapestries, or large cloth wall hangings.

In the Middle Ages, people told stories about unicorns, saying that only a pure and lovely maiden could see this magical beast. Some of the most famous tapestries from the Middle Ages show a story called "The Hunt of the Unicorn." We do not know who designed or wove these tapestries, but we do know they hung in a castle in Cluny [CLOO-nee], France, during the 1400s CE.

The detail of this tapestry, part of a series created to tell a mythic story about hunting a unicorn, shows the unicorn after it has been captured.

Islamic Art and Architecture

The Alhambra

During the Middle Ages, people from North Africa created an Islamic empire and conquered much of Spain. They developed an architectural style very different from the Gothic style. Europeans called this style Moorish, because they called the Muslim people from North Africa Moors.

On a hill overlooking the town of Granada [grah-NAH-dah], Spain, one Muslim leader built a palace that became known as the Alhambra [ahl-HAHM-bra]. Completed in the 1300s, the Alhambra was a home for the royal family. It included an enormous bath, more like an indoor pool than the bathtubs and showers we have today.

From as early as 100 BCE, Spain was part of the Roman Empire. When the Moors took over in Spain, in the 700s CE, they changed the design of buildings to suit their needs and their sense of beauty. They replaced thick Roman columns with slim, delicate ones. They smoothed the walls of buildings with plaster and drew designs on the plaster before it dried. These designs give the walls a delicate appearance, very different from the solid walls of Roman buildings. You can see this in the Court of the Lions at the Alhambra.

The Alhambra includes a courtyard called the Court of the Lions, so named because twelve fountains shaped like lions surround its large central fountain.

The Dome of the Rock

The Dome of the Rock, sometimes called the Mosque of Omar, was built for Muslims in Jerusalem in 691 CE. Muslims believe the Prophet Muhammad journeyed up to heaven from this spot (see page 132).

Here is how the Dome of the Rock in Jerusalem looks today.

Take a Look
Ask your child to think of other domed buildings he has seen. Ask him, "What role do you think the dome has in architecture?"

One of the first things you notice when you look at the Dome of the Rock is the golden dome on top of the mosque. When Muhammad met someone who didn't believe in God, he would point to the sky and ask who had made the stars and planets. Islamic mosques are built with domed ceilings that represent the sky above. Some ceilings are decorated to shine like a starry night sky.

The Taj Mahal

One of the world's most famous buildings is the Taj Mahal in India. The Taj Mahal was built in the 1600s CE as a tomb for a Muslim emperor's beloved wife. Many people consider it one of the world's most beautiful buildings.

The Taj Mahal in India, one of the world's most famous buildings, was built in the 1600s CE.

Take a Look
Look at the pictures of famous works of Islamic architecture on pages 227–229. Ask your child, "Can you point out some of the things these buildings have in common?"

Built at the end of a very long, narrow pool of still water, the Taj Mahal appears to float. When you look at it from a distance, the pool reflects its perfect symmetry, or balance. As you walk closer, the gleaming white building looms bigger and bigger. Slender minarets, or towers, stand at the four corners. Like domes, minarets are common in Islamic architecture.

Art in the Muslim World

The Qur'an is the holy book of Islam, just as the Bible is the holy book of Christianity. Muslims believe the Qur'an holds the actual words of God.

Muslims believe only God can create living things. This has led to opposition in the Muslim world to depicting living things, including people, in religious art. As a result of this belief, Muslim artists and architects decorate holy books and mosques with geometric patterns instead. Over the centuries, Muslims have made beautiful copies of the Qur'an. Some are so beautiful they are considered works of art, with elegant Arabic lettering and touches of real gold.

This illuminated page from the Qur'an, painted in the 1300s, has Arabic writing in the center and complicated decorations painted along its edges.

> **Make a Connection**
> Read more about the spread of Islamic empires in the World History chapter.

Art of Africa

Dancing Antelopes

Long ago many African people did not write down their histories. They remembered things from the past by singing songs, dancing, acting, and telling stories—and by making works of art.

In Mali, a group of people called the Bamana [bah-MAH-nah] believed that, long ago, a special being called Chiwara [chee-WAH-rah] used magical powers to teach the people to farm. To remember their ancestors and to honor the powers of Chiwara, Bamana artists carved tall wooden figures shaped like antelopes, designed to be worn on the top of the head. During planting and harvest festivals, young men dressed in costumes made of fiber, wore these tall headdresses, and performed a dance like leaping antelopes. The dance told the story of Chiwara.

Bamana artists didn't try to make their sculptures look exactly like real antelopes. Instead, they suggested the shape of the antelope's body with big, bold curves.

Portraits in Clay and Bronze

The Yoruba [YO-roo-bah] people of West Africa lived in the city of Ife [EE-fay]. From about 1000 to 1500 CE, artists in Ife carved beautiful sculptures.

Ife sculptures are made of brass (a metal) and terra-cotta (red clay baked in a hot fire). Ife artists made sculptures that looked like real people, with delicate features, dignified expressions, and eyes that stare straight ahead.

To make this brass sculpture, the artist molded the head using a mixture of sand and clay. He then covered it with a thin layer of beeswax. Next, using a knife made of bone, he molded the details of the face into the beeswax, and then covered it all with a thin layer of clay. When he put the sculpture on a hot fire, what do you think happened? The bees-

This brass sculpture probably represents the head of an Ife king.

wax melted and drained out, leaving a thin hollow space between two face-shaped shells of clay. The sculptor then poured hot melted brass into the space. After the brass cooled, he broke the clay shells. What remained was this brass sculpture.

A Portrait Mask of an African Queen

The Edo [EH-doe] people lived in Benin [ben-EEN], a kingdom southeast of Ife, in the area of today's Nigeria. The Edo people considered the king and his ancestors to be like gods, and they created sculptures to show their respect. The mask on this page, carved out of ivory, is a portrait of Idia [id-EE-a], the mother of a king who lived in Benin in the sixteenth century. The king may have worn this mask on his belt for important occasions.

In Benin, every time a hunter killed an elephant, one tusk was given to the king. Ivory carvers lived near the palace and worked for the king. They turned the tusks into pieces of art.

Like the brass and terra-cotta heads the Yoruba made, Benin masks represented real people. The artist did not make an exact copy of the person's facial features, though. The artist idealized the portrait, or made it closer to perfect than any one person can be.

This ivory mask was created to represent a queen of the Edo people in Benin (now part of the country of Nigeria). The queen's head is surrounded by bearded men, representing soldiers. Why do you think the artist placed soldiers around her head?

Art of China

Paintings on Silk

The ancient Chinese believed the spirit of nature breathes life into all things. For them, the artist's job was to capture this spirit in art. This focus on nature can be seen in all media of Chinese art.

By the end of the 500s CE, Chinese artists were capturing the spirit of nature by making paintings on scrolls—long bands of paper or silk. Chinese artists painted pictures of children, birds, flowers, and animals. By the 900s, Chinese artists painted entire landscapes, or pictures of natural scenery, on silk scrolls.

This lovely picture of flowers in bloom was painted on a silk scroll. This image was painted much later, in the eighteenth or nineteenth century, but shows the subjects and the way that much earlier Chinese artists painted as well.

Make a Connection
Learn more about ancient Chinese history and culture in the World History chapter.

The Art of Handwriting

In China, beautiful handwriting became an art form. Chinese people appreciated calligraphy (the art of handwriting) for its beauty and for the shapes and pictures in its symbols.

There are several Chinese languages, but all are quite different from English, both in the way they sound and in the way they look. Instead of letters, Chinese people use characters that stand for words. Many Chinese characters are little pictures that look something like the things they stand for. Chinese calligraphers work hard to make their characters look beautiful.

Choose one character in this example of Chinese calligraphy. Imagine making it with a paintbrush. Where would you start? What direction would you move the paintbrush? You would have to decide how hard to press down, whether to make the lines thick or thin, and how much ink to put on your brush. Calligraphers think carefully about all these things, but finally they dip their brushes into the ink and, quick as lightning, paint the characters without stopping.

Why Are Cups and Saucers Called China?

The Chinese started making porcelain [POR-suh-luhn], or fine white pottery, during the Tang dynasty, which lasted from 618 CE to 907 CE. Nobody in Europe was making such lovely pottery then, so the Europeans traded with the Chinese for their porcelain and simply called it china. It would be another seven hundred years before Europeans learned how to make porcelain. During China's Ming dynasty, which lasted from 1368 to 1644, artists got so good at making porcelain that they made six-foot-tall porcelain sculptures!

Potters in the Ming dynasty developed glazes, or shiny paints, for decorating their pottery. The most common colored glaze was this brilliant blue, made from a chemical called cobalt.

American Art

Portraits of Patriots

How would you paint a picture of the president of the United States? In a suit or in work clothes? Smiling or looking very serious? Would you paint a richly detailed background or focus on your subject's face? Would you paint exactly what you saw or leave out physical imperfections? After you answered these basic questions, you would need to make some more decisions. For example, would you use bold, eye-catching colors, or would you use browns and grays? Would

Photograph © July 2016, Museum of Fine Arts, Boston

the focus of the painting be sharp or soft? Would the light in the painting be dim or bright? These are a few of the choices portrait painters have to consider. Different artists make different decisions.

One of the first great American painters, John Singleton Copley, painted portraits of important figures in colonial New England. One of the people he painted was Paul Revere, the famous patriot. In this portrait, Revere, a silversmith and engraver, is dressed in his work clothes. He holds a silver teapot. On the table are the engraving tools he will use to decorate the teapot.

Wealthy Americans often had portraits painted of themselves and their families, especially by artists who had studied art with great European masters. Gilbert Stuart was one such artist. Stuart took art lessons from British painters when he was still a child. Later, he studied painting in London.

By 1795, Stuart was considered the premier portrait painter in America. Martha Washington hired him to paint portraits of herself and her husband.

This is one of Gilbert Stuart's many portraits of George Washington. Another of Stuart's portraits of Washington became the model for the picture on our one dollar bill.

Take a Look

Does your child remember learning about George Washington and Paul Revere? Washington was the first president of the United States. Revere was the patriot whose famous midnight ride warned colonists about the arrival of British troops at the beginning of the Revolutionary War. Ask your child to look at the portraits of Washington and Revere on pages 236 and 237 and to compare the use of light, sharpness, and shadow.

George Washington grumbled about sitting for his portrait. Later, Stuart remembered that Washington was "grave" and "sullen" at the time. What expression do you think Stuart captured in his portrait of Washington?

Unlike Copley, who carefully painted clothes, settings, and personal belongings, Stuart chose to concentrate on Washington's face. Notice the way Stuart uses the color red in Washington's cheeks to draw our eyes there. With quick, sketchy brushstrokes and softly blended colors, Stuart creates a warm, fuzzy background that frames Washington's head.

People who knew Washington said the portrait looked like him. But Stuart also idealized this portrait in some ways. He left out scars caused by smallpox and a mole under Washington's left ear. By painting Washington without physical flaws, Stuart emphasized his heroic qualities—and this is the image most of us remember when we think of the first president today.

Painting Revolutionary History

Here is the German artist Emanuel Leutze's painting of George Washington and his troops crossing the Delaware River. The actual painting is more than twelve feet high and twenty-one feet wide!

Take a Look

Have your child take a closer look at some of the other figures in the painting *Washington Crossing the Delaware*. Point out their mismatched clothes. Ask your child what these details suggest about the state of the Revolutionary army.

Every so often a painting captures a moment in history so perfectly it becomes a famous symbol of the event. *Washington Crossing the Delaware*, by Emanuel Leutze, is that kind of painting.

On the day after Christmas in 1776, Washington led his half-starved and freezing troops across the Delaware River for a surprise attack on enemy troops camped at Trenton, New Jersey. The revolutionaries' victory, one of the most important events in the war, inspired them to keep fighting. Leutze chose to paint not the actual battle, but the river crossing that preceded it.

Notice that only Washington is standing. In reality, Washington would not have stood like this—he would have risked capsizing the boat and spilling everyone into the icy water! In the painting, his profile juts into the sky, while his soldiers hunch over the oars. His face is one of the few in the picture above the horizon. The bright sky illuminates his profile, highlighting it more dramatically than any other. All of these decisions allowed the painter to turn General George Washington into a larger-than-life figure, a symbol of patriotic devotion and bravery.

Little Mountain, Great Architect

When he was a boy, Thomas Jefferson had a secret hideaway at the top of a mountain on his father's estate in Albemarle County, Virginia. Many years later, he built a house there. Jefferson designed, built, and rebuilt Monticello [mont-i-CHELL-oh, Italian for "little mountain"] over more than forty years. Also during this time, he helped lead the American Revolution and write the Declaration of Independence, and he served as vice president and president of the United States. "Architecture is my delight, and putting up and pulling down one of my favorite amusements," he once said.

If you want to see another image of Monticello, look on a nickel.

Make a Connection

In addition to borrowing from classical architecture, what else did the American colonists borrow from ancient Greece and Rome? Democracy! Read more in the Geography and History section.

Jefferson learned about architecture from books. His favorite book showed buildings that looked like ancient Greek and Roman temples. Monticello and other buildings Jefferson designed have wide, open porches with white columns and triangular pediments, or triangular roofs, above them, elements borrowed from classical temples.

Can you draw a picture of one of your favorite buildings? Think about the details you will include and leave out. What time of day will you show in the picture?

Suggested Resources

General

Children's Book of Art, by DK Publishing (DK Children, 2009)

13 Buildings Children Should Know, by Annette Roeder (Prestel, 2009)

Art of the Middle Ages

Color Your Own Book of Kells, by Marty Noble (Dover Publications, 2002)

Gargoyles and Medieval Monsters Coloring Book, by A. G. Smith (Dover Publications, 1998)

Illuminated Manuscripts Coloring Book, by Marty Noble (Dover Publications, 2013)

Medieval Tapestries Coloring Book, by Marty Noble (Dover Publications, 2004)

Islamic Art and Architecture

Arts and Culture in the Early Islamic World, by Lizann Flatt (Crabtree Publishing, 2011)

Taj Mahal: A Story of Love and Empire, by Elizabeth Mann (Mikaya Press, 2008)

The Taj Mahal: Great Structures in History, by Rachel Lynette (KidHaven Press, 2005)

The Art of African Masks: Exploring Cultural Traditions, by Carol Finley (Lerner Publishing Group, 1998)

My First Book of Chinese Calligraphy, by Guillaume Olive (Tuttle Publishing, 2012)

Twenty-Four Hokusai's Paintings (Collection) for Kids, by Stanley Cesar (2014)

John Singleton Copley: 100+ American Colonial Paintings, by Daniel Ankele (Ankele Publishing, 2011)

IV
Music

Introduction

This chapter introduces some concepts that will help children understand and appreciate music. It offers basic information about musical notation, the orchestra, vocal ranges, and Gregorian chants (in connection to the history topic addressing medieval times). It also profiles a few composers and includes the lyrics to some popular songs.

The value and delightfulness of this chapter will be greatly enhanced if children are able to listen to the classical selections described. To facilitate such listening, the Core Knowledge Foundation has assembled CD collections of the works discussed here. These are available on our website, www.coreknowledge.org.

In music, as in art, students benefit from learning by doing. Singing, playing instruments, and dancing all sharpen a child's sense of how music works. We encourage you to share good music with children by singing some of the songs presented here, attending concerts, listening to the radio, and playing CDs and music on the computer or other devices.

The Elements of Music

Make a Note of It!

People have been sharing and playing music all over the world for thousands of years. The oldest instrument ever found, a flute made of bone discovered in Germany, is thought to be more than forty-two thousand years old! Over time, people began to write music down. Musicians developed musical notation—a way to write down music so that different people, no matter what language they spoke, could read that music and sing or play it.

When composers write music down, they use special marks called notes, and they arrange the notes on a set of parallel lines called a staff. The notes on the staff below give the music for the beginning of "Twinkle, Twinkle, Little Star."

When you are learning a piece of music, you can follow the notes across the staff from left to right, just as you follow words across the page when you read.

The position of notes on the staff tells you how high or low the notes are. The higher the note sits on the staff, the higher your voice goes when you sing that note. Can you hear how your voice goes up to a higher pitch as you move from the first "twinkle" to the second one, and then up again as you sing "little"? Then the pitch of your voice comes steadily downward until you sing "are" at the same pitch as the first note.

The shape of the note tells you how long to hold each note. Did you notice that when you sing "Twinkle, Twinkle, Little Star," you hold the notes for "star" and "are" longer than the other notes? That's because these notes are half notes, while the other notes in the song are quarter notes. A half note is held twice as long as a quarter note.

Shorter and Longer Notes

The music for "Twinkle, Twinkle, Little Star" contains only half notes and quarter notes, but musicians also use other notes, some shorter and some longer. An eighth note is like a quarter note with a little flag on top.

An eighth note is held for half as long as a quarter note. When two or more eighth notes are written side by side, they are sometimes connected with a bar, like this:

A whole note is held twice as long as a half note. That means it's held for as long as four quarter notes or eight eighth notes. It looks like this:

If a composer wants to make a note last longer than a half note but not as long as a whole note, she just adds a little black dot to the right side of the note. That dot tells performers to hold the note for its original number of beats, plus another half. Composers can add a dot to any note. A dotted quarter note is held as long as a quarter note plus an eighth note.

Another special symbol can be used to show that a note should be held for a long time. Composers use a tie—a curved line that ties notes together—to tell the musician to continue to hold the first note through the time of the second.

Do It Yourself
Have your child look at the staff on this page. Ask her: "Can you find the tied notes? The dotted notes? How many of each do you see?"

Give It a Rest!

Composers also need to tell musicians when to be quiet. When a composer wants silence, he writes a mark called a rest. A whole rest lasts as long as a whole note, a half rest as long as a half note, and a quarter rest as long as a quarter note. This chart shows notes and rests of the same length.

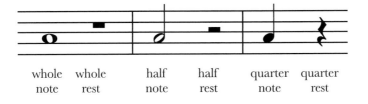

| whole note | whole rest | half note | half rest | quarter note | quarter rest |

Measures and Time Signatures

Look again at the music for "Twinkle, Twinkle, Little Star" on page 246. Do you see the vertical (up-and-down) lines that separate the notes into groups? These lines are called bar lines. They divide the music into measures. How many measures of "Twinkle, Twinkle, Little Star" are shown?

Composers use a single bar line to mark the end of a measure. They use a double bar line to mark the end of a piece of music.

See the two numbers sitting on top of each other at the beginning of the music for "Twinkle, Twinkle, Little Star"—the ones that look like a fraction? Those numbers make up the time signature. The top number tells you how many beats there are in each measure, and the bottom number tells you what kind of note represents one beat. For "Twinkle, Twinkle, Little Star," the time signature is 2/4. That 2 on top means that there are two beats per measure, and the 4 on the bottom means each beat lasts as long as a quarter (1/4) note.

Do It Yourself

With your child, clap along to the time signatures described in the lesson, including 4/4, 3/4, and 2/4. Stress the first beat of each measure. You may find it helpful to count measures like this: ONE two three four, TWO two three four, THREE two three four, FOUR two three four.

You can see that the first measure of "Twinkle, Twinkle, Little Star" is made up of two quarter notes, each of which is held for one beat: "twin-kle." But the fourth measure is a little different. It only contains one note. But this note—the one that goes with the word "star"—is held for twice as long—for two beats. So there are still two beats in this measure, even though there is only one note. Every measure in the song adds up to two beats.

When the time signature is 2/4, we say that the song is written in two-four time. Many popular songs are written in 2/4 time. But you will also see songs in 3/4 time and 4/4 time. How many quarter notes fill a measure in 4/4 time? How many eighth notes will fit in a measure in 3/4 time? As you can see, math is important for understanding music.

The Treble Clef

Musical pitches are named after the first seven letters of the alphabet: A B C D E F G. Each line and each space on the staff matches up with one of these letters.

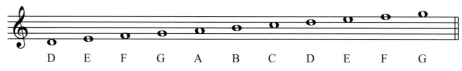

D   E   F   G   A   B   C   D   E   F   G

Do you see how the letters repeat themselves as you go from low to high? At the bottom of the staff, just below the bottom line, is D. Then you move up to E, F, and G. But there's no H. Instead, the letters start over again with A. This is because the A in the middle of the staff sounds very similar to the A at the top of the staff. The interval between the two is called an octave. If you have a piano or keyboard, pick any white key, count seven white keys to the left or right, and play both notes at the same time. Can you hear how similar they sound?

How can you remember which positions on the staff correspond with which letters? Here's one way. Notice that the letters located on the lines, from bottom to top, are E, G, B, D, and F. You can remember these letters by memorizing this sentence: "**E**very **g**ood **b**oy **d**oes **f**ine."

Another way to remember which letters go where on the staff is to look at the treble clef. The treble clef is the fancy curlicue symbol located at the beginning of the music. The treble clef is also known as the G clef because the innermost circle of the clef circles around the second line in the staff—the line that stands for G. If you remember this, you can figure out all the other notes above and below G.

The lowest note shown on the staff above is D. What would happen if the composer wanted to write a note one note lower than D? She would draw a short line segment below the staff and place the note on the line segment. This particular note has a special name. It is called middle C because the key that sounds this note is located in the middle of a piano keyboard.

> ### Do It Yourself
>
> If you have a keyboard or piano, try playing along to the notes shown throughout the lesson. This will help your child understand the concepts through experience.

Middle C

See if you can identify the notes in the first few measures of "Twinkle, Twinkle, Little Star" by letter.

The Composer's Language

Composers place notes on a staff to show how they want their music to be performed, but sometimes they give even more specific instructions.

When a composer wants the music to be played smoothly, without breaks between the notes, he writes "legato" in the music. In Italian, *legato* means "tied together." In a piece sung legato, there's little breath between notes. When the composer wants the music to be played in the opposite way, with short, bouncy sounds, he writes the Italian word "staccato." *Staccato* means "detached" or "separated."

Other notations, written in Italian words or their abbreviations, tell musicians how loudly or softly to play a piece of music.

mp	mezzo piano (moderately soft)
p	piano (soft)
pp	pianissimo (very soft)
mf	mezzo forte (moderately loud)
f	forte (loud)
ff	fortissimo (very loud)

Another instruction you may see written on music is "da capo al fine." "Da capo" means "from the beginning." "Al fine" [ahl FEE-nay] means "to the end." This instruction is often used when the composer wants the beginning of a piece repeated.

Sharps and Flats

The notes in a piece of music match the notes on a piano keyboard. The white keys on the piano all have letter names.

The black keys on a piano are important, too. They don't get their own names, though. They get named according to the keys on either side.

Find D on the piano keyboard. The black key just to the right of D is called

---

Do It Yourself

Ask your child to hum, sing, or play an instrument in the different styles mentioned in the section "The Composer's Language." Act as a conductor and call out changes in style so that your child can better hear the differences.

Do It Yourself

Help your child understand that each key on a piano matches the notes in a piece of music. With your child, use sticky notes to label eight of the white keys on the photograph of the piano keys. Starting with the leftmost white key in the image, label eight keys as follows: C, D, E, F, G, A, B, and C.

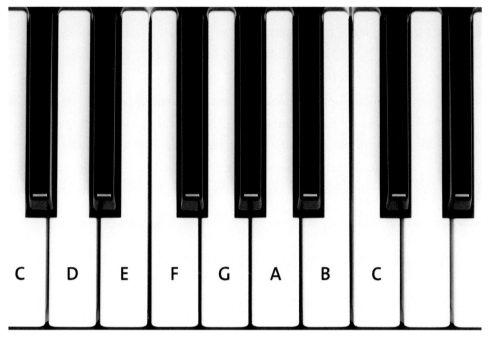

Each white key on a piano has its own letter name.

D-sharp, which can be written D♯ for short. D♯ is a little bit higher in pitch than D.

Now go back to D on the piano keyboard. The black key just to the left of D is called D-flat, or D♭ for short. D♭ is a little bit lower in pitch than D.

A black key can have two names. It can be called the sharp of a note to the left or the flat of a note to the right. No matter which name you call that note, it always sounds the same.

Listening and Understanding

What About You?
If your child has seen an orchestra before, ask him what it was like to hear the musicians warm up. Alternatively, you can find many clips online of orchestra members warming up. Watch a few clips with your child so he can see how the orchestra warms up.

The Orchestra

Half an hour before a performance, the concert hall is quiet. The stage lights shine on empty chairs, arranged in the shape of a fan, all pointing toward a platform at the edge of the stage. Ushers lead the first audience arrivals to their seats, and the hall begins to stir with quiet conversation. Soon, the musicians enter from backstage, carrying their instruments and walking to their places. Once they have settled in, the musicians begin to warm up, similar to how athletes stretch and move their bodies before a game.

The concert hall soon fills with high-pitched toots, deep rumbles, and plucked strings. To the audience it sounds a little chaotic, but soon the musicians will be ready for the concert.

From out of all the noise, an oboe sounds the note A. Soon, all the other musicians are playing the same note. Violinists draw their bows lightly across the

An orchestra is divided into groups for different kinds of instruments. How many different groupings can you spot in this orchestra?

strings of their instruments; one of the four strings makes the note A. If any string makes notes that sound off-pitch, a violinist turns the tuning pegs to adjust it.

The musicians have spent many hours practicing for the concert, and now they are ready to perform. The conductor crosses the stage, steps up on the platform, bows to the audience, turns to the orchestra, lifts his baton, and signals for the music to begin.

Fanning out in front of the conductor, the orchestra includes four major families of instruments. The string instruments are played with a bow or plucked with a finger, the woodwind and brass instruments are blown, and the percussion instruments are struck with sticks or mallets.

The conductor knows the music and every instrument's part. Even when all the instruments are playing, the conductor can hear if a note is played too high or low, too loud or soft, or out of rhythm. The conductor's job is to help all the instruments blend into a beautiful and well-balanced whole and to make sure the music is played the way the composer meant it to be played. The conductor is like a coach who tries to get all the members of the team to work together to ensure a winning performance.

Pavel Kogan is a world-famous Russian violinist and conductor. Here, he conducts an orchestra playing the music of Ludwig van Beethoven in Ukraine.

A Magical Musical Tour

Do It Yourself

YouTube is usually a good source for Benjamin Britten's *Young Person's Guide to the Orchestra*. If available, play the video for your child. Help her begin to identify instruments by their sounds.

At first, it can be difficult to figure out how an orchestra works. That's why the English composer Benjamin Britten wrote *The Young Person's Guide to the Orchestra*. In this piece of music, you'll hear the same melody, or theme, played a number of times, by different instruments of the orchestra. This makes it easier to identify each of the instrument families as they take turns. When a piece of music plays the same theme in different ways, it is called a theme and variations.

The Young Person's Guide to the Orchestra begins as the whole orchestra plays the main theme. Each of the four major families—woodwinds, strings, brass, and percussion—then plays variations on the theme. The music ends with the whole orchestra playing together again.

The woodwinds begin with the high notes of the piccolo and the sweet, clear sound of two flutes, accompanied by violins and a harp. The thoughtful-

sounding oboe comes in next, followed by the smooth and athletic clarinets, which make sounds that seem to loop all around. The bassoons, next, make the deepest, fullest sounds.

The family of strings then comes in, led by the violins. Their sound is so important to the orchestra that there are more of them than any other instrument.

These musicians are playing stringed instruments. From the left, there are two violins, a cello, and a viola.

Violas, a bit larger in size, have a deeper, often somber-sounding tone. Both the violin and the viola are held against the musician's chin while he draws a bow across the strings.

Cellos, much larger than the violas, are held upright on the floor, between the knees of the players. Cellos have a rich, warm sound. The double bass—the largest member of the string family—rumbles when it plays its lowest notes. The harp belongs in the string family, too. A harpist plucks the instrument's forty-seven strings while seated behind it.

Among the brass instruments, the horns lead the way. The trumpets come in with higher, brighter sounds. The trombone, played by sliding one metal tube in and out of another, adds a deep voice. The bass tuba has an even deeper, heavier sound.

The percussion instruments take their turn as the kettledrums, or timpani [TIM-pahn-ee], make deep, vibrating sounds you can feel as well as hear.

The tuba makes a deep, low sound.

There are many rhythmic noisemakers in this family, including bass drum, cymbals, tambourine, and triangle. Wooden blocks clapped together make a sound like the crack of a whip, commanding the whole orchestra to play together again.

Britten ends his tour of the orchestra with a fugue, in which the instruments play one after another as if singing a round. This gives us another chance to hear the distinctive qualities of each family of instruments. Now we can appreciate the role each has in the full orchestra sound. The brass instruments sing out at the end of the piece, celebrating the sounds of the orchestra. Each time you listen to this piece, you will be able to distinguish more clearly the instruments of the orchestra by the sounds that they make.

The Instrument We All Can Play

Even without music lessons, you already play the oldest, most universal, and most expressive musical instrument of all—the human voice. You can practice all the basic elements of music—rhythm, melody, harmony—simply by singing.

Everyone has a high note, a low note, and the notes in between that she can sing comfortably. The highest note and the lowest note that you can sing define your range.

Can you think of a popular American song that has such a big range from its highest to its lowest note that it's a challenge to sing every note? Many people would name "The Star-Spangled Banner," the national anthem of the United States. Think of how low your voice goes when you sing the word "say" in "O-oh say can you see?" Think of how high you have to go to sing "and the rockets' red glare, the bombs bursting in air."

Voices, High and Low

Have you noticed that, among the people you know, some sing high and some sing low? The voices of women and men are divided into three main categories of singers.

Women's voices

> High: soprano
>
> Middle: mezzo [MET-so] soprano
>
> Low: alto

Men's voices

> High: tenor
>
> Middle: baritone
>
> Low: bass

What About You?

Ask your child to identify the category into which his or her voice most likely falls. Ask, "Do you know anyone who has a deep singing voice? How about a high-pitched one?"

Composers write music with these vocal ranges in mind, and their choices can have dramatic effects.

Music of the Middle Ages

In the world history and art sections of this book, you learned about Europe in the Middle Ages. During the Middle Ages, groups of men lived in religious communities, devoting all their time and work to their religion. They were called monks, and their homes were called monasteries. Monasteries were quiet, protected places where monks could concentrate on their faith. The monks wore plain robes, gave up their personal possessions, and promised never to marry. They went to bed early and woke up before sunrise. They did a lot of physical labor, much of it to help the poor.

During the Middle Ages, few people knew how to read and write. Monks could read music as well as words, and they spent many hours carefully copying music and Latin texts by hand. (They lived in a time before computers and printing presses, when every book had to be copied by hand.)

This book contains Gregorian chants written by monks. How is the music in the book similar to written music today? How is it different?

Every day the monks came together to pray and sing. The songs they sang are called Gregorian chants, in honor of Pope Gregory the Great, who was the head of the Roman Catholic Church from 590 to 604 CE. Today, monks still sing Gregorian chants.

The words in the chants were mostly taken from the Bible. Usually, the monks sang in Latin, with no instruments playing along. Sometimes, two choirs sat across from each other, taking turns singing.

When you first hear Gregorian chants, they may sound monotonous. There are similar sounds over and over again without much variation. Modern music sounds much more complicated, with more contrast in rhythm and harmony. But strong voices singing in a candlelit church echo and blend into one bigger voice, sounding beautiful, powerful, and even a bit mysterious. Try to find a recording of Gregorian chants to hear for yourself.

George Frideric Handel (1685–1759)

George Frideric Handel [HAN-del] was born in Germany in 1685. He was interested in music as a young boy, but his father wanted him to become a lawyer, not a musician. Handel's parents would not let him have an instrument, so he smuggled a small keyboard instrument called a clavichord [CLA-vi-cord] into his house. Because he was not allowed to have an instrument, Handel had to play his treasured clavichord in secret. Later, when Handel was older, he studied music full-time, no longer having to keep it hidden.

Handel is best known for his compositions based on stories from the Bible. One of these pieces, called *Messiah* [mes-SYE-ya], is performed by an orchestra and a chorus. Soloists in all the

Handel

Talk and Think

If it is available, listen to the "Hallelujah Chorus" with your child. Ask your child if she can identify other places she has heard the music.

vocal ranges sing interlocking melodies. Each part of *Messiah* tells a different episode in the life of Jesus. For words, Handel used verses from the English Bible and a prayer book. The most famous part of *Messiah* is the thrilling "Hallelujah Chorus," in which voices proclaim the everlasting glory of God.

There is a story that when Handel's *Messiah* was performed the first time in March 1743 for King George of England, the king was so moved by the "Hallelujah Chorus" that he stood up to hear it. Whether the story is true or not, audiences have been standing up to hear that chorus ever since; such is the inspiring effect of Handel's music.

Haydn

Joseph Haydn (1732–1809)

When he was very young, Joseph Haydn [HIGH-dun] delighted his family with his singing. He soon joined the church choir where he lived. By the time he was eight, he was singing in the choir at St. Stephen's Cathedral in Vienna, Austria. He also learned to play the violin, the organ, and other instruments.

As he grew older, Haydn wrote music, played the piano to accompany singing lessons, and taught music to others. Word of his talent spread, and eventually a prince in Hungary brought him to live in his palace. There, Haydn's job was to teach, write music, and direct concerts for the prince and his many guests. He lived for nearly thirty years in the palace, where he produced music that made him famous throughout Europe.

At the prince's palace, Haydn often conducted symphonies after dinner. He composed more than one hundred symphonies and many other works. His symphonies are considered so important in the history of music that he is sometimes called the "Father of the Symphony."

A symphony is a musical composition performed by an orchestra. The word comes from the Greek words *sym*, meaning "together," and *phonos*, meaning "sound." Usually, a symphony is divided into four movements, or sections, each distinctly different from the others yet musically connected—similar to the chapters in a book.

As Haydn conducted the palace orchestra, he noticed that the quieter passages in his music lulled some guests to sleep. He decided to play a musical joke on the prince and his guests. In one symphony, the second movement begins with a gentle melody—the kind that might put a drowsy person to sleep—and then suddenly the sound of a great chord unexpectedly bursts in, breaking the quiet. Ever since, people have called Haydn's Symphony No. 94 in G the "Surprise Symphony." Have a listen!

Talk and Think
Ask your child to think of another song that has a surprising chord or melody after a gentle beginning.

Wolfgang Amadeus Mozart (1756–1791)

Wolfgang Amadeus Mozart [MOTE-sart] was also born in Austria. His father was a professional musician who could tell very early on that his son had remarkable musical talent. By the age of four, Mozart played the piano and the violin very well. By the time he was eight, he was composing symphonies!

Through much of his childhood, Mozart toured Europe with his father and

From an early age, Mozart was a great musician. Here he is playing as a child with his father, Leopold.

older sister playing music. Everywhere he went, the young boy amazed audiences. When the emperor of Austria heard Mozart play, he called him a "little wizard."

Mozart wrote musical compositions of all kinds—for the piano, for small groups of instruments, for orchestras, and for singers. He wrote several famous operas, which are plays in which the actors sing rather than speak their lines.

One of Mozart's most famous operas is *The Magic Flute*. *The Magic Flute* is a strange and beautiful love story, full of dragons, sorcerers, and spells. It tells the story of the young prince Tamino [tah-MEE-no], who sets out to rescue the beautiful princess Pamina [pah-MEE-na]. Tamino has to pass many tests, some in the company of a silly bird catcher named Papageno [pa-pa-GAY-no]. In the end, Tamino passes all his tests and is united with Pamina.

Mozart followed the rules for composing different types of music, but he enjoyed adding twists. Many of his pieces include bold musical ideas. For example, Mozart wrote twelve variations of an old French song called "Ah, vous dirai-je Maman" for the piano. The song has the

Do It Yourself

Ask your child to experiment with humming, singing, or playing familiar songs by changing the tempo. How do these changes in tempo affect the mood or feeling of the song?

same tune as "Twinkle, Twinkle, Little Star." Mozart begins with the simple melody; then he changes it around. He changes the tempo, or speed of the music. He changes the dynamics, or the intensity with which the music is played, so some versions are loud and some are quiet. Some sound proper and formal, some sound exuberant and full of fun, and one even sounds a little spooky.

Mozart said his music came to him in a kind of "lively dream." He heard all the parts at once and kept them in his head until he could write them all down. Haydn once said that Mozart was "the greatest composer known to me," and many people agree with him to this day.

Some Songs for Fourth Graders

PARENTS: Look through the songs on the following pages. With your child, sing along to the ones you know.

Auld Lang Syne

"Auld Lang Syne" is an old Scottish song, often sung on New Year's Eve. The phrase "auld lang syne" means "old long since," or "old times." In the song two old friends are talking. One asks, "Should old friends and old times be forgotten?" Then, he answers his own question, saying, "No, let's have a drink—'a cup of kindness'—for old times' sake!"

Should auld acquaintance be forgot
And never brought to mind?
Should auld acquaintance be forgot
And days of Auld Lang Syne?

For Auld Lang Syne, my dear,
For Auld Lang Syne,
We'll take a cup o' kindness yet,
For Auld Lang Syne!

What About You?
Ask your child if he has heard "Auld Lang Syne" sung or played before. Why might it be a popular song to sing on New Year's Eve?

Cockles and Mussels

In Dublin's fair city
Where the girls are so pretty,
'Twas there I first met with
Sweet Molly Malone.

She drove a wheelbarrow
Through streets broad and narrow,
Crying, "Cockles and mussels,
Alive, all alive."

Chorus:
"Alive, alive-O! Alive, alive-O!"
Crying, "Cockles and mussels,
Alive, all alive."

She was a fishmonger,
But that was no wonder:
Her father and mother
Were fishmongers, too.

They drove wheelbarrows
Through streets broad and narrow,
Crying, "Cockles and mussels,
Alive, all alive."

Chorus.

She died of the fever,
And nothing could save her
And that was the end
Of sweet Molly Malone.

But her ghost wheels her barrow
Through streets broad and narrow
Crying, "Cockles and mussels,
Alive, all alive."

Chorus.

There is a statue of the fictional Molly Malone in Dublin, Ireland, where "Cockles and Mussels" is set.

Comin' Through the Rye

If a body meet a body
Comin' through the rye,
If a body kiss a body,
Need a body cry?

Every lassie has her laddie.
None, they say, have I;
Yet all the lads they smile on me
When comin' through the rye.

New Word

After reading the lyrics to "Loch Lomond," ask your child to use context clues to guess what the word **gloaming** means. Point out that the word "gloaming" is used to describe the time of day at which the moon comes out. Help your child understand that "gloaming" means "twilight or dusk."

Loch Lomond

Oh! you take the high road and
I'll take the low road,
An' I'll be in Scotland afore ye;
But me and me true love
Will never meet again
On the bonnie, bonnie banks of Loch Lomond.

'Twas there that we parted,
In yon shady glen,
On the steep, steep side of Ben Lomond,
Where purple in hue,
The Highland hills we view
And the moon coming out in the **gloaming**.

My Grandfather's Clock

My grandfather's clock was too large for the shelf,
So it stood ninety years on the floor.
It was taller by half than the old man himself,
Though it weighed not a pennyweight more.

It was bought on the morn of the day that he was born,
And was always his treasure and pride;
But it stopped short—never to go again—
When the old man died.

In watching its **pendulum** swing to and fro,
Many hours he spent while a boy;
And in childhood and manhood the clock seemed to know
And to share both his grief and his joy.
For it struck twenty-four when he entered at the door,
With a blooming and beautiful bride.
But it stopped short—never to go again—
When the old man died.

My grandfather said that of those he could hire,
Not a servant so faithful he found;
For it wasted no time, and had but one desire—
At the close of each week to be wound.
And it kept in its place—not a frown upon its face,
And its hands never hung by its side.
But it stopped short—never to go again—
When the old man died.

It rang an alarm in the dead of the night—
An alarm that for years had been dumb;
And we knew that his spirit was pluming for flight—
That his hour of departure had come.
Still the clock kept the time, with a soft and muffled chime,
As we silently stood by his side;
But it stopped short—never to go again—
When the old man died.

New Word
Does your child
know what a
pendulum is? The
noun refers to the
long arm of a
grandfather clock,
which swings back
and forth as the
clock keeps the
time. Can your
child identify the
pendulum in the
photograph?

Waltzing Matilda

Once a jolly swagman camped by a billabong
Under the shade of a coolibah tree,
And he sang as he watched and waited 'til his billy boiled,
"You'll come a-waltzing matilda with me."

"Waltzing matilda, waltzing matilda,
You'll come a-waltzing matilda with me."
And he sang as he watched and waited 'til his billy boiled,
"You'll come a-waltzing matilda with me."

Down came a jumbuck to drink at that billabong.
Up jumped the swagman and grabbed him with glee.
And he sang as he stuffed that jumbuck in his tucker bag,
"You'll come a-waltzing matilda with me."

"Waltzing matilda, waltzing matilda
"You'll come a-waltzing matilda with me."
And he sang as he shoved that jumbuck in his tucker bag,
"You'll come a-waltzing matilda with me."

Up rode the squatter, mounted on his thoroughbred;
Down came the troopers, one, two, three.
"Where's that jolly jumbuck you've got in your tucker bag?
You'll come a-waltzing matilda with me."

"Waltzing matilda, waltzing matilda,
You'll come a-waltzing matilda with me.
Where's that jolly jumbuck you've got in your tucker bag?
You'll come a-waltzing matilda with me."

Talk and Think
Ask your child to describe the effect of the slang words on the tone and meaning of the song "Waltzing Matilda." What does she think a "billabong," a "jumbuck," or a "squatter" is? What does it mean for a "billy" to boil?

Up jumped the swagman and sprang into the billabong.
"You'll never take me alive!" said he.
And his ghost may be heard as you pass by that billabong,
"You'll come a-waltzing matilda with me."

This Australian song isn't about a woman named Matilda who liked to waltz. A matilda is a knapsack that Australian hobos carried in the late 1800s. To go "waltzing matilda" meant to walk around, looking for work, with all your belongings in your knapsack. In this song, a swagman, or hobo, stuffs a farmer's sheep into his knapsack and gets caught in the act.

The Yellow Rose of Texas

There's a yellow rose in Texas
That I am going to see.
No other soldier knows her—
No soldier, only me.
She cried so when I left her,
It like to broke my heart,
And if I ever find her,
We never more will part.

She's the sweetest rose of color
This soldier ever knew.
Her eyes are bright as diamonds;
They sparkle like the dew.
You may talk about your dearest May
And sing of Rosa Lee,
But the Yellow Rose of Texas
Beats the belles of Tennessee.

Do you think the songwriter is referring to an actual yellow rose in "The Yellow Rose of Texas"? How do you know?

Songs of the U.S. Armed Forces

Make a Connection

Ask your child to identify one of the historic places or people mentioned in "The Army Goes Rolling Along." He can read more about Valley Forge in the American History and Geography section of this book (page 183).

The Army Goes Rolling Along

Valley Forge, Custer's ranks,
San Juan Hill and Patton's tanks,
And the Army went rolling along.
Minutemen, from the start,
Always fighting from the heart,
And the Army keeps rolling along.

The Marines' Hymn

From the halls of Montezuma
To the shores of Tripoli,
We fight our country's battles
In the air, on land, and sea.
First to fight for right and freedom,
And to keep our honor clean,
We are proud to claim the title
Of United States Marine!

Air Force Song

Off we go into the wild blue yonder,
Climbing high into the sun;
Here they come zooming to meet
our thunder,
At 'em boys, give 'er the gun!

Suggested Resources

Can You Hear It?, by William Lach (Harry N. Abrams, 2006)

Do Re Mi: If You Can Read Music, Thank Guido D'Arezzo, by Susan Roth (HMH Books for Young Readers, 2007)

George Handel, by Mike Venezia (Children's Press, 1995)

Lady Treble and the Seven Notes, by Eliyana Biklou (Simply Read Books, 2010)

The Magic Flute: An Opera by Mozart by Kyra Teis (Starbright Books, 2008)

Mozart: 59 Fascinating Facts for Kids About Wolfgang Amadeus Mozart, by Andrew Gibbs (Fascinating Facts for Kids, 2013)

My First Classical Music Book, by Genevieve Helsby (Naxos Books, 2009)

The Story of the Orchestra: Listen While You Learn About the Instruments, the Music and the Composers Who Wrote the Music, by Robert Levine (Black Dog & Leventhal, 2000)

Those Amazing Musical Instruments: Your Guide to the Orchestra Through Sounds and Stories, by Genevieve Helsby (Naxos Books, 2007)

Who Was Wolfgang Amadeus Mozart? by Yona Z. McDonough (Grosset & Dunlap, 2003)

V
Mathematics

Introduction

At this age, your child will really start honing her skills with arithmetic and real-world problems. This chapter summarizes the essential math topics for fourth grade, including number sense, fractions, decimals, computation, measurement, and geometry.

Practice is key to success in learning math, but be careful this practice does not become mindless and repetitive. Daily practice should be well planned and thoughtful, with a variety of problems. The objective should be development of higher-order problem-solving skills, but these skills require a sound foundation. Taking the time to grasp basic concepts and master the fundamental operations of adding and subtracting will pay off in the long run. More advanced problem solving in later years is established on a habit of practicing early.

However, some well-meaning people still dread practicing mathematics. Does memorizing arithmetic facts or doing timed worksheets sound fun to you? You may even agree with the naysayers that math practice kills the joy of learning for children, but nothing could be further from the truth. Anxiety, not practice, kills the joy in learning. One simple way of overcoming anxiety is by practicing until the procedures feel so easy and automatic that the fear evaporates.

One effective way to practice is to have children speak out loud while doing problems, explaining their strategy and computational steps along the way. In this way, you can witness the child's mental processes and correct any misunderstandings at the source.

The brief outline of topics presented in this chapter does not constitute a complete math program. While learning this material, your child should practice with many more problems than we have included. To learn these topics thoroughly, children first need to be exposed to the basic concepts, which you can do with this book. However, then they must be encouraged to practice. Therefore, we recommend that you select a mathematics program that allows plenty of opportunities to practice, practice, practice.

The best math programs incorporate the principle of incremental learning: After you introduce a concept or skill, the child practices it through exercises of gradually increasing difficulty (including story problems). This approach often improves the child's arithmetic skills to the point where they become automatic—when she can tell you instantly what 6 times 6 equals, for example. Once they have achieved automatic command of basic operations, children will be prepared to tackle more challenging problems. Math programs that offer both incremental learning and varied opportunities for problem solving get the best results.

Numbers and Number Sense

Place Value

PARENTS: Point to the multidigit numbers without reading them out loud to see how your child pronounces them first.

Can you read this number?

$$329,425,278$$

When you read a large number with this many digits, you have to pay attention to the place value of each digit. Place value refers to the position of each digit within the number.

millions			thousands			ones		
hundreds	tens	ones	hundreds	tens	ones	hundreds	tens	ones

Beginning with the digit all the way to the right, the values of the places are: ones, tens, hundreds, thousands, ten thousands, hundred thousands, millions, ten millions, and hundred millions.

> **Do It Yourself**
>
> After reading this Place Value section, ask your child to fill in the boxes here with the number 462,977,003 and identify the place value of each digit.

As you move to the left, each place has a value 10 times greater than the place to its right. This system of writing numbers is called the decimal system.

"Decimal" means based on 10. In the decimal system, the place values are groups of 10. Whenever we have 10 of a certain place value, we write it as 1 in the next highest place value to the left. For example, there are 10 tens in 1 hundred and 10 hundreds in 1 thousand.

When reading a number, always begin with the largest place value. Let's try reading the following number:

$$\underline{4},315,825$$

In this case, start with the 4, which is one digit to the left of the second comma, which represents millions. This digit is in the millions place. So you would read the whole number 4,315,825 as "four million, three hundred fifteen thousand, eight hundred twenty-five." Now, let's try reading this number:

$$\underline{4}62,977,003$$

The 4 is three digits to the left of the second comma for millions. This digit is in the hundred millions place. So you would read 462,977,003 as "four hundred sixty-two million, nine hundred seventy-seven thousand, three." Notice how the commas make the number easier to read? They help you see the millions and thousands by separating the digits into groups of three.

The Value of Digits

Now, let's consider the number 9$\underline{3}$6,$\underline{4}$55,171. The underlined 3 is in the ten millions place. Its value is 30,000,000. The underlined 4 is in the hundred thousands place. Its value is 400,000.

Another useful way to figure out place value is to count how many of each place value the number has. For example, take 43,289. You can write the number in terms of how many ten thousands, thousands, hundreds, tens, and ones it has. It has 4 ten thousands, 43 thousands, 432 hundreds, 4,328 tens, or 43,289 ones in it. Learning to use place value in this way is especially valuable for both subtraction and division.

Commas and Place Value

You can write the numbers from 1,000 to 9,999 with or without a comma. For example, 9,672 and 9672 are the same number. However, whenever you write numbers that are 10,000 or greater, always write them with commas to mark off each group of three. For instance, you would never write 10403; always write 10,403.

Comparing Numbers

When comparing numbers, always begin with the digits that have the largest place value. For example, to figure out whether 286,563 or 97,800 is greater, you should begin at the left with the largest places.

Think: 286,563 ? 97,800
      200,000 > 90,000
      so 286,563 > 97,800

Remember that the symbol > stands for "is greater than." The symbol < stands for "is less than." A statement like "286,563 > 97,800" is called an inequality because it shows how the two numbers are not equal.

Another way to practice comparing numbers is to write a double inequality. To do this, find a number that fits between the two numbers in order to compare them. 286,563 is greater than 200,000, while 200,000 is greater than 97,800. You would write:

      286,563 > 200,000 > 97,800
      so 286,563 > 97,800

Standard Form and Expanded Form

The standard way to write a number is to express it as a single number with digits. For example, the number 8,532,706 is in standard form.

You can also write this number in expanded form by separating the digits by their place values. There are two ways to write the same number in expanded form. You can use addition to write:

$$8,532,706 = 8,000,000 + 500,000 + 30,000 + 2,000 + 700 + 6$$

You can also multiply each digit by its place value like this:

$$8,532,706 = (8 \times 1,000,000) + (5 \times 100,000) + (3 \times 10,000) \\ + (2 \times 1,000) + (7 \times 100) + (6 \times 1)$$

Using a Number Line

Comparing numbers gets easier when you use a number line. Suppose your friends have been selling lemonade during a hot summer week. They sold 7 glasses on Monday, 5 on Tuesday, 1 on Wednesday, 16 on Thursday, and 10 on Friday.

By placing these numbers on a number line, you can see which day was the best for sales. The numbers on a number line increase as you move to the right and decrease as you move to the left. Therefore, the farther to the right a number is, the larger it is. Take a look at the number line for lemonade sales below. On which day did your friends sell the most glasses of lemonade?

Negative Numbers

Positive numbers are numbers greater than 0. There is also another set of numbers that are less than 0. They are called negative numbers. Negative numbers are written with a minus sign, like −1.

Negative numbers can be a bit harder to understand than positive numbers, but they can be useful. For instance, suppose you wanted to keep track of how much money your friend Jerome owed you. Let's say Jerome owed you 5 dollars at first. Then, Jerome buys you a drink that costs 2 dollars. After Jerome buys you a drink, suppose he buys you a snack for 4 dollars. How much does Jerome owe you now?

You can use a number line to help you figure out the answer! Jerome owed you 5 dollars, but then he spent 2 dollars on a drink. Subtract 2 from 5 by moving your finger 2 notches to the left on the number line below. Then, he spent 4 dollars on a snack for you. If you move 4 more notches to the left, you move past 0 to −1. What does it mean to say Jerome owes you −1 dollar? It means you owe him a dollar!

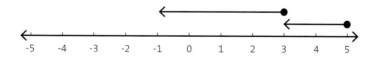

How much would you owe Jerome if he loaned you 3 more dollars?

See if you can put these numbers in order from the least to the greatest: 1, −3, 2, 0, and −5. By using the number line, you can see that the order (from left to right) is −5, −3, 0, 1, 2. Don't be fooled into thinking that −5 must be larger than −3 because 5 is larger than 3. The number line shows you that −5 is farther to the left of 0 than −3, which means it is smaller.

Do It Yourself

After reading the scenario about Jerome, ask your child to create a number line to put all of the given numbers in order from least to greatest.

Rounding

Sometimes, you do not need to know an exact value of a number. You can round numbers to estimate their value. Let's practice how to round.

When you round, you will either round up to the next-highest place value or round down to the next-lowest. To decide which way to round, always look at the digit in the place just to the right of the one to which you are rounding. For example, if you are rounding to the nearest ten, you look at the digit in the ones place. If you are rounding to the nearest hundred, you look at the digit in the tens place.

If the digit to the right is 4 or less, you round down. If the digit to the right is 5 or greater, you round up. Here are three examples:

14 rounded down to the nearest 10 → 10
(because 14 is closer to 10 than to 20)

18 rounded up to the nearest 10 → 20
(because 18 is closer to 20 than to 10)

15 rounded up to the nearest 10 → 20
(15 is halfway between 10 and 20, but when a number is halfway between two
     numbers, always round up)

Now, let's round 3,417 to the nearest thousand. When you look at the thousands place, you see the digit 3. Your choices are to round the number up to 4,000 or round it down to 3,000. The digit in the place just to the right of the 3 is a 4, so you should round down to 3,000. Notice that when you round a number to a certain place value, all the digits to the right of that place become zeros.

Perfect Squares

When you multiply a number by itself, you "square" the number. When you square a whole number, the resulting product is called a perfect square. Here are some examples of perfect squares:

$$1 \times 1 = 1$$
$$2 \times 2 = 4$$
$$3 \times 3 = 9$$
$$4 \times 4 = 16$$
$$5 \times 5 = 25$$
$$6 \times 6 = 36$$
$$7 \times 7 = 49$$
$$8 \times 8 = 64$$
$$9 \times 9 = 81$$
$$10 \times 10 = 100$$
$$11 \times 11 = 121$$
$$12 \times 12 = 144$$

> **Do It Yourself**
> Try representing this concept with physical objects. For instance, ask your child to construct perfect squares with building blocks.

Drawing pictures that represent the numbers can help you see why 9, 16, 25, and the other products above are called perfect squares.

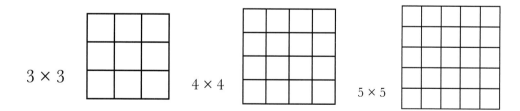

3 × 3   4 × 4   5 × 5

You can read the equation "$5 \times 5 = 25$" as "5 times 5 equals 25." Alternatively, you can say "5 squared equals 25."

Square Roots

When you are asked to find the "square root" of 25, you are really being asked what number multiplied by itself equals 25. The answer is 5, because 5 times 5 equals 25. So the square root of 25 is 5.

Let's try finding the square root again. What is the square root of 81? Remember the question is: What number multiplied by itself equals 81? Recalling the perfect squares, you should remember that 9 times 9 equals 81. Therefore, the square root of 81 is 9.

We use a special symbol to mean "square root of" that looks like this: $\sqrt{}$. We read $\sqrt{64}$ as "the square root of 64." What does $\sqrt{64}$ equal? How about $\sqrt{100}$? $\sqrt{144}$?

Roman Numerals

The numerals we use the most often are the digits 0, 1, 2, 3, 4, 5, 6, 7, 8, and 9. These digits are called Arabic numerals. But you also may encounter Roman numerals.

Here are the Roman numerals from 1 to 10. Look at them carefully, especially the numerals for 4 and 9.

I II III IV V VI VII VIII IX X

Here are the Roman numerals from 10 to 100, counting by tens:

X XX XXX XL L LX LXX LXXX XC C

Once you learn the values of the following Roman numerals, you can use these symbols to write any number into the thousands.

$$I = 1$$
$$V = 5$$
$$X = 10$$
$$L = 50$$
$$C = 100$$
$$D = 500$$
$$M = 1,000$$

Here are two rules to remember:

1. Look at the Roman numeral to the right of the other numerals. If it is equal or smaller, you add their values together.

   XV is (10 + 5), or 15.
   XXX is (10 + 10 + 10), or 30.

2. If the Roman numeral to the right is larger, you subtract the smaller one from the larger one.

   IV is (5 − 1), or 4.
   IX is (10 − 1), or 9.
   XL is (50 − 10), or 40.

Often, you will need to use both rules to write large numbers as Roman numerals. The example below shows you how to group numbers within a long Roman numeral, which helps you read it:

$$CDXLVIII$$
$$= CD + XL + VIII$$
$$= (500 - 100) + (50 - 10) + (5 + 3)$$
$$= 400 + 40 + 8$$
$$= 448$$

Make a Connection

After reading about Roman numerals, look back to the names of medieval kings on pages 123–129. Explain that the Roman numerals in these kings' names show lineage—just as you might call your son a "Jr." if he had the same name as you. As names were passed further and further along, people used Roman numerals to remember how far the succession had gone.

Sometimes, people use Roman numerals for years. For example, you might find a book published in the year MMXV:

$$M + M + XV$$
$$= 1,000 + 1,000 + (10 + 5)$$
$$= 2,000 + 15$$
$$= 2,015 \text{ (the year 2015)}$$

In what year were you born? Can you write the year in Roman numerals? What famous historical event happened in MCDXCII? How about MDCCLXXVI?

Graphs

We often receive information in numbers, which we call data. Sometimes, we make pictures using the data to help us understand what the numbers mean. A picture that represents a set of numbers is called a graph.

A bar graph is a good way to show different amounts. Suppose that your friend Charlie recorded how much it rained during one week in Seattle, Washington. We will use his data for the amount of millimeters of rain per day to make a bar graph.

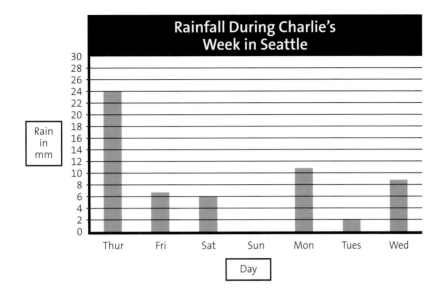

Along the bottom of the graph, we will write the days of the week. Along the left side of the graph, we will choose a convenient way to show the millimeters of rain. In this case, intervals of 2 millimeters will work. (You could show each millimeter, but the graph would be very tall.) We should also title the graph, label the information along the bottom and the sides, and draw a bar to show each day's rainfall. Above is the finished graph.

You can see right away by looking at the bars that there was far more rain on Thursday than on any other day.

A line graph can show how amounts change. Consider the prices of Mrs. Sinclair's stocks. At the end of each week for five consecutive weeks, Mrs. Sinclair found the average price per share of the stock she owned. Then she wanted to see how much the prices changed each week using a line graph.

To make a line graph, we will put the dates along the bottom of the graph. Along the left side, we will choose money amounts in inter-

Talk and Think
Think of data that a person might graph, such as a person's salary over her career or the number of pumpkins bought per day at a pumpkin patch. Ask your child to identify the best type of graph to use for each set of data.

vals that will make the graph a reasonable size and show the data clearly. We should also title the graph and label the bottom and side. Here is the finished graph:

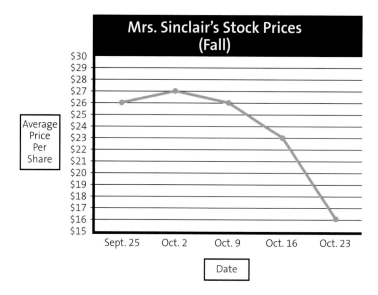

Plotting Points on a Grid

The location of a point on a grid has a specific name. This name is a pair of numbers called an ordered pair. For example, the location of point A is the ordered pair (2, 1). The first number of the ordered pair tells you how many units to go to the right of 0. The second number tells you how many units up to go from 0. To get to point A at (2, 1) from zero, you go 2 units to the right, and then 1 unit up. Point B is at (5, 3) or, in other words, 5 units to the right of 0 and 3 units up. What is the name of the location of points C and G on the grid?

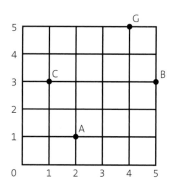

Multiplication

Multiplication Review

Multiplication is a quick way of adding the same number over and over. For instance, you can solve 4 + 4 + 4 + 4 + 4 in two ways. You can write the numbers in a column and add them all together, or you can multiply 4 times 5. Both methods will get the same result, 20. In the equation 4 × 5 = 20, the numbers 4 and 5 are called the factors, and 20 is called the product.

Do you know the basic multiplication operations from 1 × 1 to 10 × 10? Can you fill in the blanks in the following equations?

$$4 \times 8 = \underline{\hspace{1cm}}$$
$$7 \times 6 = \underline{\hspace{1cm}}$$
$$\underline{\hspace{1cm}} \times 7 = 35$$
$$\underline{\hspace{1cm}} \times 9 = 63$$

If it takes you more than a couple of seconds to solve any of these problems, keep practicing your multiplication facts—you'll get there!

A Property of Multiplication

Multiplication has a special property. This property allows you to find a product by first multiplying with one part of a number, then multiplying with the other part, and finally adding the two partial products together to find the whole product. Here is an example with 9×4. If you cannot remember that $9 \times 4 = 36$, you could figure it out this way:

$$9 \times 4$$
$$= (6 + 3) \times 4$$
$$= (6 \times 4) + (3 \times 4)$$
$$= 24 + 12$$
$$= 36$$

Because of this property of multiplication, there is an easy way to multiply numbers with more than one digit in your head. You can multiply the value in each digit separately, and then add to find the whole product. Here's an example:

$$3 \times 17$$
$$= 3 \times (10 + 7)$$
$$= (3 \times 10) + (3 \times 7)$$
$$= 30 + 21$$
$$= 51$$

To multiply 3,624 by 5, you first multiply 5 by the ones, then by the tens, then by the hundreds, and then by the thousands. Finally, you add those numbers together.

$$3,624 \times 5 =$$
$$(4 \text{ ones} \times 5) + (2 \text{ tens} \times 5) + (6 \text{ hundreds} \times 5) + (3 \text{ thousands} \times 5)$$
$$= (4 \times 5) + (20 \times 5) + (600 \times 5) + (3,000 \times 5)$$
$$= 20 + 100 + 3,000 + 15,000$$
$$= 18,120$$

There is another, quicker way to work through these stages of multiplication. First, write the two numbers to be multiplied one on top of the other by lining up the ones place. Then multiply the ones, tens, hundreds, and thousands columns, "carrying over" numbers to the next column as needed.

$$\begin{array}{r} {\scriptstyle 3\ 1\ 2} \\ 3{,}624 \\ \times 5 \\ \hline 18{,}120 \end{array}$$

First, multiply 4×5. You know that $4 \times 5 = 20$, or 2 tens and 0 ones. Write zero in the ones place and carry the two tens by writing a small 2 over the tens column. Now, move to the tens place. 5×2 tens $= 10$ tens plus the two tens carried over $= 12$ tens. Write 2 in the tens place and carry over the 1 hundred for the hundreds column. Continue to multiply and add in this way until you have multiplied each digit by the 5 and added the number carried over from the last place.

Multiples

The number 24 is a multiple of 6, because $6 \times 4 = 24$. A multiple of a number is the product of that number and any whole number. The number 36 is also a multiple of 6 because $6 \times 6 = 36$.

Here are more multiples of 6: 6, 12, 18, 24, 30 . . .

Here are some multiples of 7: 7, 14, 21, 28, 35 . . .

Here are some multiples of 10: 10, 20, 30, 40, 50 . . .

Notice that all multiples of 10 end in zero. All whole numbers that end in 0 are multiples of 10.

Here are some multiples of 2: 2, 4, 6, 8, 10, 12, 14 . . .

Notice that all the multiples of 2 are even. You can define even numbers using multiples: all even numbers are multiples of 2.

Common Multiples

The number 18 is a multiple of 6 because $6 \times 3 = 18$. But 18 is also a multiple of 9 because $9 \times 2 = 18$. As a result, we say that 18 is a common multiple of 6 and 9. Another common multiple of 6 and 9 is 36 because $6 \times 6 = 36$ and $9 \times 4 = 36$. Can you find three common multiples for 4 and 6?

Multiplying by Tens

Whenever you multiply a number by 10, you make it 10 times larger. In the decimal system, you make a whole number 10 times larger by adding a zero to the end of it. It is fairly easy to multiply by 10—just add an extra zero to the number you're multiplying.

$$
\begin{array}{r} 4 \\ \times 10 \\ \hline 40 \end{array} \qquad
\begin{array}{r} 54 \\ \times 10 \\ \hline 540 \end{array} \qquad
\begin{array}{r} 184 \\ \times 10 \\ \hline 1{,}840 \end{array}
$$

You can use this basic concept to multiply by any multiple of 10 quickly. Suppose you want to multiply 23 by 60. You already know how to multiply 23 by 6, and now you know how to multiply by 10. By combining these two skills, you can find the product:

$$23 \times 60$$
$$= 23 \times (6 \times 10)$$
$$= (23 \times 6) \times 10$$

So, the product of 23×60 is equal to the product of 23 times 6, times 10:

$$
\begin{array}{r} {\scriptstyle 1} \\ 23 \\ \times 6 \\ \hline 138 \end{array}
$$

Then, multiply 138×10, which is as easy as adding a zero: $138 \times 10 = 1{,}380$. Therefore, $23 \times 60 = 1{,}380$. Try multiplying 14×70 on your own.

Multiplying by Two-Digit Numbers

Once you know how to multiply by tens, you can multiply by any two-digit number. You just break the problem down into two parts. First, you multiply by ones, and then, you multiply by tens. After this multiplication, you add. Here's how you would find the product of 23×58.

Think: 23×58 is $(20 \times 58) + (3 \times 58)$

$$
\begin{array}{r}
58 \\
\times\ 3 \\
\hline
174
\end{array}
\quad \text{Multiply 58 by 3 ones.}
$$

Multiply 58 by 2 tens. Make sure to write a zero in the ones place.

$$
\begin{array}{r}
58 \\
\times 20 \\
\hline
00 \\
+1{,}160 \\
\hline
1{,}160
\end{array}
$$

Then add.

$$
\begin{array}{r}
58 \\
\times 23 \\
\hline
174 \\
+1{,}160 \\
\hline
1{,}334
\end{array}
$$

You can multiply larger numbers by two-digit numbers in the same way. Here's an example:

$$372 \times 48 = 372 \times (40 + 8)$$
$$= (372 \times 40) + (372 \times 8)$$

$$\begin{array}{r} 372 \\ \times 48 \\ \hline \end{array}$$

$$2{,}976 = 372 \times 8$$
$$\underline{14{,}880} = 372 \times 40$$
$$17{,}856 = 372 \times 48$$

Do It Yourself

Ask your child to multiply a few other numbers by 100, such as the number of pets he has had or the number of subjects he studies at school.

Multiplying by Hundreds

When you multiply a whole number by 100, you add two zeros to it. Multiplying by 100 is like multiplying by 10 twice.

$$100 \times 6 = (10 \times 10) \times 6 = 10 \times (10 \times 6) = 10 \times 60 = 600$$

$$\begin{array}{r} 6 \\ \times 100 \\ \hline 600 \end{array} \qquad \begin{array}{r} 87 \\ \times 100 \\ \hline 8{,}700 \end{array} \qquad \begin{array}{r} 942 \\ \times 100 \\ \hline 94{,}200 \end{array}$$

To multiply by any multiple of 100, write zeros in the ones and tens place of the product. Then, multiply using the digit in the hundreds place.

Write zeros in the ones place and the tens place.

$$\begin{array}{r} 487 \\ \times 300 \\ \hline 00 \end{array}$$

Multiply.

$$\begin{array}{r} 487 \\ \times 300 \\ \hline 146{,}100 \end{array}$$

Multiplying by Three-Digit Numbers

Now that you know how to multiply by hundreds, you can multiply three-digit numbers. First, multiply by the ones, then by the tens, and then by the hundreds. The last step is to add. Here is an example:

Multiply by 4 ones.

$$565$$
$$\underline{\times 394}$$
$$2{,}260 = 4 \times 565$$

Multiply by 9 tens.

$$565$$
$$\underline{\times 394}$$
$$2{,}260$$
$$50{,}850 = 90 \times 565$$

Multiply by 3 hundreds.

$$565$$
$$\underline{\times 394}$$
$$2{,}260$$
$$50{,}850$$
$$\underline{169{,}500 = 300 \times 565}$$
$$222{,}610 = 394 \times 565$$

Do It Yourself

Ask your child to multiply a few other numbers by 1,000, such as the number of houses on his street.

Multiplying by Thousands

When multiplying a whole number by 10, you add one zero. When multiplying by 100, you add two zeros. How many zeros do you suppose you will add when multiplying a whole number by 1,000? If you said three, you have picked up on the pattern. Multiplying by 1,000 is like multiplying by 10 three times.

$$
\begin{array}{r} 7 \\ \times 1{,}000 \\ \hline 7{,}000 \end{array}
\qquad
\begin{array}{r} 23 \\ \times 1{,}000 \\ \hline 23{,}000 \end{array}
\qquad
\begin{array}{r} 981 \\ \times 1{,}000 \\ \hline 981{,}000 \end{array}
$$

To multiply by any thousand, write zeros in the ones, tens, and hundreds places of the product. Then, multiply by the digit in the thousands place. Write zeros in the ones place, the tens place, and the hundreds place.

$$
\begin{array}{r} 64 \\ \times 2{,}000 \\ \hline 000 \end{array}
$$

Multiply.

$$
\begin{array}{r} 64 \\ \times 2{,}000 \\ \hline 128{,}000 \end{array}
$$

Multiplication with Zeros

Sometimes, you will need to multiply numbers that end in several zeros. There is a handy shortcut for multiplying numbers that end in zeros.

Let's say you wanted to multiply 300 by 500. You can do this as you would normally. Write two zeros in the product. Multiply 500 by 3.

$$
\begin{array}{r} 500 \\ \times 300 \\ \hline 00 \end{array}
\qquad\qquad
\begin{array}{r} 500 \\ \times 300 \\ \hline 150{,}000 \end{array}
$$

Alternatively, you can take a shortcut. You can rule off all the zeros at the ends of the numbers and write all four of the zeros in the product right away. Then multiply 5 by 3.

$$
\begin{array}{r} 5\,|\,00 \\ \times 3\,|\,00 \\ \hline 0000 \end{array}
\qquad\qquad
\begin{array}{r} 5\,|\,00 \\ \times 3\,|\,00 \\ \hline 15\,|\,0{,}000 \end{array}
$$

Use this strategy to multiply 2,000 by 600 and to multiply 600 by 800. What products did you get?

Do It Yourself

Have your child check his multiplication in the previous problems using estimation or by changing the order of the factors he is multiplying.

Checking Multiplication

There are two different ways of checking multiplication: by estimation or by changing the order of the factors you are multiplying. Estimation helps you know if your answer is close to the right one. Changing the order of the factors gives you an exact check.

To check a multiplication problem by estimation, round each factor to the nearest ten, hundred, or thousand. (You do not need to round one-digit factors.) Then, multiply and check to be sure the estimate is close to the answer you found originally.

To check this problem:

$$
\begin{array}{r}
254 \\
\times 49 \\
\hline
2{,}286 \\
10{,}160 \\
\hline
12{,}446
\end{array}
$$

Round both factors to the nearest ten and multiply:

$$
\begin{array}{ccc}
254 & \rightarrow & 250 \\
\times 49 & \rightarrow & \times 50 \\
\hline
& & 12{,}500
\end{array}
$$

See if the original product is close to the estimate. If it is not, go back and multiply again.

$$12{,}446 \text{ is close to } 12{,}500 \checkmark$$

Based on this estimation, you would not be able to say that your multiplication is absolutely correct, but you will know whether you are close.

You can also check multiplication by changing the order of the factors and multiplying again. To check this problem:

$$\begin{array}{r} 68 \\ \times 37 \\ \hline 476 \\ 2{,}040 \\ \hline 2{,}516 \end{array}$$

Reverse the order of the factors and multiply:

$$\begin{array}{r} 37 \\ \times\ 68 \\ \hline 296 \\ 2{,}220 \\ \hline 2{,}516 \end{array}$$

If your answer is correct, the product will be the same both times, no matter what order you multiply the factors in.

Multiplying Three Factors

You've just seen how you can check a multiplication problem by changing the order of the two factors. You can also do this when multiplying three factors. When you multiply three numbers, you can multiply them in any order, but one particular order may be easiest.

For example, consider the multiplication problem $879 \times 5 \times 6$. In this problem, you can save time if you multiply 5 by 6 in your head to get 30, and then multiply 30 by 879.

Division

Division Review

Division and multiplication are inverse operations. This means that one operation undoes, or reverses, the other. Consider the equation $10 \times 10 = 100$. You could reverse the operation by dividing $100 \div 10 = 10$. The first equation says if you combine 10 groups, each containing 10 items, you will have 100 items in total. The second says if you break that collection of 100 items into 10 equal groups, each group will have 10 items.

Before you learn the more complicated aspects of division, make sure you know the process of simple division. For example, because you know that $8 \times 4 = 32$, you should also know that the inverse operations are true: $32 \div 4 = 8$ and $32 \div 8 = 4$.

Finally, memorize these two important rules about division:

1. You cannot divide by 0.
2. Any number divided by 1 equals that number.

Factors

Talk and Think

Ask your child, "Can you think of other numbers that do not divide evenly?"

A factor is a number that divides into another number evenly and does not leave a remainder. What are the factors of 4?

$$4 \div 1 = 4$$
$$4 \div 2 = 2$$
$$4 \div 3 = \text{DOES NOT DIVIDE EVENLY}$$
$$4 \div 4 = 1$$

Therefore, the factors of 4 are 1, 2, and 4 because they all divide into 4 exactly. The number 3 does not divide 4 evenly, and so it is not a factor of 4. Try listing all the factors of 12.

Common Factors

The factors of 20 are 1, 2, 4, 5, 10, and 20. The factors of 24 are 1, 2, 3, 4, 6, 8, 12, and 24. How many factors do 20 and 24 have in common? There are three: 1, 2, and 4. Factors shared by two or more numbers are called common factors.

What are the common factors of 28 and 42? What about 30 and 45?

Prime Numbers

Every whole number larger than 1 has at least two factors. The number can be divided evenly by itself, and it can be divided evenly by 1. If a number has only two factors (itself and 1), it is called a prime number. The number 11 is a good example of a prime number. You can divide it evenly by 1 ($11 \div 1 = 11$), and you can divide it evenly by 11 ($11 \div 11 = 1$). However, you cannot divide 11 evenly by 3, 4, 6, or any other whole number. Therefore, 11 is a prime number.

The number 2 is considered the first prime number (1 is a special case). Can you identify the other prime numbers between 2 and 20? Hint: There are seven of them, not counting 2.

Composite Numbers

What do we call a number that has factors and is not prime? This is a composite number. A composite number is a number that is divisible by at least one other number besides itself and 1. The number 6 is a good example. The number 6 is evenly divisible by 1, 2, 3, and 6. Therefore, it is a composite number. Is 21 composite? How about 37?

Dividend, Divisor, Quotient

In the equation $32 \div 8 = 4$, the number before the division symbol (32) is called the dividend, the number after the division symbol (8) is called the divisor, and the number after the equals sign (4) is called the quotient. The dividend is the number you are dividing into, the divisor is the number you are dividing by, and the quotient is the result.

Three Ways of Writing Division Problems

You can write a division problem in three ways: using a division symbol, using long division, or using a fraction bar. "28 divided by 7" can be written as:

$$28 \div 7 \qquad 7\overline{)28} \qquad \frac{28}{7}$$

All three methods have the same meaning: 28 divided by 7.

Divide and Conquer

. . . .

Let's divide 33 by 5.

$$\begin{array}{r} 6 \ \ \text{R3} \\ 5\overline{)33} \\ -30 \\ \hline 3 \end{array}$$

First, we look to see if the divisor is smaller than the first digit of the dividend. It is larger (5 > 3), so we have to look at the next digit of the dividend and divide 5 into 33. We know that $5 \times 6 = 30$. But $33 - 30$ leaves a remainder of 3. So 33 divided by 5 equals 6 with a remainder of 3. We abbreviate this quotient as "6 R3."

Because multiplication and division are inverse operations, you can use your multiplication skills to check your division. To check a division problem, you multiply the quotient by the divisor and add the remainder (if there is one). Your answer should equal the dividend.

$$(\text{quotient} \times \text{divisor}) + \text{remainder} = \text{dividend}$$
$$(6 \times 5) + 3 =$$
$$30 + 3 = 33 \ \checkmark$$

You can begin to use this same form—multiplication plus addition of the remainder—as a way of writing division answers.

$$33 = (6 \times 5) + 3 \qquad 3 < 5$$

You write the inequality 3 < 5 to show that the remainder is less than the divisor. Remember that if the remainder is not less than the divisor, the quotient is too small, and you will need to go back and redo your division.

Understanding Remainders

When you solve word problems with division, you may need to think about your remainders in a different way. Suppose that 31 students are going on a school trip in vans. Each van can hold 7 students. How many vans does your teacher need?

When you divide 31 by 7, you get the quotient 4 (7 × 4 = 28) with a remainder of 3. Does the answer 4 with a remainder of 3 mean you only need 4 vans? Well, if you only had 4 vans, 3 people would not be able to go on the trip. This means 4 vans cannot be the correct answer. In this problem, the remainder tells us an extra van will be needed. Altogether, 5 vans will be needed for the trip, even though the fifth van will not be full.

Now try the following problem: Mrs. Pauli wants to make surprise baskets for a fair. She has 6 baskets and 52 treats to place in them. If she wants all the baskets to have the same number of surprises, how many treats should go in each basket? How many treats will be left over for her grandchildren?

> **Do It Yourself**
> Try asking your child to demonstrate remainders by dividing with building blocks or other small objects.

Zeros in Quotients

Sometimes when you divide, you need to write a zero as one of the digits of the quotient. Consider dividing 922 by 3.

$$
\begin{array}{r}
3 \\
3\overline{)922} \\
-9 \\
\hline
0
\end{array}
$$

Think: 0 < 3

Divide the tens. Because you cannot divide 2 by 3, write a zero in the tens place of the quotient and bring down the tens.

$$
\begin{array}{r}
30 \\
3\overline{)922} \\
-9\downarrow \\
\hline
0 \\
02
\end{array}
$$

Bring down the ones. Divide 22 by 3.

$$
\begin{array}{r}
307 \ \text{R1} \\
3\overline{)922} \\
-9\downarrow\downarrow \\
\hline
0 \\
022 \\
-21 \\
\hline
1
\end{array}
$$

Think: $1 < 3$

Check by multiplying the quotient by the divisor and adding the remainder.

$$
\begin{array}{r}
307 \\
\times3 \\
\hline
921 \\
+1 \\
\hline
922
\end{array}
$$

Practice writing your answer as multiplication and addition, followed by an inequality.

$$922 = (3 \times 307) + 1 \qquad 1 < 3$$

The Number of Digits in a Quotient

Before you begin solving a division problem, it's helpful to figure out how many digits there will be in the quotient. For example, in the problem $496 \div 3$, you know right away that there will be three digits in the quotient because you can divide 4 hundreds by 3. Another way to think of this is that $496 > (3 \times 100)$. You know the quotient will be at least 100, which is the smallest possible three-digit number.

In the problem $519 \div 6$, you know right away that the quotient will have two digits. You cannot divide the 5 in the hundreds place by 6, but you can divide 51 tens by 6. Another way to think of this is that $519 < (6 \times 100)$. You know the quotient will be less than 100.

Dividing Larger Numbers

You can use the same method to divide larger multidigit numbers by one-digit numbers. Here is an example of dividing a number in the thousands.

$$8\overline{)8254}$$

You can divide 8 thousands by 8. Begin by dividing the thousands. The quotient will have four digits.

In this problem, notice how you cannot divide 2 in the hundreds place by 8. So, first, you must write a zero in the hundreds place, bring down the 2 and the 5, and divide 8 into 25 tens.

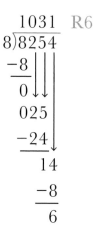

Mental Division

Sometimes you can do a division problem in your head without writing out all the steps. Here's an example.

$$3\overline{)936}$$

To solve this problem, **Think:**

9 hundreds ÷ 3 = 3 hundreds

3 tens ÷ 3 = 1 ten

6 ones ÷ 3 = 2 ones

so, $\dfrac{312}{3\overline{)936}}$

Now you've seen the process.

Try solving $8\overline{)1664}$ and $7\overline{)749}$ in your head.

Dividing by Tens

When dividing by tens, remember that division is the inverse operation of multiplication. Here's an example:

$$30\overline{)90}$$

To solve this problem, **think**: What times 30 equals 90?
Try different numbers.

$$2 \times 30 = 60$$
$$3 \times 30 = 90$$

$$\begin{array}{r} 3 \\ 30\overline{)90} \\ -90 \\ \hline 0 \end{array}$$

Think: $0 < 30$

Now try dividing 80 by 20.

Dividing by Two-Digit Numbers

When the divisor is a two-digit number but not an even ten, round it to the nearest ten to estimate what the quotient will be. Here is an example.

$$28\overline{)640}$$

Step 1:
To divide the 64 tens by 28,
round 28 to 30.
Think: What times 30 is roughly 64?

$2 \times 30 = 60$

Step 2:
To divide the 80 ones by 28,
round 28 to 30.
Think: What times 30 is about 80?

$\mathbf{2 \times 30 = 60}$
$3 \times 30 = 90$
3×30 is too large.

$$
\begin{array}{r}
2 \\
28\overline{)640} \\
-56 \\
\hline
8
\end{array}
$$
Think: 8 < 28

$$
\begin{array}{r}
22 \text{ R24} \\
28\overline{)640} \\
-56\downarrow \\
\hline
80 \\
-56 \\
\hline
24
\end{array}
$$
Think: 24 < 28

Check by multiplying the quotient by the divisor and adding the remainder.

$$
\begin{array}{r}
22 \\
\times 28 \\
\hline
176 \\
+440 \\
\hline
616 \\
+\ 24 \\
\hline
640
\end{array}
$$

Practice writing your answer as multiplication and addition, followed by an inequality.

$$640 = (28 \times 22) + 24 \qquad 24 < 28$$

Adjusting the Quotient

Sometimes when rounding the divisor to the nearest ten, the quotient you try will be too large or too small. In these cases, you will need to adjust the quotient. Here's an example:

$$36\overline{)146}$$

You cannot divide 14 tens by 36. Divide 146 ones by 36 ones instead. Round 36 to 40. You know that $40 \times 3 = 120$, which is less than 146. Try 3 as a quotient.

$$
\begin{array}{r}
3 \\
36\overline{)146} \\
-108 \\
\hline
38
\end{array}
$$

The remainder is greater than the divisor. This means the quotient you tried was too small. Make the quotient one number larger. Try 4.

$$
\begin{array}{r}
4 \quad \text{R2} \\
36\overline{)146} \\
-144 \\
\hline
2
\end{array}
$$

$$146 = (36 \times 4) + 2 \qquad 2 < 36$$

Here's a similar problem for you to try:

$$13\overline{)851}$$

Dividing Thousands

You divide numbers in the thousands by two-digit numbers in the same way.

$$\text{To solve } 32\overline{)6{,}659}, \text{ follow these steps:}$$

1. Divide 66 hundreds by 32.
2. Subtract 64 from 66. Bring down the 5 tens. You cannot divide 25 tens by 32. Write a zero in the tens place of the quotient.
3. Bring down the 9 ones. Divide 259 ones by 32. **Think**: What times 30 is roughly 259?
4. Check your work by multiplying the quotient by the divisor and adding the remainder to that product.

Check by multiplying the quotient by the divisor and adding the remainder.

$$
\begin{array}{r}
208 \quad \text{R3} \\
32\overline{)6{,}659} \\
-64 \\
\hline
259 \\
-256 \\
\hline
3
\end{array}
$$

Check.

$$
\begin{array}{r}
208 \\
\times 32 \\
\hline
416 \\
+624 \\
\hline
6{,}656 \\
+\ \ 3 \\
\hline
6{,}659
\end{array}
$$

Practice writing your answer like this:

$$6{,}659 = (32 \times 208) + 3 \qquad 3 < 32$$

Long division is a beneficial way to practice both multiplication and division. Here are a few long-division problems you can use for practice:

$$39\overline{)4{,}132} \quad 27\overline{)1{,}007} \quad 45\overline{)2{,}503}$$

Talk and Think
Ask your child, "What do you think are some advantages to being able to estimate quotients?"

Estimating Quotients

When you estimate a quotient, you can round the dividend or the divisor to a number that makes the division easy, rather than to the greatest place value. Here are two examples:

$$\text{Estimate} \quad 6\overline{)383}$$

Round the dividend (383) to 360 because you can divide 360 by 6 easily. You cannot divide 400 by 6 without a remainder.

$$\begin{array}{r} 60 \\ 6\overline{)360} \end{array}$$

$383 \div 6$ is roughly 60.

$$\text{Estimate} \quad 28\overline{)1{,}143}$$

Round the divisor (28) to the greatest place value (30), yet 30 does not go into the divided 1,000 easily. However, 30 does divide into 1,200 easily. Round the dividend to 1,200.

$$\begin{array}{r} 40 \\ 30\overline{)1{,}200} \end{array}$$

$1143 \div 28$ is roughly 40.

Solving Problems and Equations

Letters That Stand for Numbers

Sometimes, we use a letter to stand for an unknown number in math. Here's an example:

$$A = 6 + (8 \times 5)$$

In this equation and others like it, A stands for a mystery number, and your job as a math detective is to figure out what A equals. In this case, you can solve the mystery by multiplying and then adding. $8 \times 5 = 40$, and $40 + 6 = 46$. So, $A = 46$.

See if you can figure out the mystery number in this equation: $B = (8 \times 3) - 4$.

Equality Properties

Equality properties are rules that can help you solve equations like the ones above. One equality property says that equals added to equals are equal. This property can help you figure out the mystery number in the following equation.

$$Y - 25 = 15$$

The equality property of addition says that if you add an equal quantity to both sides of any equation, it will still be the same equation. Look what happens if we add 25 to both sides of this equation.

$$Y - 25 = 15$$
$$Y - 25 + 25 = 15 + 25$$
$$Y = 40$$

If you subtract 25 from Y and then add 25, the addition and subtraction cancel each other out. This leaves just Y on the left side of the equation. On the right side of the equation, you add 25 to 15 and get 40. So, you know that $Y = 40$.

Use this same technique to solve $Z - 12 = 17$ and $P - 29 = 17$.

Now let's learn another equality property: Equals multiplied by equals are equal. This property is very useful for solving equations with division. Here's an example:

$$Y \div 2 = 37$$

The equality property of multiplication says that you can multiply both sides of this equation by the same number and still have the same equation. Look what happens when we multiply by 2:

$$Y \div 2 = 37$$
$$Y \div 2 \times 2 = 37 \times 2$$
$$Y = 74$$

If we divide Y by 2 and then multiply it by 2, the multiplication undoes the division, and this leaves just Y on the left side of the equation. Meanwhile, on the right side of the equation, we multiply 37 times 2 and get 74. So, $Y = 74$.

Try to solve another similar problem on your own: $Z \div 6 = 23$.

Getting comfortable with using these equality properties will help you when you begin to study the branch of mathematics called algebra in later years.

Fractions and Decimals

Fractions

Can you read these numbers?

$$\frac{1}{2} \qquad \frac{1}{3} \qquad \frac{1}{4} \qquad \frac{1}{5} \qquad \frac{1}{6} \qquad \frac{1}{7} \qquad \frac{1}{8} \qquad \frac{1}{9} \qquad \frac{1}{10}$$

From left to right, they are: one-half, one-third, one-fourth, one-fifth, one-sixth, one-seventh, one-eighth, one-ninth, and one-tenth. These numbers are all fractions. They are all smaller than 1 but larger than 0. Each one is made up of two digits, the numerator and the denominator.

$$\frac{1}{3} \quad \begin{array}{l} \longleftarrow \text{ numerator} \\ \longleftarrow \text{ denominator} \end{array}$$

The bar in a fraction means the same thing as a division sign. These numbers are all fractions, too.

$$\frac{3}{4} \qquad \frac{3}{5} \qquad \frac{5}{5} \qquad \frac{7}{11} \qquad \frac{11}{12}$$

Can you identify the numerator and denominator in each fraction?

Do It Yourself

Come up with a few fractions of your own, and then have your child point out which ones are proper and which are improper.

Improper Fractions

When the numerator of a fraction is equal to or greater than the denominator, the fraction is called an improper fraction. Here are some examples of improper fractions:

$$\frac{5}{5} , \frac{7}{4} , \frac{12}{3} , \text{and } \frac{18}{5}$$

Let's consider the first one, $\frac{5}{5}$. When the number in the numerator equals the number in the denominator, the fraction equals the whole number 1. Remember that any number divided by itself equals 1. The improper fraction $\frac{5}{5}$ means the same thing as $5 \div 5$, which equals 1.

$$\frac{2}{2} , \frac{3}{3} , \frac{1}{1} , \frac{100}{100} , \text{and } \frac{197}{197} \text{ all equal 1.}$$

When the numerator of an improper fraction can be divided evenly by the denominator with no remainder, the improper fraction equals a whole number.

$$\frac{12}{4} \rightarrow \quad 4\overline{)12} \atop \underline{-12} \atop 0 \quad \text{so, } \frac{12}{4} = 3$$

Mixed Numbers

When the numerator of an improper fraction cannot be divided evenly by the denominator, the fraction cannot be written as a whole number. Instead, it must be written as a mixed number. Mixed numbers have two parts: a whole number and a fraction. The numbers $\frac{22}{3}$, $\frac{51}{4}$, and $\frac{11}{6}$ are all mixed numbers.

The improper fraction $\frac{18}{5}$ can be written as a mixed number. Remember that $\frac{18}{5}$ means $18 \div 5$. If you solve this division problem, you will get a whole number and a remainder.

$$
\begin{array}{r}
3 \ \ \text{R3} \\
5\overline{)18} \\
-15 \\
\hline
3
\end{array}
$$

The improper fraction $\frac{18}{5}$ is the same as the mixed number $3\frac{3}{5}$. To write the remainder as a fraction instead of R3, use the remainder (3) as the numerator of the fraction and the divisor (5) as the denominator. A remainder always shows there is a fractional part left over after the division. The quotient to each division problem you solved that had a remainder could be written as a whole number plus a fraction.

Improper fractions can always be written as either whole numbers or mixed numbers. Take a look at the improper fractions below. Which ones can be written as whole numbers? Which ones can only be written as mixed numbers?

$$\frac{9}{9} \qquad \frac{8}{3} \qquad \frac{9}{2} \qquad \frac{16}{5}$$

Equivalent Fractions

Even if two fractions have different numbers in the numerator and denominator, they can name the same amount. When fractions name the same amount, they are called equivalent fractions.

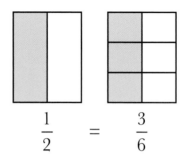

$$\frac{1}{2} = \frac{3}{6}$$

You can make an equivalent fraction by multiplying or dividing both the numerator and the denominator by the same number. Here are two examples:

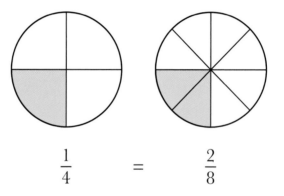

$$\frac{1}{4} = \frac{2}{8}$$

Multiply the numerator and denominator by 2.

$$\frac{1}{4} = \frac{1 \times 2}{4 \times 2} = \frac{2}{8}$$

Talk and Think

Ask your child to think of a few more equivalent fractions. Then, ask your child why it might be important to know which fractions are equivalent.

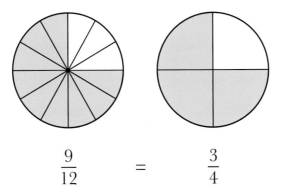

$$\frac{9}{12} \quad = \quad \frac{3}{4}$$

Divide the numerator and denominator by 3.

$$\frac{9}{12} \quad = \quad \frac{9 \div 3}{12 \div 3} \quad = \quad \frac{3}{4}$$

Can you figure out what should go in place of the question mark in the problems below?

$$\frac{2}{3} = \frac{?}{12} \qquad\qquad \frac{3}{4} = \frac{?}{100} \qquad\qquad \frac{8}{16} = \frac{1}{?}$$

Putting Fractions in Lowest Terms

A fraction is in lowest terms when its numerator and denominator have no common factor greater than 1—or, in other words, when no number larger than 1 can divide into both the numerator and the denominator. So, to put a fraction in lowest terms, divide the numerator and denominator by common factors until there is no common factor left greater than 1.

Here is an example. Put $\frac{3}{9}$ in lowest terms. You can divide the numerator 3 and the denominator 9 by 3. They both have 3 as a common factor.

$$\frac{3}{9} \quad = \quad \frac{3 \div 3}{9 \div 3} \quad = \quad \frac{1}{3}$$

The new numerator 1 and new denominator 3 have no common factor greater than 1. Therefore, the fraction $\frac{1}{3}$ is in lowest terms.

Now try putting $\frac{12}{18}$ in lowest terms. You can divide both 12 and 18 by 2.

$$\frac{12}{18} \quad = \quad \frac{12 \div 2}{18 \div 2} \quad = \quad \frac{6}{9}$$

But you can go further. You can divide both 6 and 9 by 3.

$$\frac{6 \div 3}{9 \div 3} \quad = \quad \frac{2}{3}$$

There are no more common factors greater than 1. These three fractions are equivalent.

$$\frac{12}{18} \quad = \quad \frac{6}{9} \quad = \quad \frac{2}{3}$$

The last fraction, $\frac{2}{3}$, is the only one of these equivalent fractions that is written in lowest terms.

You could have done this problem in one step by noticing that 12 and 18 have 6 as a common factor, and 6 is the greatest common factor of 12 and 18.

$$\frac{12 \div 6}{18 \div 6} \quad = \quad \frac{2}{3}$$

When you divide the numerator and denominator by their greatest common factor, you put the fraction in lowest terms in one step.

Comparing Fractions

You can compare multiple fractions with the same denominator by comparing their numerators. For example, the fractions $\frac{2}{6}$, $\frac{4}{6}$, and $\frac{5}{6}$ all have a common denominator, 6.

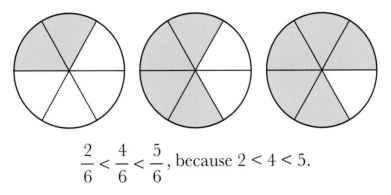

$$\frac{2}{6} < \frac{4}{6} < \frac{5}{6}, \text{ because } 2 < 4 < 5.$$

To compare fractions with different denominators, you must first give them a common denominator. Once their denominators are the same, you can easily compare them. Which fraction is larger: $\frac{2}{3}$ or $\frac{1}{6}$?

First, you need to find the equivalent fraction for $\frac{2}{3}$ with a denominator of 6. You can make an equivalent fraction by multiplying the numerator and the denominator by the same number.

$$\frac{2}{3} = \frac{?}{6}$$

What would you need to multiply the denominator 3 by to get 6? The answer is 2, because $3 \times 2 = 6$. Now, you can find the equivalent fraction by multiplying both the numerator and the denominator by 2.

$$\frac{2}{3} = \frac{2}{3} \times \frac{2}{2} = \frac{4}{6}$$

Therefore, $\frac{2}{3}$ is equivalent to $\frac{4}{6}$. You can now compare $\frac{2}{3}$ and $\frac{1}{6}$ because you have the common denominator 6.

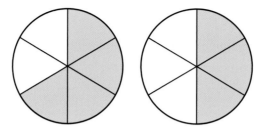

Because 4 is greater than 3, the fraction $\frac{4}{6}$ (or $\frac{2}{3}$) is greater than $\frac{3}{6}$.
Can you compare $\frac{2}{3}$ and $\frac{5}{12}$? Which fraction is larger?

Adding Fractions

You can add fractions with the same denominator by adding the numerators only.

$$\frac{2}{5} + \frac{1}{5} = \frac{3}{5} \qquad\qquad \frac{4}{9} + \frac{3}{9} = \frac{7}{9}$$

Be sure to add just the numerators. The denominators stay the same. The picture below shows why. You are adding the number of parts shown in each numerator. You are not changing the total number of parts represented by the denominator.

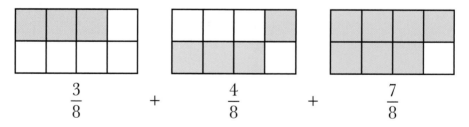

$$\frac{3}{8} \qquad + \qquad \frac{4}{8} \qquad + \qquad \frac{7}{8}$$

Practice adding other fractions that have the same denominator. Make sure you write each sum in lowest terms. If the sum is an improper fraction, write it as a whole number or a mixed number in lowest terms. Here are three examples.

$$\frac{5}{9}+\frac{7}{9}=\frac{12}{9}=1\frac{3}{9}=1\frac{1}{3} \qquad \frac{5}{12}+\frac{1}{12}=\frac{6}{12}=\frac{1}{2} \qquad \frac{7}{13}+\frac{6}{13}=\frac{13}{13}=1$$

Subtracting Fractions

You can subtract two fractions that have the same denominator by subtracting the numerators. The denominators remain the same. Here is an example.

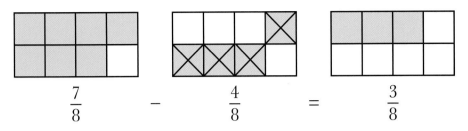

$$\frac{7}{8} \quad - \quad \frac{4}{8} \quad = \quad \frac{3}{8}$$

When you subtract fractions, make sure you write the difference in lowest terms. Here are two examples.

$$\frac{5}{16} - \frac{3}{16} = \frac{2}{16} = \frac{1}{8} \qquad \frac{5}{12} - \frac{5}{12} = \frac{0}{12} = 0$$

Notice that $\frac{0}{12} = 0$. All fractions with a numerator of 0 equal 0.

Expressing Simple Outcomes

Sometimes, we use fractions to express simple outcomes. For instance, suppose you took a survey to see how many fans at a football game were rooting for the home team and how many for the visitors. After asking a large crowd of people, you found that for every 4 fans you asked, 3 fans supported the home team and only 1 fan supported the visitors. You could use fractions to explain these outcomes. You might say that $\frac{3}{4}$ of the crowd was rooting for the home team and only $\frac{1}{4}$ for the visitors.

Suppose there are 25 students in your class, 15 girls and 10 boys. That means $\frac{15}{25}$ of the class are girls. Can you put that fraction in lowest terms? What fraction, in lowest terms, would represent the part of the class who are boys?

Decimals

You can write the fraction $\frac{1}{10}$ as the decimal 0.1. You read each the same way: "one-tenth." The period to the right of the 0 is called a decimal point. The decimal point shows that the value of the digits to its right is somewhere between 1 and 0, like a fraction. A decimal is any number that uses places to the right of the decimal point to represent a fraction of 1.

The first place to the right of the decimal point is the tenths place. You can write the mixed number $1\frac{7}{10}$ as the decimal 1.7. You read each the same way: "one and seven-tenths."

ones	.	tenths
1	.	7

The second place to the right of the decimal point is the hundredths place. You can write the fraction $\frac{1}{100}$ as 0.01. You read each the same way: "one-hundredth."

ones	.	tenths	hundredths
0	.	0	1

Now, consider this mixed number:

$$2\frac{47}{100} =$$

ones	.	tenths	hundredths
2	.	4	7

You read each as "two and forty-seven hundredths." Notice that when there are both tenths and hundredths in a decimal, you read the tenths and hundredths together in terms of hundredths. Remember to put the word "and" between the whole-number part and the fractional part of a decimal, just as in mixed numbers.

The third place to the right of the decimal point is the thousandths place. You can write the fraction $\frac{1}{1,000}$ as 0.001. You read each the same way—"one-thousandth."

ones	.	tenths	hundredths	thousandths
0	.	0	0	1

Notice that as you move from the left to the right, each place value gets 10 times smaller. In the decimal system, each place has a value one-tenth as large as the one to its left. Now try reading this mixed number and its equivalent decimal:

$$3\frac{857}{1000} = 3.857$$

You read both as "three and eight hundred fifty-seven thousandths." Notice that because there are thousandths in the decimal, you read the tenths and hundredths in terms of thousandths.

Reading and Writing Decimals

Practice writing decimals in words. The decimal 0.27 is "twenty-seven hundredths." The decimal 3.8 is "three and eight-tenths." You should also practice writing the digits for decimals that are expressed in words. "Three hundred fifty-four thousandths" is the decimal 0.354. "Five hundred and fourteen hundredths" is the decimal 500.14. Can you write "seven hundred and one thousandth"?

Practice writing decimals in expanded form, too:

176.04 = 100 + 70 + 6 + 0.04

What is 600 + 40 + 0.7 + 0.08?

Decimals as Fractions

You can write decimals as fractions and fractions as decimals. The fraction $\frac{39}{100}$ can be written as 0.39, and the decimal 0.02 can be written as $\frac{2}{100}$. Practice rewriting $\frac{25}{100}$ and $\frac{101}{1,000}$ as decimals. Then, practice rewriting 0.16 and 0.599 as fractions.

Are you ready for something more challenging? Find the decimal equivalents of the fractions that follow. You will need to convert the fractions by using a common denominator of 100.

$$\frac{1}{2}, \frac{1}{4}, \frac{1}{8}, \frac{1}{10}$$

Now try converting these decimals to fractions in lowest terms: 0.25, 0.75, and 0.875.

Rounding Decimals

You round decimals the same way you round whole numbers. To decide whether to round a decimal up or down, look at the digit to the right of the place to which you are rounding.

Round 6.85 to the nearest tenth. Look at the digit to the right of the 8 in the tenths place. This digit is a 5, so you will round up to 6.9.

Round 7.453 to the nearest hundredth. Look at the digit to the right of the 5 in the hundredths place. This digit is a 3, so you will round down to 7.45.

Rounding a decimal to the nearest whole number means rounding it to the ones place. There should be no fractional part left. Round 76.47 to the nearest whole number. Look at the digit to the right of the ones place. 76.4 is closer to 76 than 77, so you will round down to 76.

Comparing Decimals

Remember that when you compare numbers, you start with their greatest place values.

Compare 7.77 and 7.82. First, compare the ones: 7 = 7. Next, compare the tenths: 0.7 < 0.8. Therefore, you know that 7.77 < 7.82.

Compare 7.77 and 7.7. Remember that you can write 7.7 as 7.70. Then you can compare 7.77 and 7.70. Compare the ones: 7 = 7. Compare the tenths: 0.7 = 0.7. Compare the hundredths: 0.07 > 0.00. So, you know that 7.77 > 7.7.

Remember that you can add zeros to the end of decimals without changing their value. Practice comparing decimals in problems like these: Is 8.09 greater than 8.092? Is 5.12 less than 5.102?

Comparing Decimals and Fractions

You can also compare decimals and fractions. For example, compare $1\frac{7}{10}$ and 1.15. First, rewrite the mixed number $1\frac{7}{10}$ as a decimal: 1.7. Now, compare 1.7 and 1.15. Compare the ones: 1 = 1. Compare the tenths: 0.7 > 0.1. So, 1.70 > 1.15.

Is $\frac{1}{4}$ greater than 0.27? Hint: Convert $\frac{1}{4}$ to a decimal and compare the hundredths.

Reading Decimals on a Number Line

We can show decimals on a number line.

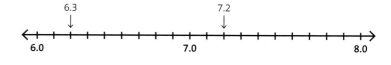

On this number line, each mark shows one tenth. The first arrow is at 6.3, three tenths past 6. The second arrow is at 7.2, two tenths past 7. You can see from the number line that 7.2 > 6.3.

> **Do It Yourself**
>
> Make your own number line with several whole numbers on it. Write several decimals for your child to place on the number line, with your guidance.

Adding and Subtracting Decimals

You add and subtract decimals the same way that you add and subtract whole numbers. Just make sure the decimal points and place values are lined up correctly. Line up the tenths with the tenths, the hundredths with the hundredths, and the thousandths with the thousandths. Make sure to put the decimal point in the right spot in your answer.

Add 0.167 and 2.346.   Subtract 1.846 from 5,072.

$$\begin{array}{r} 0.167 \\ +2.346 \\ \hline 2.513 \end{array} \qquad \begin{array}{r} \overset{4\ \ 10\ 6\ 12}{5.0\cancel{7}2} \\ -1.846 \\ \hline 3.226 \end{array}$$

Sometimes when you are adding decimals, putting in zeros helps you line up the place values correctly. It is not necessary to add zeros, however, as long as you can keep the place values straight.

Add 9.307 + 8 + 0.53 + 6.2.

One way is to put in
decimal points and zeros.

$$
\begin{array}{r}
9.307 \\
8.000 \\
0.530 \\
+6.200 \\
\hline
24.037
\end{array}
$$

Another way is to leave
the numbers as they are.

$$
\begin{array}{r}
9.307 \\
8 \\
0.53 \\
+6.2 \\
\hline
24.037
\end{array}
$$

When you subtract decimals, you will often have to put in zeros. Here is an example. When you subtract 2.63 from 5, you must write 5 with a decimal point and two zeros, to match 2.63. Then subtract.

$$
\begin{array}{r}
\overset{4\ \ 9\ 10}{5.00} \\
-2.63 \\
\hline
2.37
\end{array}
$$

Making Change

· ·

We express dollars and cents using decimals. We write "three dollars and forty-five cents" like this:

$$\$3.45$$

Suppose you are selling popcorn to raise money for your favorite club. Each box of popcorn costs $2.75. A man gives you $5.00 for one box. How much change should you give him? Line up the decimal points and do the subtraction:

$$\begin{array}{r} \$5.00 \\ -2.75 \\ \hline \$2.25 \end{array}$$

You should give the customer two 1-dollar bills and 25 cents in change. The change might be a quarter, or two dimes and a nickel, or even 25 pennies.

Measurement

Measuring Length in U.S. Customary Units

In the United States, people generally measure length using U.S. customary units. The basic units for length in this system are inches, feet, yards, and miles. The following chart shows you the U.S. customary units and their abbreviations. It also shows some equivalences among the units. An equivalence shows that two measurements that appear different actually have equal values.

1 foot (ft.) = 12 inches (in.)
1 yard (yd.) = 3 feet
1 mile (mi.) = 5,280 feet
1 mile = 1,760 yards

A ruler often measures 1 foot. To help you measure lengths more quickly, many rulers have lines that mark the inches and fractions of an inch. The longest lines on the ruler on the next page mark the inches. The next-longest lines mark intervals of half $(\frac{1}{2})$ an inch. The lines marking each quarter $(\frac{1}{4})$ of an inch are a bit shorter, and the lines for the eighths $(\frac{1}{8})$ are even shorter. The shortest marks on many rulers mark sixteenths $(\frac{1}{16})$ of an inch. Notice that only the inches are labeled. You have to be able to recognize the halves, quarters, and eighths. See if you can measure the nail that sits next to the ruler.

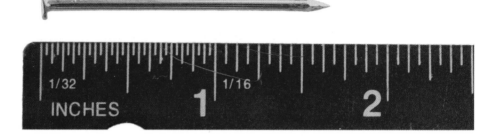

When measuring the length of a real object, we often estimate to the nearest unit. Look at the nail in the picture.

To the nearest inch, the nail is 2 inches.
To the nearest half inch, the nail is $1\frac{1}{2}$ inches.
To the nearest quarter inch, the nail is $1\frac{3}{4}$ inches.
To the nearest eighth inch, the nail is $1\frac{5}{8}$ inches.

The smaller the unit of measure, the more precise your measurement of the length of the nail will be. Find some small items and measure them to the nearest eighth of an inch using a ruler of your own.

It's also important to practice converting from one unit to another. For instance, you should be able to figure out the number of feet in one-half of a mile. You know from the table of equivalences that 1 mile equals 5,280 feet. To find $\frac{1}{2}$ any number, you divide it by 2. Because $5,280 \div 2 = 2,640$, a half mile equals 2,640 feet.

You should memorize the equivalences listed in this book. Once you have done so, you will be able to switch from one unit to another without having to look at a table.

Measuring Length in Metric Units

Not everyone in the world uses the U.S. customary units of measurement. In fact, most people in other countries use a different system of measurement called the metric system. Some important metric units for measuring length are shown below:

1 centimeter (cm) = 10 millimeters (mm)
1 meter (m) = 1,000 millimeters
1 meter = 100 centimeters
1 kilometer (km) = 1,000 meters

A meter is a little longer than a yard. A meterstick is typically divided into centimeters and millimeters. Can you measure the paper clip below?

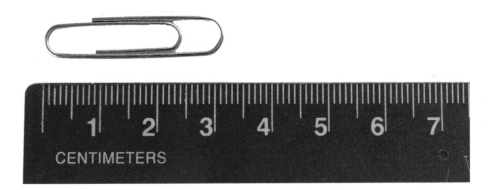

The paper clip is about 3.2 centimeters or 32 millimeters long. Take the small objects you gathered when you were measuring inches and measure them to the nearest tenth of a centimeter (the nearest millimeter).

Because the metric system is based on the decimal system, it is easy to change from one metric unit to another. The process is similar to working with place value. Here are two examples:

1. How many meters are there in 3 kilometers? Because 1 km = 1,000 m, multiply by 1,000 to change kilometers to meters. 3 × 1,000 = 3,000, so 3 km = 3,000 m.
2. How many meters are there in 400 centimeters? Because 100 cm = 1 m, you divide by 100 to change centimeters to meters. 400 ÷ 100 = 4, so 400 cm = 4 m.

Measuring Weight in U.S. Customary Units

In the United States, people measure weight using ounces, pounds, and tons.

$$1 \text{ pound (lb.)} = 16 \text{ ounces (oz.)}$$
$$2,000 \text{ pounds} = 1 \text{ ton (tn.)}$$

When a baby is born, we usually describe its weight in pounds and ounces, such as "8 pounds, 3 ounces." When a child gets older and bigger, we usually express his or her weight in pounds, estimating to the nearest pound. We might use tons if we were measuring the weight that a truck or airplane can transport.

If you have a bathroom scale in your house, you can practice weighing household items in pounds. First, weigh yourself. Then, weigh yourself holding the object. The difference between what you weigh holding the object and what you weigh by yourself is the weight of the object itself.

Practice converting from pounds to ounces and ounces to pounds. How many ounces are in 8 pounds, 3 ounces? To solve this problem, find out how many ounces are in 8 pounds, and then add 3 ounces. From the table of equivalences, you know that 1 pound = 16 ounces. So 8 pounds would be 8 × 16 ounces.

$$8 \text{ lb. } 3 \text{ oz.} = (16 \times 8) \text{ oz.} + 3 \text{ oz.}$$
$$= 128 \text{ oz.} + 3 \text{ oz.}$$
$$= 131 \text{ oz.}$$

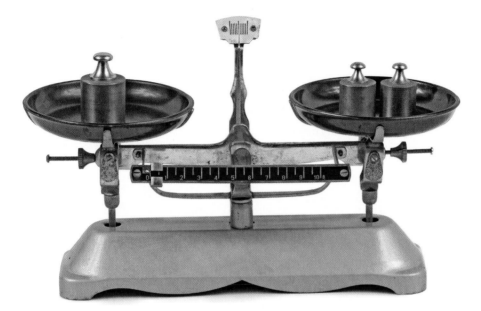

Measuring Weight in Metric Units

The main units for weight in the metric system are the milligram, the gram, and the kilogram. Here are some equivalences:

1 kilogram (kg) = 1,000 grams (g)
1 gram (g) = 1,000 milligrams (mg)
1 kilogram = 1,000,000 milligrams

What About You?
Ask your child to think about a time when she had to use units of measurement like those shown on this page.

Notice again how the metric system is based on the decimal system, with each unit 10, 100, or 1,000 times larger than another unit. There are 1,000 grams in a kilogram. You could also say that one gram equals $\frac{1}{1,000}$ of a kilogram.

If 1 egg weighs 84 grams, how much would a dozen eggs weigh? To find the answer, you multiply 84 times 12 (or one dozen). 84 × 12 = 1,008 grams. You could also express this answer as "1 kilogram, 8 grams."

Measuring Capacity in U.S. Customary Units

When cooks prepare food, they use measuring cups with different sizes. They use cups for 1 cup, $\frac{1}{2}$ cup, $\frac{1}{3}$ cup, and $\frac{1}{4}$ cup. When you buy milk or juice, you often buy a pint, a quart, or a gallon. All of these measurements tell how much liquid is inside.

Here are the equivalences for the U.S. customary measurements of capacity, also known as volume:

1 cup (c.) = 8 fluid ounces (fl. oz.)
1 pint (pt.) = 2 cups
1 quart (qt.) = 2 pints
1 gallon (gal) = 4 quarts

How many ounces of milk are in the measuring cup shown? How many cups?

Measuring Capacity in Metric Units

As with the other measurements, the metric system uses different units for capacity. The basic units are liters and milliliters:

1 liter (l) = 1,000 milliliters (ml)

If you had a 1-liter can of oil and you poured half of it into your car's engine, how many milliliters would be left?

Getting to Know the Metric System

Many foreign countries and most scientific research use the metric system. U.S. scientists and researchers have also started using this international system more and more. This is why it's beneficial to have a good sense of the metric units.

For instance, it will be helpful for you to know that a meter is a little longer than a yard, 100 kilometers is about the same distance as 60 miles, and a small bag of chips weighs about 40 grams.

Adding and Subtracting with Different Units

When you add or subtract lengths that are in different U.S. customary units, you need to regroup in different ways, unlike the decimal system.

Add the inches first.

Regroup 15 in. as 1 ft. 3 in.

$$
\begin{array}{lr}
\overset{1}{3}\text{ ft.} & 7\text{ in.} \\
+2\text{ ft.} & 8\text{ in.} \\
\hline
 & 15 \\
6\text{ ft.} & 3\text{ in.}
\end{array}
$$

You cannot take 9 in. from 4 in.

Regroup 21 ft. 4 in. as 20 ft. 16 in.

$$
\begin{array}{rr}
\overset{20}{\cancel{21}} \text{ ft.} & \overset{16}{\cancel{4}} \text{ in.} \\
-15 \text{ ft.} & 9 \text{ in.} \\
\hline
5 \text{ ft.} & 7 \text{ in.}
\end{array}
$$

You can also regroup in the same way to add and subtract feet, yards, or miles.

When you add metric measurements, you write the measurements in the same unit first. To add 2.68 liters and 27 milliliters, you can write both measurements in either liters or milliliters.

27 ml = 0.027 l   or   2.68 l = 2,680 ml

$$
\begin{array}{r}
\overset{1}{2.68} \text{ l} \\
+0.027 \text{ l} \\
\hline
2.707 \text{ l}
\end{array}
\qquad \text{or} \qquad
\begin{array}{r}
\overset{1}{2680} \text{ ml} \\
+ \quad 27 \text{ ml} \\
\hline
2707 \text{ ml}
\end{array}
$$

Always write metric measurements in a single unit before you add them.

Changing Units of Time

There are 24 hours in a day, 60 minutes in an hour, and 60 seconds in a minute. So how many minutes are there in 5 hours and 11 minutes? To find out the answer to this question, multiply 5 by 60 to find out how many minutes are in 5 hours. Then add 11 minutes. $(5 \times 60) + 11 = 300 + 11 = 311$. There are 311 minutes in 5 hours and 11 minutes.

How many minutes and seconds are there in 147 seconds?

Adding and Subtracting Time

When you add and subtract time, you may need to regroup, but in a different way from the U.S. customary units. Instead of regrouping so that 10 ones make 1 ten, when you add hours and minutes, regroup 60 minutes as 1 hour whenever there are 60 minutes or more.

What About You?

Ask your child to calculate the number of minutes in his school day.

Here is an example of adding two times: A train journey lasts 7 hours and 45 minutes. If the train leaves at 1:43 p.m., when will it arrive at its destination?

You add:
    hours   minutes

$$
\begin{array}{rcl}
1 & & \\
1 & : & 43 \\
+7 & : & 45 \\
\hline
& & 88 \\
9 & : & 28 \\
\end{array}
$$

88 minutes = 1 hour 28 minutes
Add the 1 hour to the other hours.

The train will arrive at 9:28 p.m.

You add or subtract minutes and seconds in the same way. When you subtract minutes and seconds, you may need to regroup 1 minute as 60 seconds.

Emily ran a race in 37 minutes and 22 seconds. Stella ran it in 28 minutes and 47 seconds. What is the difference between their two times in minutes and seconds?

Geometry

Planes, Points, and Segments

A plane is a flat surface that keeps going on forever in all directions. It has no thickness, only length and width. Here's a diagram of a plane.

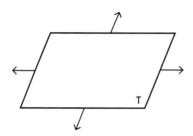

This plane, labeled T, stretches in all four directions.

Plane geometry is the study of points, lines, segments, and figures that can be drawn on a plane. Let's learn about some of these geometrical shapes.

Take a pencil and make the tiniest dot you can. In geometry, a single dot like that is called a point.

Now draw a second point and connect the two points with a ruler. This straight distance between two points is called a line segment, or just a segment.

A point is named with a single letter, and a segment is named with a pair of letters that have a line above them. The two points in the illustration below are

G and H. The segment could be called either $\overline{GH}$ or $\overline{HG}$. The bar line over the name tells us this pair of letters identifies a segment.

Lines and Rays

What's the difference between a line and a line segment? A segment has a beginning and an ending point. A line goes on forever in both directions—in other words, a line has no beginning or end.

Because it is not possible to draw a line that goes on forever, we draw arrows on both ends of a line to show that it keeps going in both directions. A line can be named for any two points along the line. This is line BE, or $\overleftarrow{BE}$.

Vertical lines run straight up and down, while horizontal lines run side to side like $\overleftarrow{BE}$. You can remember the difference by thinking horizontal lines follow the horizon from side to side.

A ray is part of a line. It has one end point and continues forever in only one direction—away from its end point. To name a ray, begin with the letter for its end point and add another point along the ray, using a bar line with one arrow. This is ray EF, or $\overleftarrow{EF}$:

Angles

An angle is formed by two rays that have the same end point. The end point is called the vertex of the angle. Here is angle WXY.

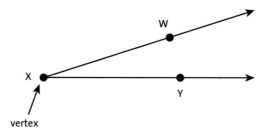

Point X is the vertex of angle WXY. When you name an angle, you always put the vertex in the middle. You can begin with either point along the rays, so this angle could also be called YXW. The word "angle" is sometimes abbreviated using a symbol like this: ∠YXW.

Make a Connection
Ask your child to look through the Visual Arts chapter to find examples of different kinds of angles in the photos.

Types of Angles

There are three kinds of angles: right angles, acute angles, and obtuse angles. Here's what they look like:

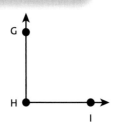

A right angle forms a square corner. ∠GHI is a right angle.

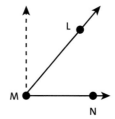

An acute angle is less than a right angle. ∠LMN is an acute angle.

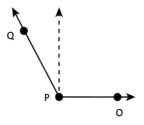

An obtuse angle is greater than a right angle. ∠QPO is an obtuse angle.

Look around you for examples of angles. What kind of angle does the corner of a windowpane form? How about the corner of a slice of pie?

Intersecting, Perpendicular, and Parallel Lines

When two lines meet, we say they intersect. Here are two intersecting lines. $\overleftrightarrow{AB}$ and $\overleftrightarrow{CD}$ intersect at point G.

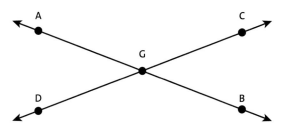

When two lines intersect to form right angles, we say they are perpendicular. $\overleftrightarrow{HI}$ and $\overleftrightarrow{JK}$ below are perpendicular lines. Where they meet, they form four right angles. $\overleftrightarrow{AB}$ and $\overleftrightarrow{CD}$ above are not perpendicular.

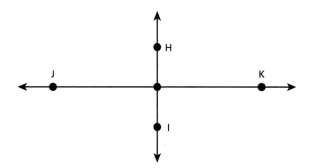

Parallel lines are lines that never intersect. $\overleftrightarrow{LM}$ and $\overleftrightarrow{NP}$ are parallel lines.

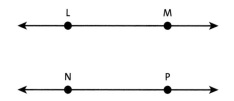

Polygons, Triangles

A polygon is a closed plane figure with three or more line segments as its sides. Polygons also have three or more angles inside them. In fact, the word "polygon" comes from a Greek word meaning "many angles."

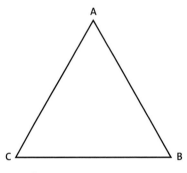

Triangle ABC

Polygons with three sides are called triangles. The prefix "tri-" means "three." All triangles have three sides and three angles. They also have three vertices, or points where the sides of a triangle meet.

The vertices of triangle ABC are points A, B, and C. We name polygons by their vertices. Triangles that have three sides of the same length are called equilateral triangles. Because their sides are all of equal length, their angles will all be equal, too. Triangle ABC is an equilateral triangle.

Quadrilaterals and Diagonals

Quadrilaterals are polygons with four sides. The prefix "quadri-" means "four," and the word "lateral" means "side." The figures below are quadrilaterals.

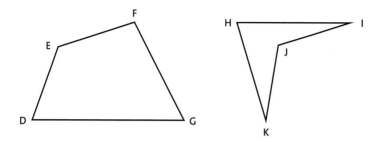

In a quadrilateral, the vertices that are not connected by a side are called opposite vertices. The line segment that joins two opposite vertices of a quadrilateral is called a diagonal.

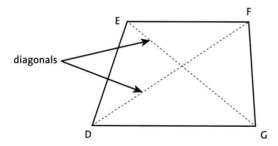

D and F are opposite vertices. G and E are also opposite vertices.

$\overline{DF}$ and $\overline{EG}$ are the diagonals of quadrilateral DEFG. Remember that you name polygons by their vertices.

Kinds of Quadrilaterals

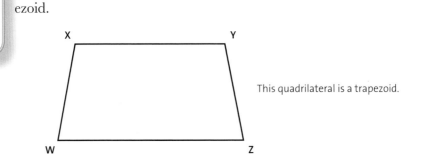

Do It Yourself

Ask your child to draw a number of different closed quadrilateral shapes using a ruler.

A quadrilateral with only one pair of parallel sides is called a trapezoid.

This quadrilateral is a trapezoid.

Quadrilateral WXYZ is a trapezoid. A line that includes segment $\overline{XY}$ is parallel with a line that includes segment $\overline{WZ}$, so we say these two sides are parallel.

A quadrilateral with two pairs of parallel sides is a parallelogram.

In a quadrilateral, sides that do not meet at a vertex are called opposite sides.

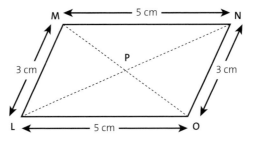

Quadrilateral LMNO is a parallelogram. $\overline{MN}$ is parallel to $\overline{LO}$. $\overline{ML}$ is parallel to $\overline{NO}$.

The opposite sides of a parallelogram are always parallel: Sides $\overline{MN}$ and $\overline{LO}$ are parallel; sides $\overline{ML}$ and $\overline{NO}$ are also parallel. Opposite sides of a parallelogram also have the same lengths: $\overline{MN}$ and $\overline{LO}$ are both 5 centimeters; $\overline{ML}$ and $\overline{NO}$ are both 3 centimeters.

Rectangles and Squares

Rectangles are special kinds of parallelograms. Rectangles are parallelograms with four right angles.

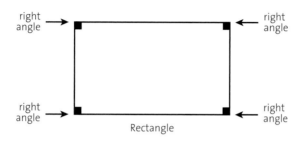

Rectangle

Rectangles can have two sides measuring one length and two sides measuring a different length. However, if all four sides have the same length, we call this special type of rectangle a square.

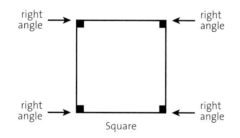

Square

Other Polygons

A polygon with five sides is called a pentagon. A polygon with six sides is called a hexagon. A polygon with eight sides is called an octagon. Here is an example of each one:

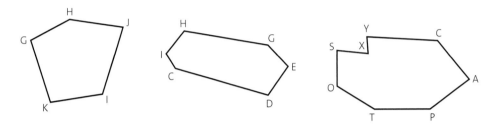

A regular polygon has sides of equal length and angles of equal measure. The pentagon, hexagon, and octagon below are regular polygons.

a pentagon   a hexagon   an octagon

What well-known traffic sign is shaped like a regular octagon? Hint: Usually it's red.

Circles

A circle is a closed plane figure but not a polygon. Polygons have line segments for sides. A circle curves in such a way that every point along the circle is exactly the same distance from the center of the circle.

A line segment with an end point at the center of a circle and another end point on the circle is called a radius. "Radius" is a Latin word, and the plural is "radii" [RAY-dee-eye]. $\overline{DR}$, $\overline{DS}$, and $\overline{DT}$ are radii of the circle at right. Because all radii of a circle have the same length, we also use the term "radius" to refer to the length of any radius of a circle.

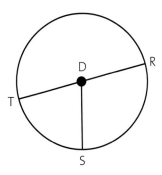

On this circle with center D, you can see three segments of equal length: $\overline{DR}$, $\overline{DS}$, and $\overline{DT}$.

A line segment that passes through the center of a circle with end points on the circle is called a diameter. $\overline{RT}$ is a diameter of the circle at right. All the diameters of a circle have the same length. The diameter of a circle is always twice as long as its radius.

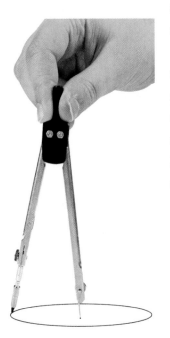

With a compass, practice drawing circles with a certain radius or a certain diameter. To do this, make a dot for the center of the circle you want to draw, and open the compass to the length of the radius of the circle. Put the point of the compass on the dot you drew. Keeping the point still, swing the arm of the compass around until it draws a circle.

Do It Yourself

Ask your child to attempt to make a perfect circle without using any instruments. It's very difficult, if not impossible!

Similar Figures

Congruent figures have both the same shape and same size. We say two figures are similar when they have the same shape but not necessarily the same size. When two figures have the same shape and size, they are both similar and congruent. All congruent figures are similar, but not all similar figures are congruent.

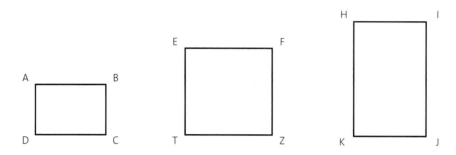

For example, rectangles ABCD and HIJK are similar. Though they have different sizes, they have the same shape. Rectangles ABCD and EFZT are not similar. They do not have the same shape.

All squares and all circles are similar, because they all have the same shape, no matter what size they are.

Talk and Think

Ask your child to think of a situation in which she might have to calculate the area of an object.

The Area of a Rectangle

The length and width of a rectangle are called its dimensions. A rectangle has two dimensions. The length of a rectangle is the length of either of its two longer sides. The width of a rectangle is the length of either of its two shorter sides.

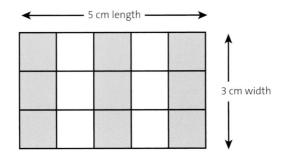

There are 5 × 3 square centimeters in this rectangle. You can find the area of a rectangle by multiplying its length by its width. This rectangle's area is 15 centimeters².

Here is the formula for the area of a rectangle. A formula is an equation written with letters that tells you a relationship that is always true. In this formula, A stands for the area of a rectangle, l for its length, and w for its width.

$$A = l \times w \qquad \text{or} \qquad \text{area} = \text{length} \times \text{width}$$

You can always find the area of a rectangle by substituting real numbers for l and w and then multiplying the rectangle's length by its width. This is one of many useful formulas in mathematics, especially for geometry.

Square Units

You always measure area in square units.

Some U.S. Customary units of area:	Some metric units of area:
mi.² (square mile)	km² (square kilometer)
yd.² (square yard)	m² (square meter)
ft.² (square foot)	cm² (square centimeter)
in.² (square inch)	mm² (square millimeter)

1. What is the area of a rectangle that is 27 feet long by 24 feet wide? To find the area of a rectangle, you multiply its length by its width. $27 \times 24 = 648$. The area of this rectangle is 648 square feet or 648 ft.^{2}

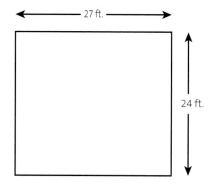

2. How many square inches are there in a square foot? Remember that there are 12 inches in 1 foot.

$$12 \times 12 = 144$$

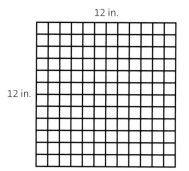

There are 144 in.^{2} (square inches) in 1 ft.^{2} (square foot). Notice that there are not 12 square inches in a square foot, even though there are 12 inches in a foot! Changing units of area is different from changing units of length. You must re-member to take into consideration the width in addition to the length. Now try a few problems with converting units of area: How many mm^2 are there in 1 cm^2? How many ft.^{2} are there in 1 yd.^{2}? How many cm^2 are there in 1 m^2?

3. You know the length of a rectangle (12 cm) and its total area (84 cm²). Find its width.

You know that 12 cm × _____ cm = 84 cm². So, you must divide the area by the length to find the width:

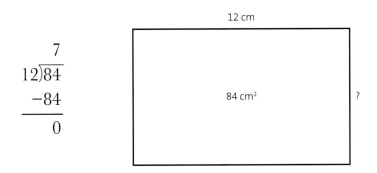

$$\begin{array}{r} 7 \\ 12\overline{)84} \\ -84 \\ \hline 0 \end{array}$$

12 cm

84 cm²   ?

The width is 7 cm.

When you know the measurement of one dimension of a rectangle and its total area, you can divide to find the measurement of the other dimension.

Volume

So far, we've only examined figures with two dimensions. These figures can be drawn on a plane. Now, let's look at three-dimensional figures. A rectangular prism looks like a box. A cylinder looks like a can of soup. A sphere looks like a ball.

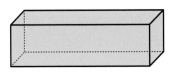

Rectangular prism

Cylinder: two flat circular faces, no vertices

Sphere: no flat surfaces

Notice that every face of the prism is a rectangle. There are six faces on a rectangular prism in all: top and bottom, left and right, and front and back.

The volume of a three-dimensional figure is how much space it occupies. You measure space in cubic units. One example of a cubic unit is a cubic centimeter. The abbreviation for cubic centimeter is cm^3.

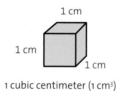

1 cubic centimeter (1 cm³)

Notice that a cubic centimeter is a cube. All cubic units are cubes.

By counting cubic units, you can find the volume of a figure—in other words, how much space it occupies. Sometimes you have to count cubic units that you know exist but cannot see.

You can count the hidden cubic units by thinking about the pattern of those you can see. On one layer of this rectangular prism, there are 8 cubes. There are two layers. $8 \times 2 = 16$. There are 16 cubic centimeters in the rectangular prism.

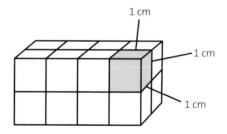

See if you can figure out the volume of the next figure. Notice that there are two sections. The top section is a cube that measures 2 centimeters on each side. The bottom section is a rectangular prism of $4 \times 4 \times 2$ cm. To figure the total volume, you'll have to count the cubic units in each section separately and then add them together.

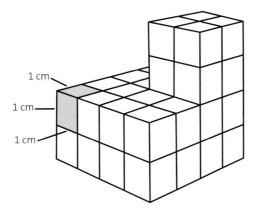

1 cm
1 cm
1 cm

Suggested Resources

A Fraction's Goal—Parts of a Whole, by Brian P. Cleary (First Avenue Editions, 2013)

Fraction Fun, by David A. Adler (Holiday House, 1997)

Fractions, Decimals, and Percents, by David A. Adler (Holiday House, 2010)

How Long or How Wide?, by Brian P. Cleary (First Avenue Editions, 2009)

How Tall, How Short, How Far Away?, by David A. Adler (Holiday House, 2000)

If You Were a Fraction, by Trisha Speed Shaskan (Capstone Press, 2008)

Millions to Measure, by David M. Schwartz (HarperCollins, 2006)

Multiplying Menace: The Revenge of Rumpelstiltskin, by Pam Calvert (Charlesbridge, 2006)

Perimeter, Area, and Volume: A Monster Book of Dimensions, by David A. Adler (Holiday House, 2013)

Shape Up!, by David A. Adler (Holiday House, 2000)

The Action of Subtraction, by Brian P. Cleary (First Avenue Editions, 2008)

The Mission of Addition, by Brian P. Cleary (First Avenue Editions, 2007)

The Multiplying Menace Divides, by Pam Calvert (Charlesbridge, 2011)

Working with Fractions, by David A. Adler (Holiday House, 2009)

VI
Science

Introduction

This chapter treats children to the wonder of the circulatory and respiratory systems, electricity, atoms, chemistry, geology, and meteorology. It also profiles several eminent scientists.

To supplement this chapter, you can take your child to science museums and do simple experiments. Many books of fun, safe experiments are available.

Children should also be encouraged to view the world scientifically: to ask questions about nature and seek answers through observation; to collect, count, and measure; to start a rock collection, monitor weather conditions, or fly a kite to learn about wind.

Hands-on experience is so important that some educators now reject the very idea of teaching young children about science from books. But book learning about science *content* should not be neglected altogether, as it helps bring system and coherence to a young person's developing knowledge of science *concepts* and provides essential building blocks for later study. Book learning also provides knowledge that simple observations will not likely explain; for instance, books can teach us about things that are not visible to the unaided eye, such as white blood cells, subatomic particles, and continental drift. Both kinds of experience are necessary to ensure that gaps in knowledge will not hinder later understanding.

The Human Body

Circulation and Respiration

Put your hand on your chest and feel your heartbeat. Now, take a deep breath and feel the air expanding in your chest. Every time your heart beats, blood pumps through a network of blood vessels, from the heart to all the parts of your body. Every time you breathe in, air flows down your windpipe and fills your lungs. Oxygen in that air travels from your lungs into your bloodstream, ready to feed the cells in your body.

The heart and the blood vessels are parts of your body's circulatory system. The lungs and windpipe are parts of your respiratory system. These two systems work together to keep you alive. To understand them, though, let's study them separately.

The Heart

The heart is a powerful muscle. It works every second of every day, from the moment you are born until the day you die. Most of the time, you don't even know it is working. But if you sprint up some stairs, you can feel it working harder, thump-thump-thumping as it pumps blood through your body.

Your heart is about the size of your fist. It is divided into four chambers. The top two chambers are called the atriums; the bot-

> **What About You?**
> Have your child make a fist with her hand so that she can see the approximate size of her heart.

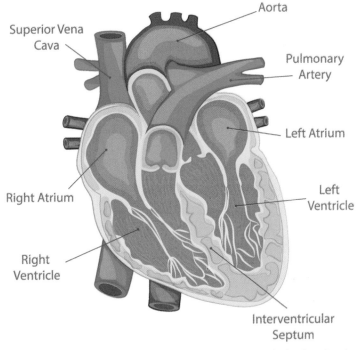

Aorta

Superior Vena Cava

Pulmonary Artery

Left Atrium

Right Atrium

Left Ventricle

Right Ventricle

Interventricular Septum

This drawing shows the heart cut in half so you can see inside the four chambers.

tom two are called the ventricles. Valves in between the ventricles and atriums open and close to allow the blood to flow through the heart.

Blood needing oxygen comes into the heart through the right atrium. It squeezes through a valve and into the right ventricle. From there, it flows out to the lungs for a new supply of oxygen. From the lungs, it flows back into the left atrium of the heart, squeezes through a valve into the left ventricle, and then is pumped out of the heart through the aorta, the biggest blood vessel of all. The aorta divides and branches out to take the blood to all the different parts of the body.

The Blood Vessels

The heart pumps blood through your body in hollow, stretchy tubes called blood vessels. The blood vessels that carry the oxygen-rich blood away from your heart are called arteries. The blood vessels that carry blood back to your heart for more oxygen are called veins.

Smaller blood vessels, called capillaries, branch off from arteries and veins. The tiny capillaries bring blood in contact with the cells in the body. Capillary walls are so thin that nutrients, oxygen, and waste products pass back and forth through them easily. Capillaries connect arteries and veins. They are the end points of arteries, through which oxygen and nutrients are delivered, and the starting points of veins, which pick up and carry waste materials away.

If you look in the mirror and gently pull down your lower eyelid, you can see some capillaries. See those tiny red squiggles on your eyeball? Those are capillaries.

Blood Pressure and Heart Rate

Each time the heart pumps, the stretchy blood vessels swell and shrink as the blood courses through them. The pumping heart causes a pushing force that moves blood through the

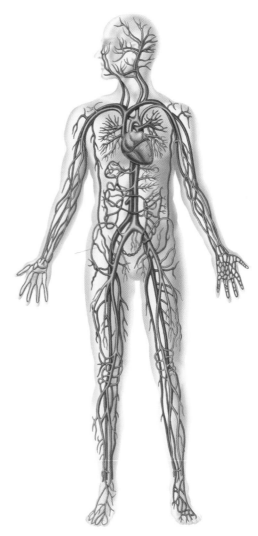

This diagram shows the circulatory system. Arteries are shown in red, and veins are shown in purple.

body. This force is called blood pressure. Blood pressure is one of the things that nurses and doctors check to make sure your circulatory system is working properly.

A doctor taking a girl's blood pressure

Your pulse, or heart rate, indicates how often your heart squeezes to pump blood through your body. To measure your heart rate, press your fingertips on the pulse point on your wrist. Use a watch with a second hand and count the number of pulses or beats in thirty seconds. The average human heart rate is about ninety pulses a minute, so you will probably count about forty-five beats in half a minute.

But what happens to your heart rate when you exercise? Hop on one leg ten times, and then wave your arms over your head ten times. Then measure your heart rate again. When you exercise, your cells use lots of oxygen and soon need more. That's why exercise makes you breathe harder and makes your heart pump faster.

Talk and Think
Ask your child if he has ever had his blood pressure taken. If so, does he know what the resulting numbers mean? A blood pressure measurement consists of two numbers: for example, 120/80, read as "120 over 80."
• The first number records systolic pressure: the force of blood on the arteries each time the heart beats.
• The second number records diastolic pressure: the force of blood on the arteries when the heart relaxes between beats.

What Is Blood and Why Do We Need It?

Blood never stops moving through your body. It delivers nutrients from food and oxygen to the cells in organs, muscles, bones, and nerves. It picks up waste materials from the cells in your body and carries that waste to organs that can process it. Cells give off a gas called carbon dioxide, which blood carries back to the lungs. When you breathe out, you release carbon dioxide.

If you look at blood under a microscope, you can see tiny objects of several different shapes, all floating in a thin, clear liquid. The liquid part of the blood is called the plasma. The most common shapes you would see floating in the

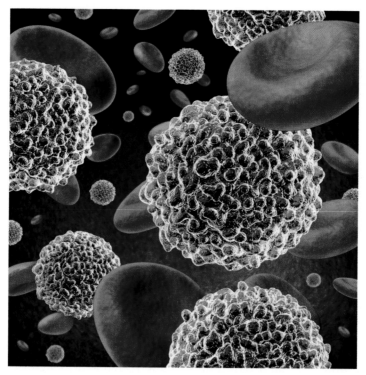

This image of red and white blood cells shows them as they would appear under a microscope—magnified to many times their real size. The red blood cells look like doughnuts with the centers not quite punched out. The round cells with the bumpy surfaces are white blood cells.

plasma are the red blood cells. There are more than twenty-five trillion—that's 25,000,000,000,000—red blood cells in one person's body. Red blood cells contain a substance called hemoglobin. It's the hemoglobin that does the work of carrying oxygen and carbon dioxide.

Looking through the microscope, you would also see white blood cells. White blood cells are like a special forces team that travels in the blood, ready to fight disease at a moment's notice. When an infection develops, white blood cells attack.

If you have ever had a cut, then you've seen platelets in action. Platelets are tiny solids in the blood. Their job is to help stop bleeding. Platelets make blood coagulate, or get thicker, so a scab develops, protecting the wound while it heals.

Cleaning the Blood

Because your red blood cells work hard, they last only for about four months before they die and are replaced by new ones. Red blood cells die at a rate of eight million a second! That means a lot of dead red blood cells are floating in your blood right now.

Removing those dead blood cells is one of the jobs of the liver, your body's largest internal organ. (Your body's largest organ is your skin.) The liver breaks down dead cells and reuses what it can as nutrients. The spleen, another cleansing organ, helps filter your blood and remove harmful wastes.

Understanding and Preserving Your Heart

For a long time, people did not know that the heart pumps blood in a circuit through the body. One of the men who helped us understand this was an English doctor named William Harvey (1578–1657).

Harvey suggested that the heart was at the center of a blood-circulating system. For a while, no one believed him. A few years later, though, the newly invented microscope was used to investigate his claim. Through the microscope, doctors watched blood flowing in the tail of a live fish and realized Harvey had been right.

Jogging is a good way to keep your heart healthy.

Today we know much more about the circulatory system and how to keep it healthy. For example, we understand that exercising makes your heart muscle grow stronger and can help you live longer.

Eating smart is another key to a healthy heart. If you eat more fat than your body can use, it may build up on the inside of blood vessels like crud in an old sink pipe. Then less blood flows through and less oxygen gets to the fingers and toes, brain, and heart. When the heart does not receive enough oxygen, heart muscle cells die. The result is called a heart attack.

What's Your Blood Type?

In 1900, an Austrian doctor named Karl Landsteiner discovered that not everyone has the same type of blood. For years, doctors had been trying to perform transfusions—that is, giving badly injured people blood from another person. It seemed like a good idea, but the patients often died.

Dr. Landsteiner noticed that when he mixed blood from two different people in a lab, the blood cells would often clump together and clot. After many experiments, Dr. Landsteiner concluded that there were several different groups of blood: group A, group B, and group O. His colleagues later identified a fourth: group AB. Additionally, each blood group contains two types: positive and negative. Therefore, there are eight different blood types. One type of blood may not flow well in the veins of a person with a different type of blood. As a result of Dr. Landsteiner's work, doctors understand that people donating and receiving blood have to have compatible blood types.

The Lungs

You breathe in and out more than twenty thousand times a day. Each time, you replenish the oxygen in your body's systems and release carbon dioxide that your body cannot use. Your lungs and respiratory system work together with your heart and circulatory system to keep you healthy and keep your cells alive.

What About You?

Ask your child if she knows her blood type, and if not, tell her. Ask her to explain why it is important to know one's blood type. Point out that people with group O blood are "universal donors" because they can donate blood to anyone: group O blood flows well in everyone's veins. In contrast, people with group AB blood are "universal receivers" because they can receive blood from anyone, though they can donate blood only to other people in group AB.

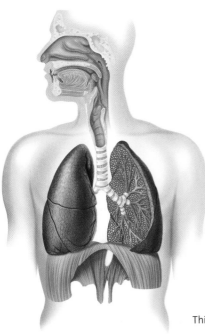

Inside your chest, on either side of your heart, are two inflatable sacs called lungs. They are like warm, wet sponges inside. They expand and contract as your breathing fills them with air and then pushes the air out again. Take a deep breath and imagine the air filling those two warm, wet sacs inside your chest.

As you take a breath, air flows through your nose or mouth and travels down the windpipe, or trachea [TRAY-kee-ah]. The air moves past the voice box and into tubes inside your lungs called bronchi [BRON-kye]. Bron-

This diagram shows the respiratory system.

chi branch into smaller and smaller tubes. At the very ends of the tiniest bronchi are air sacs called alveoli [al-VEE-oh-lye]. These alveoli contain tiny capillaries where the respiratory and the circulatory systems meet. Hemoglobin in red blood cells absorbs the oxygen from the breath you took and carries it to all the cells in your body.

The process happens in reverse, too. As blood circulates through your body, it picks up carbon dioxide, which is of no use to your body. When the red blood cells carrying the carbon dioxide reach the capillaries in the alveoli, they unload the waste products into the lungs. When you breathe out, you get rid of the unneeded gas.

Breathing in and out happens because of the diaphragm [DIE-uh-fram], which is a stretchy sheet of muscle underneath your lungs. When the diaphragm arches down, it opens up space in your lungs, and air rushes in to fill them. When the diaphragm arches up, it pushes the lungs together and forces air out of them through the windpipe.

What About Smoking?

Smoking cigarettes is one of the worst things you can do to your lungs and heart. Every pack of cigarettes carries a warning, like this:

Surgeon General's Warning: Smoking causes lung cancer, heart disease, emphysema, and may complicate pregnancy.

When a person inhales cigarette smoke, four thousand different chemicals invade the lungs. Some of these chemicals are poisons that cause lung cancer. Cigarette smoke also contains sticky black tar. When the nooks and crannies of a smoker's lungs become clogged with tar, the alveoli can become so stiff with goo that they cannot expand and pass oxygen to the blood. With less of their lungs working, smokers cannot exercise without running out of breath. Their hearts pump harder and harder, but less oxygen reaches their cells.

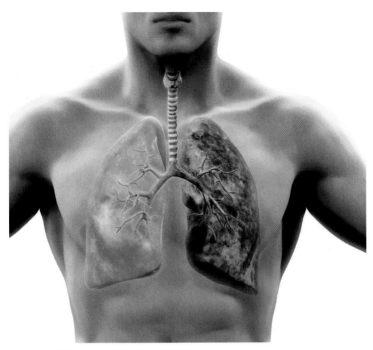

Healthy (left) and unhealthy lungs (right)

Elizabeth Blackwell

Sometimes a person's whole life can change in an instant. Elizabeth Blackwell's life changed one afternoon in 1844 when she was twenty-three. Blackwell went to visit a friend who was dying. The dying woman asked her why she did not think of studying medicine. When Blackwell reminded her friend that there were no women doctors, the woman sighed and said that if she had been treated by a "lady doctor," she might not be dying.

At that time, it was not considered proper for women to talk about or know anything about their

Elizabeth Blackwell

bodies. Elizabeth Blackwell's sick friend had been so ashamed to mention her internal problems to a man that she hid her pain for too long. When she finally sought treatment, it was too late to save her life.

Blackwell couldn't get the dying woman's suggestion out of her mind. She decided to try to become a doctor. She wrote to twenty-nine medical schools asking for admission. Most didn't even reply, and several of the ones that did were very rude. Friends suggested that she dress up as a man to attend medical school, but Blackwell wanted to be accepted for what she was. Finally, a small medical college in upstate New York said yes. Blackwell graduated in 1849 at the head of her class, the first woman in the United States to receive a medical degree.

No American hospital would hire Dr. Blackwell, so she went to work in European hospitals. When she returned to the United States, she opened her own clinic, the New York Infirmary for **Indigent** Women and Children. The clinic's patients were very poor; few had ever seen a doctor before.

Dr. Blackwell worked at her clinic, wrote articles, and made speeches teaching women about nutrition for babies, the need for exercise and clean air, and the importance of cleanliness. Her clinic grew into an institution that included a medical college for women. Over the next ninety years, more than one million patients were treated at the clinic she helped start.

Dr. Blackwell made many sacrifices. She even lost an eye from infection after caring for a sick baby. Nevertheless, she remained determined to teach women to care for their bodies and those of their children. She was also determined to open new career opportunities for other women. Today, almost three hundred thousand women doctors in the United States follow in her footsteps.

> **New Word**
>
> The word **indigent** describes people who are very poor. Ask your child why Dr. Blackwell might have chosen to work with indigent women and children, and what challenges she might have faced at her clinic.

Charles Drew

Charles Drew was born in Washington, D.C., in 1904. When Drew was fifteen, his sister died of tuberculosis. As he watched her condition deteriorate, Drew wished he could do something to help. It was then that he first thought about the possibility of becoming a doctor.

Charles Drew treating an air raid victim

There was only one problem with this idea: Drew was African American. In those days, much of American society was segregated, or separated, along racial lines: black people and white people went to different schools and could not sit together in restaurants or on buses. Only a handful of colleges would accept African American students—and medical school would be another hurdle beyond college. But Charles Drew managed to succeed against the odds.

In high school, Drew was a strong student and an outstanding athlete. Eventually, he was offered a scholarship to Amherst College. At Amherst, Drew was a star quarterback, the most valuable player on the baseball team, the captain of the track team, and the national high hurdles champion. He could probably have become a professional athlete, but he remained interested in science and medicine. In 1928, he entered a medical school in Canada and began his lifelong study of blood.

Earlier in this section, you learned a little about blood and the various substances it contains. But much of what we know today was not known in the 1930s and 1940s when Dr. Drew was studying blood. Doctors knew that people who lost a lot of blood could be given new blood in a procedure called a blood transfusion, but it wasn't easy to get a blood transfusion in 1940. There was no way to keep blood fresh or take it to where people might need it. Dr. Drew discovered that if he removed the solid cells (like red blood cells) in blood and kept only the liquid part, called plasma, the blood could be stored for a long time. It could then be used in transfusions whenever and wherever it was needed. After making this discovery, Dr. Drew set up the first blood bank in New York City.

When World War II broke out overseas, many people were wounded and needed blood transfusions. Dr. Drew suggested sending plasma instead of whole blood. He started collecting blood, separating the plasma, and shipping it safely to injured people. His work saved thousands of lives.

In 1941, Dr. Drew became the first director of the blood bank of the American Red Cross. He led efforts to collect blood for our country's soldiers and sailors. But the U.S. Army told the Red Cross to keep blood donated by black people separate from blood donated by whites. Some white people disliked blacks so much that they did not want to get any "black blood," even if it might save their lives. Dr. Drew explained that this was not right because there is no such thing as "black" or "white" blood. Blood is blood. But no one listened. This made Dr. Drew very angry. To make his point, Dr. Drew resigned from the Red Cross in protest. The Red Cross continued to segregate blood on racial grounds through World War II, but civil rights reformers eventually persuaded the organization to stop this racist practice.

After resigning from the Red Cross, Dr. Drew returned to Washington, where he taught medicine at Howard University and became famous as a surgeon. In 1943 he received a special award from the National Association for the Advancement of Colored People (NAACP). He died in 1950 after a tragic car accident.

By using his talents to help other people, Dr. Charles Drew set an example for people of all races. He demonstrated that it is what you achieve in life, not the color of your skin, that shows your true worth as a person.

Chemistry

Cutting a Cube

Have you ever wondered what would happen if you tried to cut something into smaller and smaller pieces? Could you go on doing this forever? Or is there some "smallest" piece, beyond which you cannot go?

Take a look at the big cube below.

Now, imagine using a blade to cut the cube in half along all three directions so that the big cube becomes eight smaller cubes. Next, cut each of the small cubes into eight smaller cubes. How many cubes do you have now? If you said sixty-four, you are correct!

How many rounds of cutting can we do? Eventually, we will have to use a different cutting technique, because our blade will

> ### Make a Connection
> With your child, review the information about volume in the Geometry section of this book (pages 353–355). Then, ask your child which of the three cubes on this page, if any, has the greatest volume. Your child should realize that each cube is divided into a different number of pieces, but all three cubes have the same volume: They take up the same amount of space.

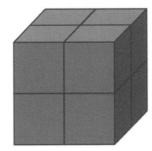

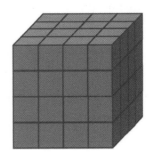

be too thick. But no matter what we do and no matter what the cube is made of, we can only cut it a certain number of times until it cannot be cut again. After that, we will have reached the very smallest piece of the material that still has the properties of that material. This smallest piece is called an atom.

Atoms are extremely small. A human hair has a width of about one hundred thousand atoms! Not all atoms are the same size. For example, an aluminum atom is larger than a helium atom. But even the largest atoms are far too small to see with your eyes.

Do It Yourself

Locate two magnets to demonstrate how magnets repel and attract each other. Before you give the magnets to your child, mark the sides of the magnets that attract each other "A" and the sides that do not attract each other "R." Then, give the magnets to your child. First, have your child put the two sides marked "A" together. Have her explain what happened to the magnets when she put them together. Then, have her attempt to put the sides marked "R" together. Have her explain the reaction of the magnets this time. Explain to her that protons and electrons work in a similar manner.

What Are Atoms Made Of?

As small as atoms are, you might suppose they are the smallest things in the universe. Not really. An atom is simply the smallest part of a material that has the same properties of that material. But atoms themselves are composed of even smaller things!

All atoms, whether helium or aluminum or hydrogen or oxygen, are composed of tiny particles called protons, neutrons, and electrons. Protons and neutrons are tightly packed in the center of the atom, called the nucleus. Electrons are found outside of the nucleus. Protons have positive electric charge (shown by the symbol +), electrons have negative electric charge (−), and neutrons have no charge at all. Just as the north pole of one magnet repels the north pole of another magnet, positive electric charges repel each other. Negative electric charges also repel each other. But just as the north pole of one magnet will attract the south pole of another magnet, positive and negative electric charges attract each other.

Drawing an Atom

Maybe you're wondering what all these parts look like. It would be helpful if we could draw a scientifically accurate picture of atoms. Unfortunately, it is impossible to draw a completely accurate picture of an atom. Any picture we try to draw of an atom shows some characteristics correctly but shows other characteristics incorrectly.

This is one possible way to draw the simplest atom: that of hydrogen. A hydrogen atom has only one proton and one electron. Most hydrogen atoms have no neutrons, though some have one or two neutrons.

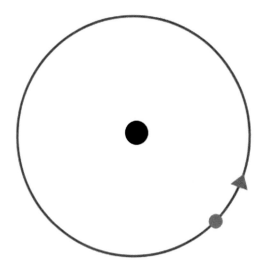

Some things about this drawing are accurate. For example, it shows the proton in the nucleus at the center and the electron moving outside the nucleus. But scientists now realize some things about this picture are incorrect. They have learned that the electron is more like a fuzzy cloud of negative charge that surrounds the nucleus. The electron does not really move around and around the nucleus, and it does not just exist at one particular distance from the nucleus. It can exist at a lot of different distances at the same time—so drawing it like a planet orbiting a star is misleading.

So maybe we should draw a hydrogen atom more like this:

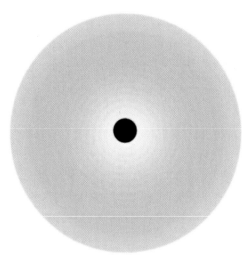

Do you see the trouble we are having? Scientists know the electron is more like a fuzzy cloud, but they also know it obeys certain laws as it moves. In fact, the electron cloud sort of spins. But how do we draw that?

Pictures are still helpful, though. For purposes of this chapter, we will use the simple, not-quite-right picture of electrons in orbit around a nucleus. At least this kind of drawing helps us keep track of the number of particles contained in the atom.

Larger Atoms

Hydrogen is the smallest atom. The second-smallest atom is helium. Helium has two electrons, one more than hydrogen has. How many protons do you think a helium atom has? If you said two, you are correct! This is because all atoms are electrically neutral—which is a way of saying that there are equal numbers of positive and negative charges, and they cancel each other out, just as positive two plus negative two equals zero. Because a helium atom has two electrons (negative charges), it must also have two protons (positive charges) to make all the charges exactly cancel out or equal zero.

The next question is: How many neutrons does a helium atom have? It is not possible to guess how many neutrons an atom has because neutrons have no electrical charge. But through careful experiments, scientists have determined that most (but not all) helium atoms have two neutrons. About one out of every million helium atoms has only one neutron. But all helium atoms have two electrons and two protons.

There are different types of atoms, such as hydrogen and helium, but there are not different types of electrons, protons, and neutrons. Scientists think that all electrons are exactly the same. It doesn't matter whether they come from hydrogen, helium, or any other atom—from atoms on Earth, Mars, or a star in a far-away galaxy. All electrons are identical. And the same is true for protons and neutrons.

Because of this, all atoms of a given type are identical. For example, all "regular" helium atoms (the ones with two neutrons) are identical.

Can We Break Open an Electron?

You might be saying to yourself, "I thought atoms were the smallest thing. But it turns out that they can be broken into electrons, protons, and neutrons. Can these particles be broken into pieces, too?"

That's a good question. At present, scientists think that electrons cannot be broken into anything smaller, but that protons and neutrons can be broken into smaller particles called quarks.

Can quarks be broken into still smaller particles? Scientists don't know. Science is an ongoing discipline, and we don't have all the answers yet.

Different Kinds of Atoms

Atoms are also called elements. Do you remember our definition of an atom as "the smallest particle of a material that has the properties of that material"? Each material is called an element.

This word may be new to you, but the idea isn't. When you see a piece of aluminum foil and ask what it is made of, the answer is "aluminum." Aluminum is an element. Do you know what a soda or juice can is made of? Aluminum. Aluminum foil and aluminum cans are made of the same element. (In reality, most aluminum products that you buy contain tiny amounts of other elements, but we still call them aluminum. A pure element contains atoms of only that element.)

Atoms are labeled as elements according to the number of protons they contain. The diagram on the next page shows a single atom of each of the first six elements. Notice how each atom has one proton more than the previous atom?

These are only the first six elements. Scientists have discovered more than one hundred elements. After carbon, the next two are nitrogen (N) and oxygen (O). Other elements you may know about are copper, silver, gold, and uranium.

Take a Look
With your child, review the periodic table of the elements. You can find many examples available for free online. Have your child identify elements that she recognizes and brainstorm or research things that contain those elements.

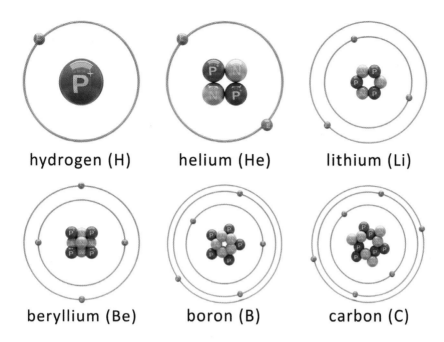

| hydrogen (H) | helium (He) | lithium (Li) |
| beryllium (Be) | boron (B) | carbon (C) |

This chart shows a single atom of each of the first six elements. The red circles stand for protons; notice their positive charges. The blue circles stand for electrons; notice their negative charges. The yellow circles stand for neutrons; notice their lack of charge.

Atoms: Keeping Their Identity

You have learned that all atoms of an element have the same number of protons and electrons. However, an atom may gain or lose electrons without changing its identity. For example, a lithium atom that loses an electron becomes a lithium ion. Because it now has more protons than electrons, the lithium ion has a positive charge. However, lithium atoms and lithium ions are still lithium because each still has three protons. You have also learned that atoms of the same element may have different numbers of neutrons. The most common atoms of lithium have three protons and three neutrons. However, the most common atoms of beryllium have four protons and five neutrons.

Few things are made of only one element. Many are a combination of two or more elements. For example, the smallest particle of water is made of two hydrogen atoms and one oxygen atom. Because it is made of three atoms, two of one element and one of another, we can't call water either an atom or an element. We call this smallest unit of water a molecule because it contains multiple atoms that combine to make up a particle of something new.

There are millions of other substances made of molecules, such as sugar, salt, alcohol, and gasoline. Even odors consist of molecules. When you smell perfume, some of the molecules of the perfume are traveling through the air and into your nose. That's how you smell things! Many substances, like milk, paint, and concrete, are mixtures of different kinds of molecules. Living things are the most complicated of all. Trees, flowers, fish, dogs, and human beings are made up of many different kinds of molecules. And, in living beings, these molecules don't always stay in the same configuration. The molecules in you or in your dog are constantly breaking apart, moving around, and recombining, forming new molecules.

Yet everything we have been talking about here is made of electrons, protons, and neutrons. Take those three basic units and combine them in many, many, many different ways and you get the huge variety of stuff that makes up the universe.

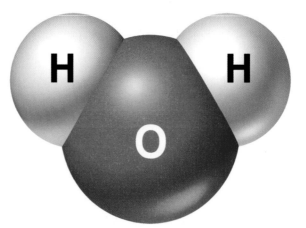

Here's a simple way of drawing a water molecule. This picture shows two small hydrogen atoms, labeled H, attached to a single, larger oxygen atom, labeled O.

Measuring That Stuff

To measure the amount of a substance, scientists use the term "mass." In the metric system, mass is measured in kilograms. For example, a 12-fluid-ounce can of soda has a mass of about 0.38 kilogram. An object's mass is the same everywhere in the universe, as long as it doesn't lose any molecules or pick up any extra ones.

At first, mass might sound like weight, the number you get when you stand on the scales to find out how heavy you are. But weight depends on how much gravity there is, and mass is the same no matter what the gravity. For example, a can of soda will weigh less on the moon than on Earth because there is much less gravity on the moon. But the mass of the can of soda is the same at either location.

A can of soda weighs about one-sixth as much on the moon, even though its mass remains the same.

There is another measurement scientists make to describe the stuff they're studying. They ask how much space an object occupies, and they call their answer volume. In the metric system, volume is often measured in liters. You can measure the volume of a liquid simply by pouring it into a graduated cylinder, but solids can be trickier. There are two common ways to measure the volume of a solid: calculate it with geometry or determine it through a process called water displacement. With geometry, you can measure the height and the area of the base of a soda can and use those numbers to calculate its volume. Or, using water displacement, you can submerge the unopened can in water and measure how much it makes the level of the water rise. Both methods will give you the same answer: The volume of a standard-size can of soda is about 0.375 liter.

If we know both the mass and the volume of an object, we can calculate another measurement important to scientists: density. Density is mass divided by volume. Objects with more density have more mass packed into the same space. For example, pour out the liquid from a soda can and pack it full of rocks. Now the can has the same volume but higher mass and, therefore, higher density.

You can measure the volume of an object by submerging it in water and comparing the water levels before and after the object was added.

Because water is so common on Earth, it is used as the basis for density in the metric system. Liquid water has a density of exactly one kilogram per liter.

But which do you think is denser, liquid water or ice? If you said liquid water, you are correct. When water freezes, the molecules move apart slightly. The mass stays the same, but the volume increases. Because density is mass divided by volume, freezing water makes its density decrease. Ice is a little bit less dense than water. This is why ice cubes float in a glass of water.

Ice floats in liquid water because ice is less dense.

Can there be a volume, or space, in which there is no matter at all, not even air? Yes. It is called a vacuum. You can imagine a vacuum in your mind, but it is rare to find a perfect vacuum in the real world. Even in outer space, a few atoms float around. When a certain space contains many fewer atoms than normal, we can call it a partial vacuum.

Solutions

You may have noticed that oil and water don't mix very well. Even if you shake a bottle containing oil and water, they separate again when you put the bottle down. One way of explaining this is to say that water molecules stick to each other really well, but they don't stick to oil molecules very well.

But what if you put a spoonful of sugar into a glass of water and stir it up? If you stir long enough, the sugar seems to disappear. Unlike oil, sugar molecules blend well with water molecules. Sugar is one of a certain kind of molecule that attracts water molecules well. The water molecules pull apart the sugar molecules, which then mingle in between those water molecules.

When this happens, we say the sugar has dissolved in water. We call this mixture of water and dissolved sugar a solution. We call the water the solvent and the sugar the solute. The sugar is still there, in solution, even though you can't see it!

Of course, you can't go on adding sugar to the solution forever. A solvent (in this case water) can dissolve only a certain amount of a solute (in this case sugar). When the maximum amount of a solute is dissolved in a solvent, we say that the solution is saturated. What do you think will happen if you add more sugar to a saturated solution?

> **Do It Yourself**
> Encourage your child to test her hypothesis by stirring sugar into a small glass of water until no more sugar dissolves. Once the solution is saturated, additional sugar will sink to the bottom of the glass. With your child, try mixing other household materials with water—for example, salt, cornstarch, and baking soda—to see what is soluble and what is not. Test what effect heating the water has on its ability to dissolve each material. Be sure to supervise your child throughout this experiment.

Electricity

Zap!

Someone knocks at the door. You shuffle across the carpet to open it. But when you touch the doorknob, you feel a zap on your fingertip. What's going on?

While unloading the clothes dryer, your sister's socks keep sticking to your pajamas. Why is that?

You're in your bedroom in the dark, and when you take off your sweater, you see tiny sparks. Where did they come from?

Your little sister scoots down a plastic slide at the park, and when she gets to the bottom, her hair is standing on end all over her head. What happened to her hair? Is she just having a bad hair day?

The answer to each of these questions lies in the movement of tiny electrons.

Static Electricity

. . . .

Electrons, as you remember, are the tiny particles that zip around the nucleus of an atom. Electrons have a negative electrical charge, while protons in the nucleus have a positive electrical charge. Attraction between the opposite charges keeps electrons from flying free of the atom, but it doesn't hold them very tightly. When objects rub together, electrons can get knocked loose and go off on their own.

For instance, as clothes tumble together in a dryer, electrons from atoms in some pieces of clothing rub off onto other pieces. Your sister's fuzzy socks might lose electrons while your pajamas pick them up. The socks end up with more protons than electrons, and thus more positive electrical charge than negative electrical charge. The pajamas, on the other hand, end up with more electrons than protons. They become negatively charged. That means the socks and the pajamas develop opposite charges—and, as you've learned already, opposite charges attract each other. That's why the socks and the pajamas cling together in the dryer.

When rubbing, or friction, makes an electrical charge build up, that charge is called static electricity. As you take off your sweater, it rubs against your shirt, picks up extra electrons, and builds up a charge. The sparks you see in the darkness are electrons flowing away in a sudden discharge of static electricity.

The zap you felt from the doorknob is discharged static electricity, too. As you rubbed your feet against the carpet, your body picked up extra electrons, which flowed to the doorknob when you reached for it. In the same way, when your sister scooted down the plastic slide at the park, her body picked up extra electrons. Since each of her hairs had the same charge, they repelled one another. The farthest they can get is by standing on end away from one another. This is why her hair looked that way!

Making Light out of Electrons

When you turn on a light, you are causing electrons to flow through an electric circuit. It all happens instantaneously, with just the flick of a light switch. Let's see what is really happening at the level of the electrons.

Here is an example of a simple circuit, consisting of four parts:

1. a circular copper wire
2. a lightbulb
3. a battery
4. a switch

The battery is the source of energy. It has a positive pole and a negative pole. When the switch is turned on, electrons travel through the wire, mak-

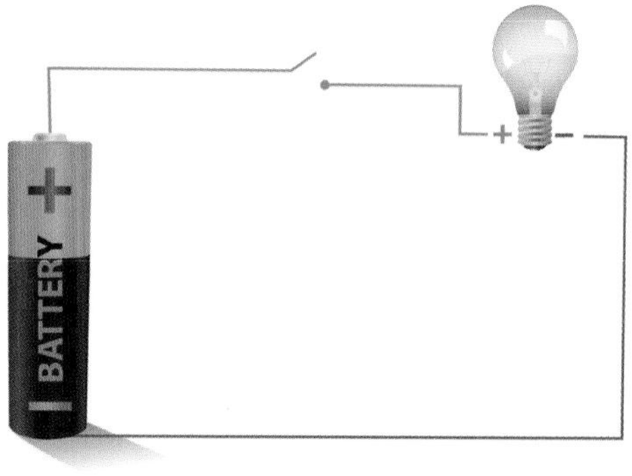

Take a Look

With your child, talk through each part of the diagrams showing the open and closed circuits, tracing your fingers along the path that electrons follow. Then, have your child flip a light switch in your home on and off. Ask your child if he can explain what is happening with each flip of the switch.

An open circuit stops the flow of electricity.

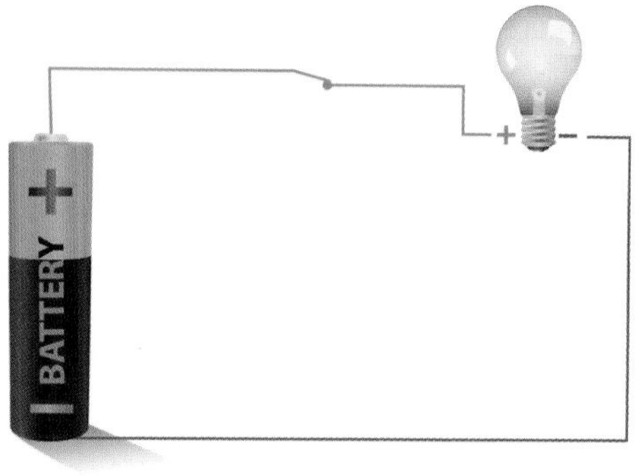

A closed circuit allows electricity to flow around the circuit.

ing the full circuit from the negative pole of the battery, through the lightbulb and the switch, and back to the positive pole of the battery. This is called a closed circuit, because the electrons go in a complete circle.

When the switch is turned off, the circuit is broken and the flow of electrons stops. This is called an open circuit, because the electrons do not travel in a complete circuit.

If you can find an incandescent lightbulb, like the one pictured, take a look inside. Do you see the two wires sticking up? Stretched between them is a very fine wire called a filament. When you turn on the switch and create a closed circuit, electrons travel through the circuit and into the lightbulb. When the electrons reach the filament, they begin to pile up because the filament is a very narrow passageway for them. It's as if traffic moving in eight lanes had to merge onto a one-lane bridge.

This electric traffic jam is caused by resistance—the narrow filament resists the large flow of electrons. As the crowd of backed-up electrons presses ahead, they cause the atoms in the filament to vibrate, get hot, and glow. Thanks to resistance, lightbulbs turn electrons into light.

Conductors and Insulators

Most household wires that carry electrical current are made of copper, the same metal used to make pennies. Electrons move readily from atom to atom in copper, so electricity flows well through copper. That makes copper a good conductor of electrical current. Other metals make good conductors, too.

Some materials are poor conductors of electrical current. These materials are called insulators. Electricity will not flow through them.

You see examples of conductors and insulators every day. Anything that you plug into a wall socket for electricity uses a wire made of both a conducting material and an insulating material. The wire is probably copper inside, but the part you see on the outside is made of plastic or rubber. The copper conducts the electricity, but the plastic or rubber insulates it from your hands. Thanks to the insulation, you don't get a shock when you touch the wire.

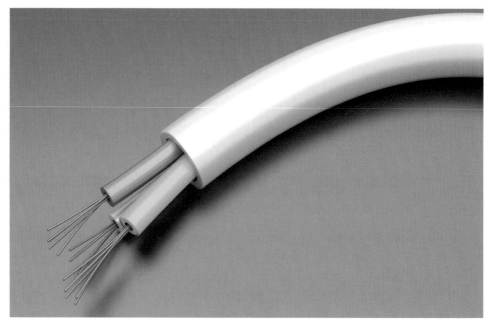

The electrical cords for televisions, radios, and other electrical appliances contain insulating materials and conducting materials.

The last thing you want to do is to become a conductor of electricity! Respecting the power of electrons could save your life. Never fiddle around inside electrical appliances when they are plugged in. Water is a good conductor, so it is especially important not to touch light switches or appliances when your hands are wet or when you are in water. In other words, don't use your hair dryer while you are in the bathtub. The shock could kill you!

Insulation also prevents bare wires from touching each other. When bare wires touch, current can flow between them and take a shortcut instead of completing the full circuit. This causes a short circuit. Current in a short circuit moves through a smaller loop while doing less work. Energy from speeding and bumping electrons builds up. As too much current flows through the wires, they become hotter and hotter. The situation can get dangerous because the wires can get hot enough to start a fire. Some good safety measures include replacing worn-out electrical cords, keeping pets from chewing on cords, and keeping cords away from heaters and places where they can be rubbed or pinched.

Overloading a circuit by plugging in too many appliances can cause wires behind the walls to heat up, too. Safety devices such as fuses and circuit breakers are designed to interrupt the circuit if too much current threatens to heat up the wiring. A fuse is a tiny glass tube surrounding a thin metal strip. If too much current runs through the fuse, the metal strip melts, breaking the circuit and stopping the flow of electricity before the wires get too hot.

Plugging too many appliances into a circuit creates a safety hazard.

Electromagnets

Electric current can be switched on and off by opening and closing a circuit. Some magnets can be turned off and on in the same way. They are called electromagnets.

If you were to take an iron nail and wrap an electrical wire around it about ten times, then connect it to a circuit, you would be making a very simple electromagnet. When you close the circuit (or turn the system on), the current flows through the wire coiled around the nail. That movement of electricity creates a magnetic field that changes the ordinary nail into a magnet. The more times the wire is coiled around the nail, the stronger a magnet that nail becomes. Switch off the electric current, and the nail loses most of its magnetic force of attraction. It becomes an ordinary nail again.

Magnets that can be turned on and off are useful in many ways. Television receivers, loudspeakers, metal detectors, and motors and brakes in some cars depend on electromagnets to work. Cranes move tons of steel using powerful

This Chinese maglev train flies along its magnetic track at speeds up to three hundred miles per hour.

electromagnets. They can use those magnets to pick up loads and, with a flip of the switch, drop those loads.

Electromagnets are also used in special trains called maglevs (for "magnetic levitation"). Instead of using wheels that run on a track, maglev trains use electromagnets that run along a guide rail. Electric current flows through the electromagnets. The magnetic pole in the tracks is opposite to the pole of the train's magnets, so magnetic force pushes the train cars off the tracks. They hover above the guide rail and glide smoothly along at high speed.

What About You?

Has your child ever been on a train that runs on rails? Ask her to talk about whether the ride was noisy and bumpy. Would a maglev train have these problems? Why or why not?

Michael Faraday

Many scientists start out by asking questions that begin, "What would happen if . . . ?" Michael Faraday (1791–1867) was one of the greatest "what if" question-askers of all time. This man's curiosity led him to discoveries about the nature of electricity that changed the world.

Faraday was the son of a poor English blacksmith. He had very little schooling and at age thirteen was sent off to work as an apprentice to a bookbinder. For years, Faraday made the most of his job by reading all the books that came into the shop to be bound. Faraday also attended public lectures and kept a journal of his thoughts.

At one series of lectures by the famous scientist Sir Humphry Davy, Faraday wrote down everything the speaker said and bound it up into a beautiful book for Davy. Not long after,

Michael Faraday

Davy was temporarily blinded by an explosion in his laboratory. He sent for Faraday and asked if he would be his right-hand man and help with experiments. In return, Faraday would be allowed to use the laboratory and equipment for his own experiments. Faraday made the most of this opportunity. This would be his lab for the next fifty years.

Faraday's most famous experiments had to do with electricity and magnetism. Another scientist had noted that a magnet would move when an electric current was sent through a nearby wire. This gave Faraday an idea. If the current could move the magnet, then maybe the magnet could move the current. He wondered, "What if electricity and magnetism are really two examples of the same force and can be converted back and forth?"

To test this idea, Faraday set up an experiment to see if the movement of a magnet could produce an electric current. He made a coil of wire and attached it to a current detector. When he moved a magnet in and out of the coil, a current was produced. Next, he attached a copper disc to two wires and spun the disc between the two poles of a horseshoe magnet. This made a steady current through the wires. Faraday had built the first electrical generator!

Faraday is remembered as one of the greatest scientists of all time. His discoveries gave other scientists and inventors the knowledge they needed to invent electric motors, generators, the telegraph, the telephone, and just about every other electrical device we use today.

Faraday was also one of the first scientists to think that it is important to share scientific experiments with everyone, not just other scientists. He held events especially for children to show them his experiments. Sometimes his experiments did not go as he had expected. Then he would say, "The failures are just as important as the successes." Michael Faraday was always learning, even from his failures.

Make a Connection

Have your child review the information about electromagnets on pages 390–391. How does this information demonstrate the importance of Michael Faraday's discoveries to contemporary life?

Geology

The word "geology" comes from the Greek word *gaia*, which means "Earth." Geology is the study of Earth, its matter, and its history. A geologist is a scientist who studies these topics.

Layers of Planet Earth

Have you ever wondered what it would be like to journey down, down, down to the center of Earth? To get there, you would have to dig a hole 3,872 miles deep, through several different layers.

The top layer—the layer on which you live—is called the crust. The crust is about twenty-five miles deep on average, though some sections are nearly fifty miles thick; other sections are fewer than five miles thick. Earth's crust is made of dirt on top of solid rock.

Once you dig through the crust, you reach a very hot second layer called the mantle. Like the crust, the mantle is made up of rock. Here, however, it is so hot that sections of rock melt and flow like thick syrup, which geologists call magma. Earth's mantle is 1,800 miles deep.

Continuing down toward the center of Earth, you come to the third layer— the core. Earth's core consists of an outer layer and an inner layer. The outer core, made of searing-hot liquid metal, is nearly as thick as the mantle.

Deeper still, you reach the inner core at Earth's center, estimated to be about the size of the moon. Here at the inner core, the temperature is hotter than at the surface of the sun! Yet unlike the outer core, the inner core is solid. The pressure from all the layers of Earth around the inner core keeps it from melting.

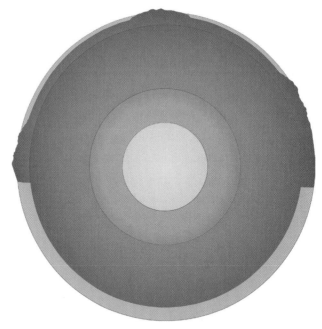

Layers of the Earth

Earthquakes

It was early morning on April 18, 1906, in the city of San Francisco, California. Eva Campbell was fast asleep when her bed began to lurch violently across the room. Her whole house was trembling: "It rocked like a ship on a rough sea. . . . Quiver after quiver followed . . . until it seemed as if the very heart of this old earth was broken and was throbbing and dying away slowly and gently."

On that terrible morning, San Francisco was destroyed by one of the most destructive earthquakes ever to take place in the United States. Many people died, crushed by falling buildings or trapped in fires that started when gas lines broke.

The San Francisco earthquake of 1906 destroyed many buildings.

An earthquake is a sudden and violent shaking of Earth's crust. Earthquakes can be strong enough to shake buildings and bridges off their foundations, to open cracks big enough that cars fall into them, and to cause huge avalanches. On the other hand, some earthquakes are so mild that people don't even notice them. In fact, an earthquake happens somewhere in the world every thirty seconds.

Geologists record the vibrations from earthquakes with machines called seismographs. Seismographs measure tremors underground and plot them like a graph. To compare the magnitude, or strength, of different earthquakes, geologists often use a chart called the Richter [RIK-ter] scale.

The Richter scale gives scientists a way to compare earthquakes. An earthquake measuring 2 on the Richter scale is ten times stronger than an earthquake rated 1. No earthquake has ever measured greater than 9 on the Richter scale. The magnitude of such an earthquake would be equal to an explosion of two hundred million tons of dynamite!

The Richter scale was developed in 1935. Today, many geologists prefer the moment magnitude scale. The moment magnitude scale and Richter scale produce similar numbers for most earthquakes. However, the moment magnitude scale produces more precise results for powerful earthquakes. It has recorded several earthquakes with moment magnitudes greater than 9.

Earth's Moving Plates

Talk and Think

Ask your child, "How do you think the movement of tectonic plates affects the way that Earth looks over time?"

Earth's crust is something like a big, messy jigsaw puzzle made of many pieces called plates. Some of the pieces fit together well. Some fit more loosely. Some of them lie on top of each other.

The boundary line where two plates meet is called a fault. Deep cracks in Earth's crust sometimes occur at faults. San Francisco sits right on top of a fault called the San Andreas Fault, which runs the length of California. The movement of plates along this fault is one reason why California experiences so many earthquakes.

It feels as if the ground we stand on is solid and motionless, but in fact the

From the air, you can see parts of the San Andreas Fault in California. The fault runs between the white arrows in this photograph.

plates that make up Earth's crust move. They push, pull, and rub against one another.

What makes the plates move? Like rafts on water, Earth's plates float on the magma of the mantle. When magma moves, so do the plates. Magma is always circulating. Hotter magma rises to the surface, cools, and then sinks. These movements jostle the plates.

The sliding of rock against rock in Earth's crust can cause pressure to build up over time until suddenly—*crack!*—rock fractures, stored energy is released, and the ground trembles. We call the release of this energy an earthquake. An earthquake's epicenter is the place on Earth's surface that is directly above where the earthquake begins.

Sometimes an earthquake happens on the ocean floor. Its energy pushes seawater into a giant wave called a tsunami [tsoo-NAH-mee]. A tsunami can travel more than four hundred miles per hour. As it approaches shore, where the water is shallower, it grows taller and taller, pushed by the energy behind it. A tsunami can grow as tall as a ten-story building before the curling wall of water crashes down on land.

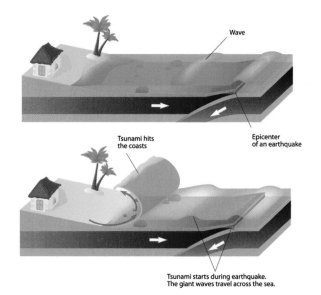

Earthquakes beneath the ocean can send gigantic waves, called tsunamis, tumbling toward land.

Volcanoes

Volcanoes are like safety valves for the planet's furnace. They release built-up pressure from inside Earth. Volcanoes form when hot magma from the mantle squeezes up through weak spots in Earth's crust, usually where plates meet. The volcano erupts when that incredibly hot liquid comes gushing out of the ground. Once it flows out of a volcano, magma is called lava. A volcanic eruption can keep going for hours, days, or even months. Ash and hunks of fiery rock spew from the opening in the ground, and over time they pile up and harden into a mountain.

Sometimes volcanoes erupt quietly, without a lot of noise and explosions. Glowing-hot lava oozes out from the opening on top and runs down the sides of the volcano. Other times volcanoes erupt violently, flinging hot lava, gases, and pieces of rock into the air. Volcanoes often erupt many times over the course of centuries, sometimes quietly and sometimes explosively, building up a mountain of layers of hardened lava, cinders, and ash.

World-Famous Volcanoes

Mount Vesuvius, on the western coast of Italy, erupted in 79 CE and buried the ancient Roman cities of Pompeii and Herculaneum in ash and cinders. Twenty thousand people were killed. The tons of ash that entombed Pompeii kept it almost perfectly preserved for centuries. Archaeologists digging in the area more than 1,500 years later unearthed the entire town, complete with houses, shops, restaurants, temples, signs, and paintings. Even the bodies of people who had lived in Pompeii were well preserved, trapped and hardened by ash.

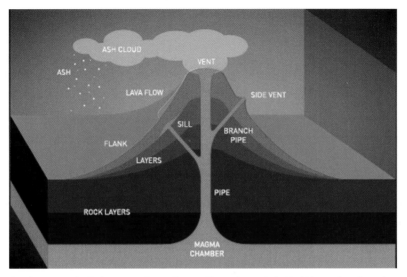

A volcano erupts; hot magma forces its way through cracks in Earth's crust and erupts on the surface as lava.

A Volcano's Status

An active volcano is one that is erupting or is expected to erupt sometime in the future. "Dormant" describes a volcano that has not erupted for a while, and no one knows for sure whether it will ever erupt again. "Extinct" describes a volcano that has not erupted since humans have been recording history and probably never will again.

Krakatoa, a volcano on an Indonesian island, erupted in 1883 with an explosion so powerful that it was heard almost three thousand miles away. Volcanic ash shot seventeen miles up into Earth's atmosphere, darkening the skies for almost twenty hours. The force of the eruption created a hundred-foot tsunami that took the lives of thirty-six thousand people on the nearby islands of Java and Sumatra. The ash Krakatoa sent into the atmosphere changed the color of sunsets around the world for months after the eruption.

When Mount Saint Helens in Washington state erupted in 1980, 230 square miles of forest were blown down or burned. Temperatures reached 1,100 degrees Fahrenheit near the blast. The winds from the blast were measured at more than six hundred miles per hour, and trees were flattened for fifteen miles around. Rocks as big as a hilltop tumbled down, filling up a valley 150 feet deep—the largest landslide in recorded history. Hot ash, three feet thick, blanketed the area nearest the volcano.

Mount Saint Helens erupted in 1980, sending huge clouds of volcanic ash into the air.

Despite all this devastation, life has returned to Mount Saint Helens in the years following the eruption. Plants have sprouted through the ash. These plants have created a little bit of humus [HYOO-mus], or decaying matter from plants and animals, in which more seeds, brought by the wind, have taken root and begun to grow. Scientists predict that by 2200, a forest will cover Mount Saint Helens once again.

Hot Springs and Geysers

In some places in the world, a lot of volcanic activity is going on under Earth's surface. Magma that is forcing its way up through the crust heats up water that has percolated down through cracks. Sometimes the hot water bubbles up to the surface and forms steamy ponds called hot springs. Sometimes, Earth's underground shape makes that hot water shoot up into the air, creating geysers. Geysers form when water collects in underground caves and chambers. The water gets hotter and hotter, until finally it boils and turns to steam. Just like the steam pressure that makes a teakettle whistle, the force of this underground steam blasts through the cracks in Earth's crust.

Each time it erupts, Old Faithful, in Yellowstone National Park, sends tens of thousands of liters of hot water into the air.

Yellowstone National Park, in the state of Wyoming, sits on a hot spot of underground volcanic activity. When you visit Yellowstone, you can see explosions of water and steam from underground. One famous geyser at Yellowstone sends a hissing fountain of water and steam 160 feet into the air. It erupts regularly, and so it is called Old Faithful.

Drifting Continents

If you could go back in time three hundred million years, before the time of the dinosaurs, and look down from space, Earth would look very different. Geologists think that, back then, the continents we know today were crowded together in one giant landmass. They have named that landmass Pangaea [pan-JEE-uh], a word made up from the Greek for "all the world." Over a hundred million years, the supercontinent of Pangaea gradually broke into pieces. Oceans flowed in between the newly formed continents.

Even though the continents drifted only a few inches apart each year, a few inches per year for millions of years adds up to a lot of changes. Geologists call those changes continental drift.

These maps show how the plates of Pangaea drifted to the location of our current continents.

Building Mountains over Time

From space, Earth looks like a smooth blue-and-white marble. But down here on the planet, we know its surface is anything but smooth. The land is wrinkled and bumpy. Mountains poke up from every continent and from the ocean floor. Scientists divide mountains into several categories based on how they were formed.

Dome-Shaped Mountains

Volcanoes can build mountains by spitting out piles of lava, cinders, and ash. Volcanic mountains can also form without an eruption. Magma beneath Earth's surface swells and pushes up a mountain-sized bump. Before it finds a vent, or a path to the surface, the magma cools and hardens into dome-shaped mountains. The Black Hills of South Dakota and Wyoming are dome mountains.

Folded Mountains

Imagine a dish towel spread on the table. Now picture what happens when you push the edges toward the center. The more you push, the more the towel wrinkles and crumples into folds. The same kind of thing has happened to Earth's crust in different places, making formations called folded mountains. Earth's tallest mountains, the Himalayas, formed forty-five million years ago when two crustal plates collided deep beneath an ancient ocean. The tremendous force of the impact made the colliding crust bend and fold into mountains and valleys. You may have a hard time believing that the Himalayas were once part of an ocean floor, but scientists still find fossils of ocean creatures embedded in the rock on the mountains' peaks! The Alps in Europe are folded mountains, too, and the Appalachians in the eastern United States are part of a very old chain of folded mountains.

Fault-Block Mountains

Sometimes when plates collide on a fault line, the rock is brittle. Then the crust doesn't bend and fold but instead cracks into huge blocks. As the two plates keep pushing against each other, the blocks on one side of the fault slowly lift up into a tilted ridge. These are called fault-block mountains. The Sierra Nevada Moun-

The Grand Tetons in the western United States are fault-block mountains.

tains, which run through northern and southern California and western Nevada, are fault-block mountains.

Making Rocks

Mountains are made of rocks, but what are rocks made of? Rocks are made of chemicals called minerals. There are more than two thousand kinds of minerals on Earth. Some rocks are made of a single mineral, and others are combinations. To classify a given rock, geologists consider how it was formed.

Rocks that were made from cooling magma and lava are called igneous [IG-nee-us] rocks. The name comes from *ignis*, the Latin word for "fire." Heavy, speckled granite; light, powdery pumice; black, glassy obsidian—even though they all look different, these are all igneous rocks. They started as hot magma and cooled into rock.

Rocks that were made when layer upon layer of sand and debris settled down

When this lava flow from a volcano in Hawaii cools and hardens, the rocks will be igneous rocks.

Take a Look
Have your child look at a photograph of a lava flow and predict what the rocks will look like when the lava cools and hardens. You may wish to search online for photographs of obsidian—an igneous rock that commonly forms from volcanic eruptions—and compare the photographs with your child's prediction.

together are called sedimentary rocks. Their name comes from the Latin word *sedo*, which means "settle down." Over millions of years, layers of sediment pressed down in the bottom of ancient oceans and rivers. The pressure cemented tiny grains together into rock. Limestone is a sedimentary rock, made mostly of the compressed bones and shells of millions of tiny sea creatures. Sandstone is another sedimentary rock.

Sedimentary rocks often form distinct layers. Each layer contains minerals—and sometimes fossils—from a different time period.

The last family of rocks is called metamorphic [met-uh-MORE-fick] rock. This family gets its name from the Greek words *meta*, meaning "change," and *morph*, meaning "form"—because metamorphic rocks are rocks that have changed form.

What About You?

Ask your child if he has ever seen a piece of marble, sandstone, pumice, obsidian, or any other rock that is mentioned in this section. Most people have. Some public buildings are built out of marble, and you can buy pumice stones at the drugstore! Ask your child what special characteristics he has noticed in these rocks.

Some metamorphic rocks have changed through heat. When magma collects underground, it heats the surrounding rock to such high temperatures that the minerals get cooked. They change into new minerals, and the rocks containing them change form. Others have changed through pressure. Immense weight, like the weight of a mountain, can press down and change minerals. For example, marble—used for its beauty in sculpture and buildings since the time of the ancient Greeks—is a metamorphic rock. Heat and pressure underground turn limestone into the rock we know as marble.

From Boulder to Rock to Pebble to Soil

While plate movement is building mountains up, other forces are wearing them down. Wind, water, ice, and plant roots crack and crumble rock over time, taking huge boulders and turning them into fist-size rocks, then pebbles, then sand, and finally into tiny particles that contribute to Earth's soil. This process is called weathering.

Imagine a boulder on a mountainside. After a million years, a little crack appears in its surface. When it rains, water trickles into the crack. On chilly nights—and there are many chilly nights on the top of a mountain—the water in the crack freezes and expands. Like a wedge, that ice pushes the sides of the crack in the boulder wider and wider apart. The cycle of freezing, thawing, and freezing again works on the crack until it becomes a network of cracks. Particles of dust and dirt carried by wind and water settle into those cracks. Seeds blown by the wind land in the soil collected in the cracks. The seeds sprout, and as the plants grow, their roots push against the sides of the cracks and make them wider still. Then one sunny day, a jagged piece of the boulder cracks off and somersaults down the side of the mountain, crashing into other boulders in its path and chipping pieces off them. That's the first step in the boulder's journey from big rock to future soil.

How long does it take for an entire mountain to crumble away? Geologists have calculated that a mountain gets approximately three inches shorter every thousand years.

Make a Connection

Using the division skills she learned in the Division section, help your child calculate how many years it will take for Mount Everest to crumble completely away. The height of Mount Everest is on page 105.

The ocean weathers rocks as well. Have you ever noticed that most of the pebbles on a beach are round and smooth? Rocks and sand tumble together in the surf, grinding off all the rough edges. Over time, the action of the waves turns rocks into pebbles and then into sand.

Water, wind, plants, and ice all cause physical weathering. But rock also gets weathered by chemicals that occur naturally in Earth. When water mixes with certain gases from the atmosphere, for example, it sometimes results in a weak acid, which can eat away at the surface of rocks. Some plants also produce weak acids, which seep into the ground and affect the rocks around them. These are examples of chemical weathering.

Erosion

Weathering is just one way that Earth's surface changes. Another way has to do with gravity. Because of gravity, soil and rocks are constantly tumbling down slopes, hills, and mountains. Wind and water also carry materials as they flow over the land. These processes contribute to erosion, the movement of sediment—rocks, pebbles, sand, and soil—from one part of Earth's surface to another.

Suppose a small pebble slides down a mountain slope, and heavy rains wash it into a stream. The pebble is carried by rushing water over a waterfall and down the mountain, where the stream dumps it into a river. The pebble falls to the river bottom, where it is pushed along by the current. It tumbles among other pebbles, rocks, sand, and soil. Gradually, it becomes a rounder, smoother, and smaller pebble than it was when it began its journey, its sharp edges worn away by the constant rubbing against other pebbles and sand on the riverbed.

As the pebble approaches the sea, it may be deposited on one of the islands at the river's delta or be swept out to sea.

Talk and Think
With your child, brainstorm ways that erosion has shaped the land where you live. Consider how sediments may have tumbled down hills and been carried away by wind, water, and ice.

Every day, erosion is happening on Earth. Streams and rivers carry millions of tons of sediment from land to ocean daily. Why don't the oceans fill up with sediment? The answer: because nature recycles.

Over millions of years, layers of sediment are squeezed into sedimentary rock on the ocean floor, which has as many mountains and valleys as Earth's surface above water. The deepest undersea valleys are places where Earth's plates meet. There, sedimentary rock is pressed down into the mantle, where it melts into magma. The magma circu-

Although erosion is a natural process, human activities can worsen its effects. The construction of hotels and other buildings has contributed to erosion that is gradually eating away at this beach.

lates under Earth's crust, and when it finds weak spots, it shoots up as lava, which builds up new mountains—and the cycle begins again.

Wind can also change rock and soil on Earth's surface. Windblown sand, especially in desert areas, works like a sandblaster over time, smoothing sharp rock edges or carving away softer rock on cliffs and mountainsides. Wind can carve unusual rock formations, creating caves, mesas, towers, and arches.

Ice is a rock carver, too. Huge masses of ice and snow called glaciers [GLAY-shurs] form on high mountains and in very cold regions. Glaciers are like rivers of ice. Even though they seem frozen solid and motionless, glaciers creep slowly downhill. Stones trapped by glaciers scrape the ground beneath them and carve grooves in the rock. Large glaciers carve out the landscape.

About ten thousand years ago, Earth emerged from the ice ages, a period of

The Saskatchewan Glacier in Canada is part of a series of connected glaciers called the Columbia Icefield, which formed many years ago during the ice ages.

more than a million and a half years when colossal glaciers, nearly two miles thick, moved over much of what is now North America, northern Europe, and northern Asia. The glaciers gouged out huge areas as they advanced and grew. At the end of the ice ages, when the glaciers melted, the holes gouged out by the glaciers filled up with water. Today we call some of those water-filled, glacier-made holes the Great Lakes!

Layer upon Layer

If you were to dig a hole in the ground, going down many feet, you would see several layers of different colors of soil.

The top layer, probably darker than the rest, is the topsoil. Topsoil contains tiny pieces of weathered rock mixed with humus. Air and water move through the tiny spaces between grains of topsoil. Plants spread broad networks of roots in the topsoil, and their roots help hold the soil down and prevent erosion. As

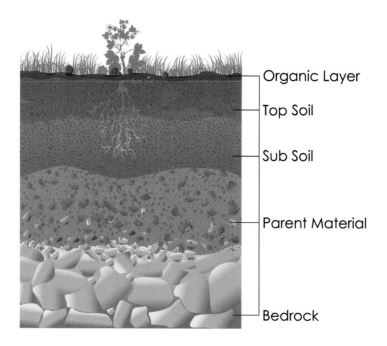

Organic Layer

Top Soil

Sub Soil

Parent Material

Bedrock

plants die, they decay and add to the humus, which will feed future plants—another one of nature's many recycling projects.

Beneath the topsoil, the next layer down is called the subsoil. It is made mostly of weathered rock and clay, with very little humus. While topsoil replenishes itself every year, it takes hundreds of thousands of years for the subsoil to form. Some tree roots grow long enough to reach the subsoil.

Under the subsoil is a layer made of solid rock, called the bedrock. Bedrock is far enough underground to be well protected from wind, water, and freezing temperatures, and so it generally has not weathered into soil. However, bedrock is often the parent material, or source, of the minerals found in a particular section of soil.

Meteorology

The Fascinating World of Weather

The sky darkens with threatening storm clouds. Suddenly, there's a brilliant flash, a crackle—and then a kaboom! Thunder rumbles around and rattles the windows. "It must be the angels' bowling night," someone says, or "That's Thor, the Viking god, in his big boots clomping across the sky." All around the world, all through history, human beings have made up stories to explain the powerful forces that we witness as weather.

Human beings have also spent centuries making a scientific study of the weather. The study of weather is called meteorology, coming from the Greek word *meteoros*, meaning "high in the air," and the suffix "-ology," meaning "study of." The people who study weather are called meteorologists.

Layers of Air

Weather happens because our planet is wrapped in layers of air, called the atmosphere, and because the sun is constantly bombarding Earth with energy. Without an atmosphere, Earth would look like the moon: a waterless, lifeless hunk of rock. Our atmosphere is constantly absorbing energy from the sun, and that energy moves around from place to place, creating weather.

Earth's atmosphere is commonly divided into five layers: the outermost layer, the exosphere [EKS-oh-sfeer]; the thermosphere [THERM-oh-sfeer]; the mesosphere [MEZ-oh-sfeer]; the stratosphere [STRAT-oh-sfeer]; and the lowest layer, which touches Earth's surface, the troposphere [TROH-poh-sfeer].

When you breathe, you are inhaling air from the troposphere. But clouds are also in the troposphere. Most of Earth's weather happens in the troposphere. The boundary between the troposphere and the stratosphere is called the tropopause.

The stratosphere, from seven to thirty miles above Earth's surface, contains a tiny amount of a gas called ozone, which protects us from ultraviolet radiation, part of the energy that comes from the sun. The boundary between the stratosphere and the mesosphere is called the stratopause.

> **What About You?**
>
> Has your child ever experienced a sunburn? Explain that ultraviolet (UV) rays from the sun cause sunburns, and that people who absorb too much UV radiation are at greater risk of developing skin cancer. If you have a bottle of sunscreen at home, show it to your child. Point out the sun protection factor (SPF). The number should be greater than 15.

The Ozone Layer

Ozone in the stratosphere absorbs ultraviolet (UV) radiation from the sun, which in high quantities can be very harmful, even deadly, to many creatures on Earth. In the 1970s, scientists discovered that ozone levels over Earth's Southern Hemisphere decreased significantly each spring. This "hole" in the ozone layer allows unhealthy amounts of ultraviolet radiation to reach Earth. Scientists determined that ozone holes are caused by human activities that release certain chemicals into the atmosphere. These chemicals react with and destroy ozone. In response, countries around the world have agreed to reduce or ban the use of these chemicals. If people continue to honor these agreements, scientists think, the ozone layer will eventually repair itself.

The mesosphere, from thirty to fifty miles above Earth's surface, acts as a protective shield in another way. Perhaps you have seen shooting stars streaking across the night sky. These are caused by meteoroids, hunks of rock streaking through space at incredible speeds. Sometimes they come so close to Earth that they enter the atmosphere. But when they rub against air in the mesosphere, all but the largest rocks heat up so intensely that they burn to cinders before reaching Earth. We call these burning streaks meteors. The boundary between the mesosphere and the thermosphere is called the mesopause.

The thermosphere, from 50 to 430 miles above Earth's surface, is constantly showered by X-rays, ultraviolet radiation, and electrons thrown off by the sun. So much energy from the sun reaches the high levels of the thermosphere that temperatures can climb above 3,000 degrees Fahrenheit! The boundary between the thermosphere and the exosphere is called the thermopause.

Between the thermosphere and empty space is the exosphere. In this layer, which extends up to 6,200 miles above Earth's surface, satellites orbit the planet. The relatively few particles of matter in the exosphere move very quickly—some manage to escape Earth's gravity and exit the atmosphere completely.

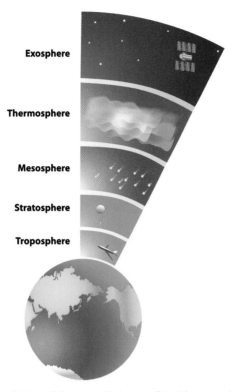

Exosphere

Thermosphere

Mesosphere

Stratosphere

Troposphere

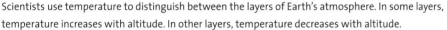

Scientists use temperature to distinguish between the layers of Earth's atmosphere. In some layers, temperature increases with altitude. In other layers, temperature decreases with altitude.

Have you ever climbed into a car that has been all closed up on a hot, sunny day? Then you know what it's like when the sun's energy shines into a place and gets trapped inside. It gets hot!

In much the same way, the sun's energy shines into Earth's atmosphere. Sunlight passes through the layers of the atmosphere and warms up the land and the oceans. Some of the sunlight bounces back into the atmosphere and heats up gases in the air. The gases absorb the heat energy, holding it in Earth's atmosphere rather than allowing it to return to space. Thanks to that process, Earth is a comfortable place for life, instead of a freezing cold planet.

As you might imagine, changes to the atmosphere can dramatically affect the weather. Read the following narrative to learn about one particularly sudden change.

Mount Tambora: An Eruption to Remember

"Mom, do you think Mount Tambora will erupt today?" Cinta asked excitedly.

"Well, I certainly hope not! Volcano eruptions are very dangerous," Cinta's mother, Iman, replied with a serious look on her face. Cinta and her mother were visiting the famous volcano Mount Tambora on Sumbawa, the small Indonesian island they called home.

"I know, I know! But you have to admit it would be cool to see the red-hot magma spurting out of the mouth of a volcano," Cinta shot back.

"You mean red-hot lava, Cinta," her mom corrected. "It's called magma when it's inside the volcano. Once magma is forced through Earth's crust out of the volcano, it becomes lava."

"Mom, I did not come here for a science lesson. I really came hoping to see a volcanic eruption!" Cinta exclaimed.

"Cinta, did you know that about two hundred years ago Mount Tambora erupted? And that eruption affected not only our ancestors here in Sumbawa, but also people thousands of miles away in the United States and Switzerland?" Cinta's mom replied.

"No, I didn't. How do you know about that?" Cinta asked.

"Well, my grandfather used to tell me a story about his grandfather Joko, who lived during the 1815 eruption. My grandfather studied the eruption and learned how that one event had drastic effects on places and people thousands of miles away, for days, months, or years to come," Iman explained.

"Wow, can you tell me the stories that your grandfather told you?" Cinta asked excitedly.

"Sure, let's find a place to sit at the base of the volcano, and I'll tell you all about it," Iman said as she and Cinta spread out their blanket and goodies for a picnic. Then, Iman began to tell her story.

"One day in 1815, Joko, my great-great-grandfather, was riding his pony across the vast grassland of Sumbawa, not far from where we are sitting right now. He heard a thundering roar. Joko didn't know what to think. Was Sumbawa being attacked by cannons? Were his people in danger? Joko gathered himself and rode back toward his village to warn everyone."

"I bet I know what was happening," Cinta interrupted. "I bet that Mount Tambora was erupting!"

Cinta's mom continued, "And you guessed correctly! What was happening was far worse than an invasion. The next thundering roar knocked Joko off his pony. It was the loudest, most violent thing he had ever heard. It was as if Earth itself had been torn asunder. He looked up and saw a stream of red and black gushing miles into the air from Mount Tambora to the north. The fourteen-thousand-foot-high volcano had erupted. Deadly flows of hot rock and gas, called pyroclastic flows, streamed like avalanches down the sides of the volcano at more than a hundred miles per hour. There was no escape. Ten thousand people died instantly."

"But how did Joko escape?" Cinta asked with wide eyes.

"Luckily, Joko was able to grab the mane of his pony and hop back on. Then, he raced as far away from the volcano as possible. Others were not as lucky. Slabs of volcanic rock violently ejected from the eruption, trapping boats in the harbor. Joko and the other survivors didn't know it then, but Sumbawa had just gone through what is now considered the most destructive volcanic eruption in recorded history. The last blast of the volcano sent smoke and gas twenty-five miles into the air. The top of the volcano was literally blown off, leaving behind a giant crater, called a caldera, almost four miles wide," Cinta's mom said with sadness in her voice.

"So after the volcano finished erupting, everything went back to normal, right?" Cinta asked hopefully.

"Unfortunately, little one, you are wrong. The worst was not yet over. The sky was black with ash that blocked out the sun. Ash continued to rain over the island for days. Homes collapsed under the weight of the ash, and the water became bad to drink. Forests and crops were completely destroyed. Those who survived and stayed on the island starved. In total, about ninety thousand people in the immediate area died as a result of the 1815 eruption of Mount Tambora."

"If all those people died, how did Joko survive?" Cinta wondered.

"Well, Joko and his family escaped Sumbawa and moved to one of Indonesia's other islands. But even people on neighboring islands weren't safe. The eruption triggered a tsunami. The waves reached as high as thirteen feet before crashing down on the islands, flooding the land and killing the people. The Sumbawa we know and love today was almost completely destroyed."

"Wow!" Cinta exclaimed as she looked at Mount Tambora with wonder. "I didn't know one volcano could cause so much destruction."

"Now you know why I wasn't as excited as you were about seeing an eruption today. But Sumbawa is not the only place that felt the effects of the eruption. Have you ever heard of a man named Thomas Jefferson?" Iman asked.

"He was a president in the United States, right? He was one of the authors of the Declaration of Independence!" Cinta answered.

"That's exactly right. And almost a year later, and ten thousand miles away, Thomas Jefferson felt the effects of the Mount Tambora eruption," Iman explained.

"No way!" Cinta exclaimed.

"Yup. On a late spring day in 1816, Thomas Jefferson walked outside to check the crops on his Monticello plantation in Virginia. Five years had passed since Jefferson stepped down as president of the United States. It was an unusually cold day, almost unbearably so. He peered into a wooden bucket and saw that the water had turned to ice. 'How could that be?' Jefferson thought. It was the middle of May! The lawn at Monticello was covered in white flecks of frost. Jefferson shivered and ran inside to grab his fur coat."

"A fur coat in the middle of May?" Cinta interrupted.

"Yes, it was a most unusual May. Frost had killed most of Jefferson's fruit and tobacco crops. Of all the years he spent recording the weather, he couldn't remember a colder May. Several hours later, in the middle of the day, he looked at his thermometer—53 degrees Fahrenheit. Jefferson went inside to check his records, and what he found astonished him. On average, the temperature was 10 degrees colder than in previous years. It remained cold all summer at Monticello. Frost stayed on the ground in Virginia through June, and Jefferson heard of snowfall in Pennsylvania as late as July. That summer, Jefferson took out a $1,000 loan to make up for the failure of his crops. Thousands of other farmers on the East Coast of the United States moved west in search of better farmland. They called 1816 'the year without summer.'"

"A year without summer is a year I can't even imagine. It's hot most of the year here. I can't imagine a year without heat! What other places felt the effects of the eruption?" Cinta asked.

"Let's see. Four thousand miles away in 1816, at Lake Geneva in Switzerland, Lord Byron was having guests over at his summerhouse. Byron was an English aristocrat and, at the time of his trip, had just become a national celebrity after publishing the first part of his poem *Childe Harold's Pilgrimage*. Byron enjoyed living a life of excess and was once described as being 'mad, bad, and dangerous to know.'"

"He sounds cool!" Cinta said.

"He was very cool because at Lake Geneva, Byron was also experiencing the year without summer. Farther north, in Ireland, a potato famine left people starving. Wheat crops were failing all over Europe due to the cold. In later years, it was the worst famine of 1800s Europe. However, Lord Byron had more pressing concerns than famine; he needed to show his guests a good time. Byron looked out over the lake being splattered with cold rain. It wasn't that he was worried about entertaining his guests—that came naturally enough to him. What he needed was to find something that fit the dreary mood. Byron watched as lightning dashed the ground around the deep blue lake. Across the lake was Byron's favorite attraction, the Château de Chillon, a medieval castle that seemed to rise out of the ethereal waters. The dungeon of the magnificent fortress had once been a place of unspeakable horrors. Lightning struck again. Byron pictured the castle's dark cells and rusted chains, and the ghosts that walked among them."

"Spooky! It sounds like the scene of a ghost story!" Cinta exclaimed.

"Exactly! Byron thought so, too. He suggested that the group should read ghost stories to one another. Byron gathered his guests by candlelight and began to read. Taken by the mood, Byron began writing his own stories. Then, he came up with a brilliant idea. He challenged his guests to come up with their own horror stories. The rain and thunder continued for days. The nightmares of Byron and his guests on those cold nights became their stories. What resulted were some of the most important horror stories ever written. During this fateful vacation, Mary Shelley wrote *Frankenstein,* and John Polidori wrote *Vampyre,* the inspiration for *Dracula.*"

"But what did the Mount Tambora eruption have to do with Thomas Jefferson, Lord Byron, and the 'year without summer'?" Cinta asked, puzzled.

"You see, the blast of the volcano so many months before was actually responsible for the 'year without summer.' This was because much of the gas and ash launched up into the sky by the volcano stayed there and mixed with the air. The sun-blocking ash traveled around the world on the wind, dimming the sky wherever it went. The loss of sunlight caused global cooling, which briefly knocked the planet's climate out of balance. Crops failed, resulting in worldwide famine. People in the United States moved west, fueling westward expansion. The eruption of Mount Tambora also caused the temperature to drop at Lake Geneva, leading Mary Shelley to write *Frankenstein.*"

"It's pretty amazing that the volcano's eruption affected so many lives for years. Guess what, Mom?" Cinta asked.

"What?" her mom replied.

"I hope I never live to see Mount Tambora erupt!" Cinta exclaimed.

"Now that's one thing we can agree on!" her mother replied with a smile.

Uneven Heating

When you look at the weather maps in the newspaper or watch the weather report on television, you can see that weather isn't the same everywhere on Earth—it isn't even the same in different towns in the same state! From warm breezes and gentle rains to hurricanes, blizzards, and ice storms, weather is always changing. It changes because Earth is heated unevenly and because heat energy moves around in the atmosphere.

The sun doesn't shine with the same intensity on every region of Earth. It shines on the area near the equator the most directly of all, so the air around the

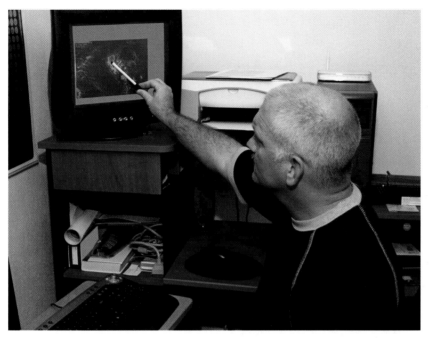

Meteorologists watch high- and low-pressure areas to predict tomorrow's weather.

equator heats up the most. It shines the least directly at the North and South Poles, so the air at the poles stays the coldest. These differences in temperature make the air in the atmosphere move around.

Have you ever noticed that when you open an oven, hot air rises up to your face, but when you open a refrigerator, cold air spills down on your feet? Hot air rises and cold air sinks. As air is heated, its molecules spread out. It becomes less dense. It is lighter and puts less pressure on Earth. When we talk about a mass of warmer, less dense air in the atmosphere, we call it a low-pressure air system. Cooler air contains molecules that are denser, or closer together. It puts more pressure on Earth, and we call it a high-pressure air system.

Near the equator, low-pressure air systems rise, spread apart, and move toward Earth's poles. At the same time, high-pressure air systems sink and move toward the equator, filling the spaces left vacant as low-pressure air moves away. Before long, the intensity of the sun at the equator heats up the high-pressure systems, transforming them into low-pressure systems, and the cycle continues. This continual exchange of warm and cool air creates wind.

Winds

A famous poem asks, "Who has seen the wind?" No one, of course. But we certainly see what wind can do. Meteorologists have developed ways to describe wind by measuring its speed and direction. For instance, a north wind at twenty miles per hour is a wind coming from the north and moving as fast as a car travels when it drives twenty miles per hour.

A wind that blows ten or twenty miles per hour is called a breeze. If the wind gusts up to forty or fifty miles per hour, it is called a gale. If it travels seventy-five miles per hour or faster, it qualifies as a hurricane.

To measure wind speed, meteorologists use an instrument called an anemometer that looks like a pinwheel, with three arms and a cup at the end of each arm. Wind blows into the cups and makes the pinwheel spin. By counting its spins during a certain time period, meteorologists can measure the speed of the wind.

Do It Yourself

Challenge your child to use craft materials to make a simple anemometer. A common method is to use drinking straws and pushpins to attach paper cups to a pencil eraser. When wind blows into the cups, they will spin around the eraser. Stronger winds will cause the cups to spin more quickly.

An anemometer measures wind speed. The faster it spins, the faster the wind.

Weather Patterns

Some wind patterns continue their movements almost all the time and in the same general direction. These winds are called Earth's prevailing winds. They are our strongest, most persistent winds, and they shape big weather patterns. Different parts of the globe experience different prevailing winds. During the Age of Exploration, Christopher Columbus and other explorers and traders used the prevailing winds known as trade winds to carry them across the Atlantic Ocean.

There are many other weather patterns that remain generally constant in certain areas of the world. Average temperatures, the amount of rainfall or snowfall, and the average amount of moisture in the air (that is, the humidity) all determine the climate of every region in the world. Climate is the average weather pattern for a region. Climate is influenced not only by weather patterns but also by geological factors, such as whether the region is a large landmass or a group of islands, whether it is flat or mountainous, and whether it is near a body of water. The world has many different climates. Each climate supports a different group of plants and animals and a particular kind of human community.

Tropical climates occur in places near the equator. Temperatures stay hot, and day length changes little throughout the year. Polar climates occur near the North and South Poles. Temperatures stay cold, even below freezing, and there is extreme variation in day length between seasons. Imagine how different the animals, plants, and human habitations must be in these two climates.

> **What About You?**
>
> Ask your child to describe the climate where you live. Begin by asking questions about weather patterns. How hot does it get during the summer? How much precipitation does your area receive during the winter? But remind your child that "weather" refers to the atmospheric conditions at a given moment, whereas "climate" refers to conditions over long periods of time.

Do It Yourself

With your child, go outside. Using the information and photographs on this page, try to identify the clouds in the sky. Do this each day for a week and see how many different types of clouds you can identify. Many clouds combine characteristics of cumulus, stratus, and cirrus.

Cloud Families

Clouds can look like fat gingerbread men or two-headed, fire-breathing dragons or your aunt Louise. No two clouds look just the same, but scientists sort clouds into categories according to their shapes. Identifying clouds can help you understand—and even predict—the weather. Here are three common types of clouds.

Cumulus [KYOOM-yuh-luss] clouds form on sunny days when updrafts of warm, wet air rise to a cooler level. Cumulus clouds in the sky usually mean fair weather.

Stratus clouds look like flat sheets that can stretch out to the horizons, blocking out sunshine. They are often a signal that rain is on the way.

Cumulus Clouds

Stratus Clouds

Make a Connection

Read the poem "Clouds" on page 8. Which of these cloud types is most like a sheep?

Cirrus Clouds

Cirrus [SIHR-us] clouds ride highest in the troposphere, where the air is coldest. Made of ice crystals, they look like wispy curlicues. Cirrus clouds often come to fair skies before a rain.

When Push Comes to Shove

Air masses with different levels of humidity and different temperatures are moving constantly above Earth's surface. They don't always mix. Often they collide. As you can imagine, a lot of things can happen when wet, low-pressure air meets dry, high-pressure air. The boundary where one air mass meets another is called a front.

Sometimes a cold air mass wedges in under a warm air mass. The boundary between them is called a cold front. The cold air below forces the warm air to rise swiftly. The warm air cools rapidly, and its water vapor forms heavy clouds full of precipitation. These conditions result in thunder, lightning, and rainstorms, followed by bright, clear weather.

Sometimes a warm air mass overtakes a cold air mass. The boundary between them is called a warm front. The low-pressure mass of warm air rides up on top of the cold air and slowly pushes it out of the way. These conditions result in stratus clouds and a long, steady rain.

Lightning and Thunder

Dark, massive clouds signal the approach of one of nature's loudest and most dazzling sound and light shows: a thunderstorm. As a cold front moves through an area, especially during spring and summer, it plows up warm, humid air. The moist air piles up higher and higher into towering, flat-topped clouds called thunderheads. A thunderhead may extend miles into the atmosphere.

At the top of thunderheads, condensed droplets quickly cool into ice crystals. Strong air currents jiggle the ice crystals up and down inside the cloud. As the ice crystals crash, bump, and rub against one another, electrons loosen and zing around as static electricity, just as they do when your socks and pajamas tumble against each other in the clothes dryer.

Electrons that have been bumped loose collect in the bottom of the cloud, giving it a negative charge. That negative charge interacts with the positive charge of Earth itself. Electrons zing down toward the positively charged ground. When the two charges meet—*crackle! zap!*—energy is released in a giant electrical discharge. The brilliant white flash of lightning that we see is a powerful electrical current flowing through the air.

A lightning bolt heats up the air around it five times hotter than the surface of the sun. That air expands *fast*—and vibrates the air all around it violently. Those vibrations reach our ears when we hear the thunder that so often accompanies lightning.

Light travels much faster than sound. The flash of a bolt of lightning travels to our eyes at 186,000 miles per second. The sounds from the same event—the clap of thunder accompanying the lightning bolt—travel only one-fifth of a mile per second.

Lightning strikes over the ocean

You can use this information to make a rough estimate of how far away lightning has struck. As soon as you see a flash of lightning, count the seconds until you hear the thunder. Divide the number you reached by five and you have the distance in miles between you and the bolt of lightning.

Tornadoes

The most dangerous thunderstorms are the ones that create tornadoes—whirling, funnel-shaped clouds that reach down to Earth's surface and suck things up. Tornadoes can be so powerful that they pick up freight trains and toss them around.

A tornado tears across the Great Plains

Meteorologists think that tornadoes are caused by the interaction of warm, humid updrafts (or swift winds moving upward from Earth's surface) and cool downdrafts (swift winds moving from the sky down to Earth's surface). They do not know exactly why the air begins to spin around and form the funnel cloud. To find out, scientists track tornadoes and post measuring instruments in their paths. They hope the data they collect will help them understand more about tornadoes.

Hurricanes

Hurricanes form over tropical oceans in areas of low pressure. Warm, moist air rises rapidly from the warm water and forms clouds. More warm, moist air rushes in to replace the rising air.

Make a Connection
Have your child look at the geography of the United States on page 99. Explain that tornadoes often form in the Great Plains, while hurricanes often form along the Gulf Coast. Encourage your child to connect the geography to the meteorology by explaining why each region is more likely to produce a certain kind of severe weather.

Powerful winds whip past trees during a hurricane

Air gets sucked up faster and faster, creating storm clouds and a tall, spiraling column of wind. The column of wind pulls more and more moisture from the ocean, growing larger and picking up speed. The eye of the hurricane is a hole in the storm at the center of the spiral. In the eye, the air pressure is very low and the winds are calm.

To track hurricanes and learn more about them, meteorologists fly airborne laboratories directly into the storms. They fly in jets equipped with instruments designed to photograph and measure the storms from high above.

Forecasting the Weather

When you wake up in the morning, do you sometimes wonder what you ought to wear—long pants or shorts, a rain jacket or a sun hat? How do you decide? Chances are you listen to the weather report. Meteorologists predict how hot the day will be, whether it may rain or snow, and how low the temperature will drop after the sun goes down in the evening.

How do people forecast the weather? To predict the weather, people need both a general knowledge of weather patterns and specific information about what's happening at the present moment. A complicated network of instruments placed all over the world—and above the world—creates pictures of air masses as they move in Earth's atmosphere. Weather balloons carry instruments high into the atmosphere. Radar equipment sends out signals that bounce off rain and ice crystals inside clouds to create pictures of clouds and measure how fast they are moving. Every three hours at six hundred weather stations around the United States, weather watchers record temperature, humidity, air pressure, wind speed, and wind direction.

Even with all this information, meteorologists cannot always be certain what the weather will bring tomorrow.

Reading a Barometer

Air moves from areas of high pressure into areas of low pressure, and as it moves, the weather changes. The gauge on a barometer (seen here) tells whether the air where you are has high or low pressure. When the barometer is falling, it means that air pressure is getting lower. Clouds will probably move in, and rain or snow may fall. When the barometer is rising, it means air pressure is getting higher, and you can expect clear skies and less humidity.

Suggested Resources

The Human Body

The Amazing Circulatory System, by John Burstein (Crabtree Publishing, 2009)

The Circulatory System, by Kristin Petrie (ABDO Publishing, 2007)

A Drop of Blood, by Paul Showers (HarperCollins, 2004)

The Heart: Our Circulatory System, by Seymour Simon (Collins, 2006)

The Heart and Circulation, by Carol Ballard (Arcturus Publishing, 2005)

Lungs: Your Respiratory System, by Seymour Simon (Collins, 2007)

The Remarkable Respiratory System, by John Burstein (Crabtree Publishing, 2009)

The Respiratory System, by Susan Glass (Perfection Learning, 2004)

Smoking, by Dr. Alvin Silverstein, Virginia Silverstein, and Laura Silverstein Nunn (Franklin Watts, 2003)

Chemistry

Atoms and Molecules: With Puzzles, Projects, and Problems, by Phil Roxbee-Cox (EDC Publishing, 1993)

Chemistry: Getting a Big Reaction, by Simon Basher (Kingfisher, 2010)

The Elements: A Visual Exploration of Every Known Atom in the Universe, by Theodore Gray (Black Dog & Leventhal, 2012)

The Lonely Electron: A Story About Atoms, Electrons, and Making Friends, by Paige Harris (Blue Ink Publishing, 2013)

The Periodic Table: Elements with Style!, by Simon Basher (Kingfisher, 2007)

What Are Atoms?, by Lisa Trumbauer (Children's Press, 2005)

Electricity

Charged Up: The Story of Electricity, by Jacqui Bailey (Nonfiction Picture Books, 2004)

Conductors and Insulators, by Chris Oxlade (NA-h, 2012)

Explore Electricity! With 25 Great Projects, by Carmella Van Vleet (Nomad Press, 2013)

Nick and Tesla's High-Voltage Danger Lab: A Mystery with Electromagnets, Burglar Alarms, and Other Gadgets You Can Build Yourself, by Bob Pflugfelder (Quirk Books, 2013)

What Is Electricity?, by Lisa Trumbauer (Children's Press, 2004)

Geology

Best Book of Fossils, Rocks, and Minerals, by Chris Pellant (Kingfisher, 2000)

Earth (A True Book), by Elaine Landau (Children's Press, 2008)

Earthquake!, by Cynthia Pratt Nicolson (Kids Can Press, 2002)

Earthquakes, by Seymour Simon (HarperCollins, 2006)

Earthquakes, by Sally Walker (Carolrhoda Books, 1996)

Earthquakes (A True Book), by Ker Than (Children's Press, 2009)

Escaping the Giant Wave, by Peg Kehret (Aladdin Paperbacks, 2004)

Everybody Needs a Rock (For the Junior Rockhound), by Byrd Baylor (Aladdin, 1985)

Extreme Earth Records, by Seymour Simon (Chronicle Books, 2012)

Find Out About Rocks and Minerals: With 23 Projects and More than 350 Photographs, by Jack Challoner (Armadillo, 2013)

High Tide in Hawaii, by Mary Pope Osborne (Random House, 2003)

How Does an Earthquake Become a Tsunami?, by Linda Tagliaferro (Raintree, 2009)

How Does a Volcano Become an Island?, by Linda Tagliaferro (Raintree, 2009)

Inside Volcanoes, by Melissa Stewart (Sterling, 2011)

Janice VanCleave's Earth Science for Every Kid: 101 Easy Experiments That Really Work, by Janice VanCleave (Wiley, 1991)

Mount St. Helens: The Eruption and Healing of a Volcano, by Patricia Lauber (Simon & Schuster, 1993)

The Krakatau Eruption (A True Book), by Peter Benoit (Children's Press, 2011)

Meteorology

Clouds, by Sir Ryan Dale (Ryan Dale Deardorff, 2013)

Clouds, by Marion Dane Bauer (Simon Spotlight, 2013)

Clouds, by Anne Rockwell (HarperCollins, 2008)

The Everything Kids' Weather Book: From Tornadoes to Snowstorms, Puzzles, Games, and Facts That Make Weather for Kids Fun!, by Joe Snedeker (Adams Media, 2012)

Hurricanes!, by Gail Gibbons (Holiday House, 2010)

Hurricanes, by Seymour Simon (HarperCollins, 2007)

The Kids' Book of Weather Forecasting, by Mark Breen and Kathleen Friestad (Ideals, 2008)

Lightning, by Seymour Simon (HarperCollins, 2006)

Tornadoes!, by Gail Gibbons (Holiday House, 2010)

Tornadoes, by Seymour Simon (HarperCollins, 2001)

Weather, by Seymour Simon (HarperCollins, 2006)

Weather Words and What They Mean, by Gail Gibbons (Holiday House, 1992)

What Will the Weather Be?, by Lynda DeWitt (HarperCollins, 2002)

Science Biographies

Charles Drew: Doctor Who Got the World Pumped Up to Donate Blood, by Mike Venezia (Children's Press, 2009)

Charles Drew: Pioneer of Blood Plasma, by Linda Trice (McGraw-Hill Companies, 2000)

Dr. Charles Drew: Medical Pioneer, by Susan Whitehurst (Child's World, 2001)

Elizabeth Blackwell: America's First Woman Doctor, by Trina Robbins (Graphic Library, 2006)

Elizabeth Blackwell: Girl Doctor, by Joanne Landers Henry (Aladdin, 1996)

Michael Faraday: Spiritual Dynamo, by Derick Bingham (Christian Focus Publications, 2010)

Who Says Women Can't Be Doctors? The Story of Elizabeth Blackwell, by Tanya Lee Stone (Henry Holt, 2013)

Wow! Charles Drew! Medical Pioneer, by Elke Sundermann (CreateSpace, 2012)

Illustration and Photo Credits

front elevation," Benjamin Henry Latrobe, 1817. Library of Congress, Prints and Photographs Division, LC-DIG-ppmsca-96502

Page 201: SuperStock/SuperStock

Page 204: Words & Numbers

Page 205: © Bettmann/CORBIS

Page 209: Buyenlarge/Buyenlarge

Page 210: Jacob Wyatt

Page 211: "Dorothea Lynde Dix." Library of Congress, Prints and Photographs Division, LC-USZ62-9797

Page 212: "The bloomer costume," N. Currier, 1851. Library of Congress, Prints and Photographs Division, LC-USZC2-1978

Page 213: "Sojourner Truth," c. 1864. Library of Congress, Prints and Photographs Division, LC-DIG-ppmsca-08978

Page 219: Gail McIntosh

Page 221: Natalia Bratslavsky/Shutterstock

Page 222: Nick_Nick/Shutterstock

Page 223: PHOTOCREO Michal Bednarek/Shutterstock

Page 224(a): LiliGraphie/Shutterstock

Page 224(b): ostill/Shutterstock

Page 225: The Virgin and Child, c. 800 AD (20th century). A 20th-century copy of the illustrated manuscript, produced by Celtic monks around 800 AD. Illustration from *The Book of Kells*, described by Sir Edward Sullivant, Bart, 4th edition, published in London in about 1920. Photo credit: HIP/Art Resource, NY

Page 226: The Unicorn in Captivity, from the Unicorn Tapestries, Netherlands, 1495–1505. The Cloisters, Metropolitan Museum of Art, New York. Image © Corbis

Page 227: Fotografiecor.nl/Shutterstock

Page 228: photo.ua/Shutterstock

Page 229: RuthChoi/Shutterstock

Page 230: Qu'an manuscript. Calligrapher: Ahmad ibn al-Suhrawardi al-Bakri,

Islamic. Attributed to: Iraq, Baghdad, Ilkhamid period (1256–1308), 1307–1308. Image copyright © The Metropolitan Museum of Art. Image source: Art Resource, NY

Page 231(a): © Charles & Josette Lenars/CORBIS

Page 231(b): Brass head with a beaded crown and plume, Ife, Nigeria. Yoruba, probably 12th–14th century AD. © The Trustees of the British Museum/Art Resource, NY

Page 232: Pendant Mask: Iyoba. Made by the Edo people, Benin. 16th CE. Image copyright © The Metropolitan Museum of Art. Image source: Art Resource, NY

Page 233: Christie's Images Ltd./Christie's Images Ltd.

Page 234: Chen Jiru. Poems for Dong Qichang. Album of eight double leaves; ink on paper. Image copyright © The Metropolitan Museum of Art. Image source: Art Resource, NY

Page 235: © Royal Ontario Museum/CORBIS

Page 236: Paul Revere, John Singleton Copley, 1768. Photograph © 2016 Museum of Fine Arts, Boston.

Page 237: *George Washington*, Gilbert Stuart, begun 1795. Image copyright © The Metropolitan Museum of Art. Image source: Art Resource, NY

Page 238: *Washington Crossing the Delaware* (copy after the Emmanuel Leutze painting in the Metropolitan Museum, NY), Eastman Johnson. Photo credit: Art Resource, NY

Page 239: Thomas Jefferson's home "Monticello" in Charlottesville, Virginia, Carol M. Highsmith [between 1980 and 2006]. Library of Congress, Prints and Photographs Division, photograph by Carol M. Highsmith, LC-DIG-highsm-14859

Text Credits and Sources

Poems

. . . .

"George Washington" by Stephen Vincent Benét. From *A Book of Americans*, by Rosemary and Stephen Vincent Benét. Copyright © 1933 by Rosemary and Stephen Vincent Benét. Copyright renewed © 1961 by Rosemary Carr Benét. Reprinted with permission of Brandt & Hochman Literary Agents, Inc.

"The Rhinoceros" from *Candy Is Dandy, the Best of Ogden Nash* by Ogden Nash, published by Carlton Books, 1994. Copyright © 1933 by Ogden Nash, renewed. Reprinted by permission of Curtis Brown, Ltd.

"Humanity" from *The Collected Poems of Elma Stuckey* by Elma Stuckey. Copyright © 1988; all rights reserved. Reprinted by permission of Sterling Stuckey.

"Dreams" from *The Collected Poems of Langston Hughes* by Langston Hughes, edited by Arnold Rampersad with David Roessel, Associate Editor, copyright © 1994 by the Estate of Langston Hughes. Used by permission of Alfred A. Knopf, an imprint of Knopf Doubleday Publishing Group, a division of Random House LLC. All rights reserved. Reprinted by permission of Harold Ober Associates Incorporated.

"Things" from *Honey, I Love*, by Eloise Greenfield. Text copyright © 1978 by Eloise Greenfield. Used by permission of HarperCollins Publishers.

"Fog" from *The Complete Poems of Carl Sandburg* by Carl Sandburg. Copyright © 1970 by Carl Sandburg. Reprinted by permission of Houghton Mifflin Harcourt Publishing Company. All rights reserved.

"the drum" from *Spin a Soft Black Song: Poems for Children* © 1971 by Nikki Giovanni. Reprinted by permission of Farrar, Straus, and Giroux LLC. All Rights Reserved.

"The Ecchoing Green," by William Blake, from *Songs of Innocence* (1789).

Stories

. . . .

"The Fire on the Mountain" from *The Fire on the Mountain and Other Stories from Ethiopia and Eritrea* by Harold Courlander and Wolf Leslau. Copyright © 1978 by Harold Courlander and Wolf Leslau. Reprinted by permission of The Emma Courlander Trust.

"The Wonderful Chuang Brocade" from *The Magic Boat and Other Chinese Folk Tales* by Dr. M. A. Jagendorf and Virginia Weng, copyright © 1980 by M. A. Jagendorf and Virginia Weng. Used by permission of Vanguard Press, an imprint of Penguin Random House LLC. All rights reserved.

Songs

. . . .

"The U.S. Air Force," by Robert Crawford. Copyright © 1951 by Carl Fisher, Inc. Copyright renewed. All rights assigned to LLC. All rights reserved. Used with permission.

Index

About the Editors

E. D. HIRSCH, JR., is the founder and chairman of the Core Knowledge Foundation and professor emeritus of education and humanities at the University of Virginia. He is the author of several acclaimed books on education issues including the bestseller *Cultural Literacy*. With his subsequent books *The Schools We Need and Why We Don't Have Them*, *The Knowledge Deficit*, and *The Making of Americans*, Dr. Hirsch solidified his reputation as one of the most influential education reformers of our time. He and his wife, Polly, live in Charlottesville, Virginia, where they raised their three children.

JOHN HOLDREN is senior vice president of content and curriculum at K12 Inc., America's largest provider of online education for graders K–12. He lives with his wife and two daughters in Greenwood, Virginia.